LIVING IN UTOPIA

To our families:
Evan, Jennifer, Ivan and Kieran
Debbie, Marc, Kerry, Hilary, Mike, Jackie and Conrad

Living in Utopia
New Zealand's Intentional Communities

LUCY SARGISSON
University of Nottingham, UK

LYMAN TOWER SARGENT
University of Missouri-St Louis, USA

WITHDRAWN

ASHGATE

Published by
Ashgate Publishing Limited
Gower House
Croft Road
Aldershot
Hants GU11 3HR
England

Ashgate Publishing Company
Suite 420
101 Cherry Street
Burlington, VT 05401-4405
USA

Ashgate website: http://www.ashgate.com

British Library Cataloguing in Publication Data
Sargisson, Lucy, 1964-
    Living in Utopia : New Zealand's intentional communities
    1.Communal living - New Zealand 2.Communal living 3. Utopias
    - New Zealand - History
    I.Title II.Sargent, Lyman Tower
    307.7'7'0993

Library of Congress Cataloging-in-Publication Data
Sargisson, Lucy, 1964-
    Living in utopia : New Zealand's intentional communities / by Lucy Sargisson and Lyman Tower Sargent.
        p. cm.
    Includes bibliographical references and index.
    ISBN 0-7546-4224-0
    1. Collective settlements--New Zealand. 2. Collective settlements. 3. Utopias--New Zealand--History.
I. Sargent, Lyman Tower, 1940- II. Title.

HX780.4.A3S27 2004
307.77'0993--dc22   2004009638

ISBN 0 7546 4224 0

Printed and bound in Great Britain by MPG Books Ltd, Bodmin, Cornwall.

Contents

List of Tables

Acknowledgements

Lyman Tower Sargent undertook the initial work of compiling the first list of intentional communities in New Zealand during 1995–96, and he wishes to thank those who made that year of research possible – the College of Arts and Sciences of the University of Missouri-St Louis and the Stout Research Centre for the Study of New Zealand Society History and Culture, Victoria University of Wellington. Those who have helped him specifically with his research on New Zealand intentional communities include the staffs of the Alexander Turnbull Library, the National Library of New Zealand Te Puna Matauranga O Aotearoa, and the Hocken Library, Dunedin. Individuals at other libraries who provided information include Fiona Corcoran of the Hamilton Public Library, Lynley Fowler of the Wanganui District Library, Mrs Tiena Jordan of the Whakatane District Museum and Gallery, Heather Knowles of the Macmillan Brown Room at the University of Canterbury Library, Mrs Gale Lockwood of the Waihi Arts Centre and Museum, Ann Milton-Tee of the Gisborne Museum and Arts Centre, Eris Parker of the Cambridge Museum, Mrs Jinty Rorke of the Tauranga Museum, Elizabeth Sharpe of the Whanganui Regional Museum, Stephanie van Gaalen of the Nelson Provincial Museum and David Verran of the Auckland Research Centre of the Auckland City Libraries. Individuals who assisted with advice, information, and less tangible forms of support include Ian Burn, Peter Callister, Michael Crawshaw, Raewyn Dalziel, Brian Easton, Miles Fairburn, Maurice Goldsmith, Margaret Hayward, Jonathan Hunt, Murray S. Martin, Elizabeth McLeay, Julienne Molineaux, Arnold Parr, John Pocock, Frank Rogers, Andrew Sharp, James Traue, Christina Tuitubou, Carole Van Grondelle, Lydia Wevers, Gareth Winter and Dianne Yates. He would also like to thank the members of Chippenham and Creekside for allowing him to visit them and Keith Langford of the Timatanga Community for providing him with information on the community as it then existed.

The following individuals provided particular assistance in the second stage of his research in 2000 – Margareta Gee and other staff members of the Alexander Turnbull Library, the staff of the Beaglehole Room of Victoria University Library, Nigel Roberts for his memories of the early years of Creekside, Hilary Stace for sharing her research on The School of Radiant Living and the Department of Politics at Victoria University for providing an appointment that allowed the research to go ahead.

Lucy Sargisson's pilot study in 2000 was funded by a grant from the University of Nottingham's Research Committee and a Personal Research Fund from the School of Politics at Nottingham University. Her fieldwork in 2001 was co-funded by a Personal Research Grant from the British Academy (Award No:SG3144) and a Personal Research Grant from the University of

Nottingham. Thanks to Bill Metcalf for providing documents and to members of the Society for Utopian Studies for comments on drafts.

She thanks all those people across New Zealand who allowed her to visit and stay in their homes, and to join, for a time, in their lives. These people are too numerous to mention by name but especial thanks go to Dave Welch of Chippenham. The pilot study would have been impossible without the help of the Ward family (Philip, Clare, Anthea, Theodora, Marcus and Ann) and Colleen Tiller. Thanks to Clare Giffard, Marie Beech, Clare and Philip Ward, and Pam and David Giffard for putting her up. Many people provided help, from loans or gifts of useful things (Maurice Goldsmith and Elizabeth McLaey, and Phil), to time (Paki Harrison, Cam and Margaret Hunter, Barry Brickell, Heath Black, Jeanette Fitzsimons, Cyril Ngamane), to friendship (Robina McCurdy, Udaya).

Thanks are also due to students and colleagues at the School of Politics at Nottingham University, Sarah Nolan for her patience in transcription, Colin Rowan, friends too numerous to list, her family and lastly to Chris Pierson, for his powers of endurance.

Preface

Utopia is the good place that is no place. Utopian imaginings of a better world exist, for the most part, in the world of fiction or theory. Examples include Thomas More's *Utopia* (1516), B.F. Skinner's *Walden Two* (1948) and, more recently, David Harvey's *Spaces of Hope* (2000). What happens then, when we try to realise utopia? What happens when we try to realise our dreams for a better world, a better way of being? Some imagine that dystopia will result and that the world will resemble a fiction such as George Orwell's *Nineteen Eighty Four* (1949) or, more recently, Margaret Atwood's *Oryx and Crake* (2003). This book seeks to explore utopian phenomena that are not constrained to the world of fiction and that exist in the world here and now. These are intentional communities. We are concerned to learn about people's experiments with their daily lives through the creation of communities that aim to realise a desire for a better way of living.

Four countries have temporarily had policies supporting the development of intentional communities, previously known, among other things, as utopian experiments and communes. Two, Australia and Israel, developed their policies as aspects of settlement and nation building; one, the United States, developed one in direct response to economic depression; and one, New Zealand, developed one because it might help channel the energies of disaffected youth. The issue that inspired New Zealand is significantly different from those that inspired the other countries, and the choice of a solution that is often connected with utopianism, illustrates the central role that utopianism played in New Zealand history. The New Zealand experiment, the Ohu Movement discussed in Chapter 4, while inspiring hundreds if not thousands of young New Zealanders, was an almost complete failure. The Murray River Settlements in Australia and the New Deal Resettlement Colonies in the United States were partial successes. The Kibbutz Movement in Israel, an inspiration of the Ohu Movement, is, of course, on going, although currently troubled.

There are many myths about intentional communities. The most important myth for our purposes is the one that says they do not exist any more. There are in fact thousands in the world today (see Bunker, Coates, Hodgson and How (eds) and *Communities Directory*). What might be called a myth of scholarship is the identification of success and longevity, an equation that was developed by Rosabeth Moss Kanter in her important book *Commitment and Community* (1972) and was widely adopted without further analysis. It fits some communities but does not reflect the intentions of most of those founded in the last quarter century; a long life in a community or even for the community is simply not a primary goal for many contemporary community members. A related myth is that most late twentieth century communities are failures on this measure. Ironically, just as scholars are rejecting the success=longevity equation, many of the communities founded in the 1960s and 1970s are approaching or passing their 30th anniversary. Since Kantor used 25 years as her measure of 'success', these communities that reject her measure are now 'successes' by it. And this applies to New Zealand communities as well.

From very early in the settlement process in the United States there were groups who settled with the explicit intention of forming a community withdrawn from other settlers to practice a particular way of life, usually based on religion. The earliest of these settled in Delaware in 1659 and other groups were established regularly at least until the middle of the nineteenth century and the Civil War, with a scattering of similar groups up to the present.

Some groups immigrated to New Zealand with the intention of establishing intentional communities, although most disintegrated shortly after arrival. In the nineteenth century the New Zealand government encouraged the establishment of 'Special Settlements' of this and other sorts, but while some were tried, none lasted as integrated communities. In the 1970s the New Zealand government actively discouraged such immigrant settlements even when New Zealand citizens supported them.

Intentional communities come in all shapes and sizes. Most communities are searching, and most members say that it is a continuing search for a life that is better on a number of dimensions than life outside the community. Life in community is not easy; many people try community life and find it or that particular community not for them. As a result people living in community urge those interested in joining to visit a number to experience various settings and groups of people before applying for membership. And most communities have a probationary period where both the individual/family and the community can get to know each other in the strains and joys of daily community life before a long-term commitment is made.

New Zealand today has communities of all types. While it was our goal to include all communities in existence in New Zealand in 2001, we knew that probably we would not succeed, and we did not. But we have representatives of all the major categories.

There are many people in New Zealand who have spent part of their lives in community and many others who are currently living in community. As a result, communal life has undoubtedly affected many aspects of New Zealand life. In addition, communities have provided the space for experimentation with a range of issues from architecture to sexuality.

Utopias lie at the heart of politics, society and everyday life. They tell us about people's dreams and desires. They stem from discontent and yet they gesture towards different and better ways of being. Intentional communities, groups of people who have chosen to live and sometimes work together for a common purpose beyond relationship or family, are, in some senses, concrete utopias. They are physical, observable spaces in which people try to create a context in which their everyday lives are closer to their utopia. This book links intentional communities and utopia throughout.

While some bow to the importance of utopianism is made in many studies of New Zealand, as, for example, in the title of Les Cleveland's politics textbook, *The Politics of Utopia* (1979), there has been virtually no mention of intentional communities in any of the literature on New Zealand or, with a few exceptions, the literature on intentional communities. New Zealand communities are striking because they often contradict what the literature on intentional communities leads us to expect. For example, anarchist communities do not generally last, but they do in New Zealand. Urban communities are short-lived, but not in New Zealand. Communities that survive usually do so by finding new members as the founders and early members inevitably leave. Thus, regular turnover in membership is the standard experience of long-lived communities, but this is much less true in New Zealand. Religious communities generally last; secular ones generally do not. In New Zealand, both last. Today, there are many long-lived intentional communities in the world, but an unusually large number of New Zealand intentional communities have lasted 20, 30, even 60 years.

New Zealand has a special place in the history of utopianism. It has historically been viewed as a land of opportunity attracting settlers, conquerors and colonisers. Paradise, Eden, and Heaven on Earth, this beautiful and abundant land has been, for many, a place in which to try to create a utopia. It is, we believe, home to more intentional communities per capita than any other country in the world and this book offers the results of the first academic survey of these, comprising discussions drawn from the experiences of over 50 intentional communities. Some are secular, some are religious, some are political, and some concerned primarily with lifestyle. We draw out lessons from this multitude of living utopian experiments and offer them to anyone who is interested in different ways of living together. As well as telling the story of the New Zealand experience, then, this book offers transferable lessons in community, cooperation, and social change.

In this book, we survey the history of New Zealand intentional communities, present a picture of New Zealand intentional communities at present, provide some answers to why these communities contradict the received wisdom on intentional communities, and, finally, look at the perennial problems that are the result of community life and the way the New Zealand communities have solved or failed to solve them. This section will, we hope, be of use to our friends living in community, without whom this book could not have been written.

Chapter 1

Introductions

Introduction

When most people are unhappy with something in their society, they either simply accept it, through apathy or because they believe, rightly or wrongly, that they have no ability or power to effect change, or they try, individually or collectively, to bring about change in the direction they desire. Others physically withdraw. Some do so because they want to lead their chosen life immediately rather than wait for change to take place; others do so because they believe that their way is the right way for a chosen few. They may withdraw by changing societies; if the country is large enough, they migrate internally to a part where they believe life will be better; or they may attempt to create that better life within the confines of the larger society but in various ways separate from it. This book is about this last form of withdrawal.

Such withdrawal has a long and diverse history. Around the time of Christ, the Essenes were a withdrawn Jewish sect in Palestine, and similar Christian communities developed early in the history of Christianity and evolved into the formal orders of monks and nuns that have now existed for centuries. Parallel developments occurred in other religions, most notably Buddhism and Hinduism. Such communities developed both through persecution and from the belief that it was the only way to practice the good religious life as understood by a particular set of believers. And different understandings of the good life led and continues to lead to the establishment of new religious communities.

Just as it is impossible to date the first religious community with any real precision, it is unclear when the first secular withdrawn community was established. As religion became less central in the lives of many people, communities came into existence designed to practice a good life that was less focused on religion and at some point religion became a matter left up to individual members. Sometimes this process took place in long-lived communities that were established as religious communities but continued as secular ones or ones that are religious in a way that leaves the characteristics of the religion undefined. But most often religious and secular communities have developed on different bases and had little to do with each other.

What to Call these Communities

Over the centuries of their existence these communities have been given many different labels. They have been called (and this long list is almost certainly incomplete) intentional communities, intentional societies, communal societies, cooperative communities, practical utopias, communes, withdrawn communities, enacted communities, experimental communities, communal experiments, alternative societies, alternative lifestyles, communitarian experiments, socialist colonies, collective settlements, mutualistic communities, communistic societies, utopian societies, concrete utopias and utopian experiments.

The differences in these labels reflect both political and scholarly judgments and, more recently, the desire of those living in such communities for a neutral term that does not suggest a particular political perspective, as, for example, communistic societies does, or that sets too high a standard, as, for example, utopian societies might appear to do. Both scholars and members have moved toward intentional community, members because it is seen as neutral and scholars because it is neutral and inclusive. Still, it is common to see other terms used, with commune the most common alternative label. Commune has the advantage of being widely recognised but the disadvantage of calling up a particular era in the history of such communities, the sixties and seventies. Another term, peculiar to both New Zealand and a particular moment in time, ohu, will be discussed at length in Chapter 4.

Past Scholarship

While there were earlier descriptions of individual communities, scholarship on such communities appears to have begun in 1841 when Mary Hennell wrote a study that was published initially as an appendix to Charles Bray's, *The Philosophy of Necessity; or, The Law of Consequences; As Applicable to Mental Moral and Social Sciences* (2: 495–663). While later editions of Bray's book were published without the appendix, Hennell's essay was published separately in 1844 as *An Outline of the Various Social Systems and Communities which have been Founded on the Principle of Co-operation*.

After Hennell's initial work, communities were most often presented in one of two ways, either through antiquarian or genealogical studies of individual communities (often by descendants) or through what might be called travelogues in which the author visited (or learned about) a number of communities and reported on them, often with no pretence of objectivity but sometimes with some sympathy. Both approaches provide sources for contemporary scholarship, albeit sources that must be used with care.

Works of the first sort were sometimes flawed by a desire to present the community in the best light and deliberately obscured practices that did not fit the authors' understanding of what was right. This led in some cases to the destruction of documents that showed the community in other than the desired manner, but such studies also ensured that material survived that might have been destroyed through ignorance and that memories were recorded that would otherwise been lost.

The travelogues also provide information that we might not have otherwise. The descriptions themselves are important, and the authors both reproduced documents and collected them, which in some cases ensured their survival. Also, others with documents recognised their value and kept them, simply because these accounts had been published.

The most important collector of documents did not himself publish a study, but the A.J. Macdonald collection, now at Yale University, provided the basis for John Humphrey Noyes's *History of American Socialisms* (1870) and much later scholarship. The most important of the travellers were John Finch, whose 'Notes of Travel in the United States' was published in 22 instalments in *The New Moral World* in 1844 and was read by Friedrich Engels (see Feuer); William Alfred Hinds, whose *American Communities* was first published in 1878 with expanded editions in 1902 and 1908; and Charles Nordhoff, whose *The Communistic Societies of the United States* (1875) is probably the best of these works.

Although communities continued in the late nineteenth and early twentieth centuries (see Fogarty 1990), interest in them waned, and there was little good scholarship except on the best-known communities like New Harmony, Oneida and the Shakers. The one exception was *History of Cooperation in the United States* (1888), which included six chapters by various authors on cooperation in different regions of the United States with some material on intentional communities.

This study reflected a change in both terminology and substance that lasted for some decades. Although the word *cooperation* (often hyphenated) had been used in the past it became the most general term in the late nineteenth and early twentieth centuries. It was regularly used to apply to communities, but it most often referred to producer or consumer cooperatives, cooperative housing and movements like cooperative housekeeping. Such organisations did not have the goal of creating entirely new communities, but they did intend to significantly improve the lives of their members. And in some instances groups created cooperative communities, and studies like the collective work *History of Cooperation in the United States* and Charles Gide's *Communist and Co-operative Colonies* (1930) reflect this.

The first steps toward the development of modern scholarship was the publication of various studies by Henrik Infield in the late 1940s and early 1950s and the publication in 1950 of Arthur Bestor's *Backwoods Utopias*, which is one of the classics of the field. Since the 1950s was a time when anything that could be construed as close to communist attracted negative attention, communal scholarship developed slowly, only taking off with the explosion of communes in the 1960s.

However, these scholars often excluded the largest group of such communities, Roman Catholic and Anglican convents and monasteries, and only recently have scholars begun to pay attention to these communities as part of the same phenomenon as the other communities they did study. Why was this? First, there was ignorance of the history of Roman Catholic and Anglican monasticism. Most of the communities that were studied tended to be rebelling against the established order, and Roman Catholic and Anglican communities were seen as part of that established order and, therefore, it was assumed that they were different in kind. But any student of these Roman Catholic and Anglican communities knows that they were often embattled, rebelling against previous community types and practices, and were frequently rejected by those in power within the church hierarchy.

In addition, Roman Catholic and Anglican communities tended to see themselves as different in kind from the other religious and secular communities and were reluctant to allow themselves to be studied as living communities by outsiders. Thus, what studies there were tended to be historical or written by insiders for insiders. But this changed.

Part of the impetus for the change came from the changed language used to describe communities. While studies by Braunfels, Hillery and Morrow, and Horn and Born used words and phrases like 'commune', 'utopian community', utopian experiment', and 'communitarian experiment', these did not seem to apply to convents and monasteries. At the same time, other descriptors like 'withdrawn community' should have signalled their inclusion. When 'intentional community' became accepted, it was clear that scholarship had excluded the largest group of such communities.

Another phenomenon added to the impetus for change. In the so-called 1960s, many people were attracted to Eastern religions, particularly Buddhism and Hinduism. As a result, Buddhist monks began to come to Australia, Europe, New Zealand and North America to teach, and they ultimately established monasteries. Hindu teachers and gurus also established ashrams in these areas, and these ashrams were quickly recognised as having great similarities to religious communes as, somewhat less quickly, did the Buddhist monasteries. Having admitting one form of monastic order to the fold, it was impossible to exclude Western forms with the same name.

A third phenomenon was the revolution that took place within the Roman Catholic Church with Vatican II. Nuns in particular saw their lives transformed. And both the men and women who joined Catholic orders were more likely to have extensive experience of the world, including intentional communities, than the previous generations had. And they became aware of the similarities themselves and in many cases began to think of themselves as living in intentional communities and became scholars on their own communities using the same tools and language as scholars of other intentional communities. As a result, today there are scholarly studies like Lawrence J. McCrank's 1997 article surveying American religious orders and the 1997 study of their own community by the Sisters of the Servants of the Immaculate Heart of Mary.

What is an Intentional Community?

There is no universally agreed upon definition of the term intentional community, and definitions in the literature vary, but there is common ground amongst the definitions (an account of past definitions can be found in Sargent 1994, 30–32). For instance, Marguerite Bouvard builds upon the work of The Federation of Intentional Communities, which identified size and organisation as key factors, and identifies social change as a key function:

> A loose definition of intentional community was adopted by the F[ederation of] I[ntentional] C[ommunities] in 1953. It sets as criteria for community a minimum size of three families or five adults, an organisation sufficient to assure a recognisable geographic proximity of members to insure continuous fellowship. Among the basic concepts of community articulated by the FIC are: sharing in a whole way of life; the importance of the spirit animating community; and the necessity of active participation in community for the maturity of the person and of the social order. At that time intentional community was conceived as the seed of a new social order inspired by the principles of mutual concern, pooling of resources, democratic and nonviolent methods and a concern for balance between the worth of the person and the social whole. (Bouvard, 100)

This is a common view and definitions often refer to size and shared goals (LeWarne, 4; Zablocki, 7), as well as work and group life (Abrams et al., 45). For some, an economic tie is necessary before a group can be called an intentional community (Fogarty 1980, ix), and others focus on the deliberate creation of alternatives (Wagner 'Sex Roles', 4). The simplest definition comes from Andy Wood:

> Very generally, communal living can be described as situations in which people knowingly and willingly share aspects of living accommodation and material goods. (Wood, 6)

For Rosabeth Kanter, a utopian community can be identified by certain organisational features and shared goals but for her, the key component of such a community is commitment (Kanter, 2–3).

Building on past scholarship, one of us proposed the following definition:

> I shall define an intentional community as a group of five or more adults and their children, if any, who come from more than one nuclear family and who have chosen to live together to enhance their shared values or for some other mutually agreed upon purpose. (Sargent 1994, 14–15)

This has been our benchmark, although experience has shown that size is not a reliable criterion and this study includes small groups in order to take into account embryonic communities and communities in a temporary lull or terminal decline. It is important to take into account both intentional and community (Shenker 1981). Intentional communities are *communities*, and this includes both collective activity and shared physical space (Metcalf 1995). And they are *intentional*, sharing a collective endeavour. And so, the working definition used in this project is simple and inclusive, encompassing a wide range of experiments in community including communes, eco-villages, religious houses and residential cooperatives. Intentional communities are groups of people who have chosen to live (and sometimes work) together for some common purpose (Sargisson 2000). Their *raison d'être* goes beyond tradition, personal relationships or family ties.

All the definitions run up against the fact that some groups of people say they constitute an intentional community when they do not meet the criteria spelled out in any definition. Others groups say they are not intentional communities when they clearly do meet the criteria. And that has proven no less true in New Zealand than elsewhere.

New Zealand

The act of immigrating to a new country is certainly an act of withdrawing from society to establish a new and, hopefully, better life, but not all colonisation schemes are community based or have a vision of creating a better society than that in the old country. The colonisation of New Zealand *did* have such visionary schemes; therefore, the history of intentional communities in New Zealand is virtually identical with the history of New Zealand. Still, the colonisation schemes as designs to create better communities with specific goals were short-lived, as were some other attempts to create communities in early New Zealand.

Thus, the earliest history of intentional communities in New Zealand is erratic and moves in fits and starts. There were various schemes and plans to establish communities but most never got beyond the planning stage, and, as we shall argue, the tension between the desire for individual betterment and community participation undermined those that got started. There were Roman Catholic communities established; there were state schemes to help immigrants and reduce unemployment; there were groups who immigrated to New Zealand with the goal of establishing intentional communities but few did; and other groups that discussed founding such communities without doing so; and there was a late nineteenth century community founded in Christchurch, the Federative Home or Wainoni, that was a radical experiment in communal living.

But other than the Roman Catholic and Anglican communities, the continuous history on intentional communities begins in the early 1930s with the founding of Beeville near Morrinsville, which lasted into the 1970s and in 1965 spawned Wilderland, which still exists today, and influenced the development of many later communities. The second community, Riverside, was founded in the early 1940s and continues to the present, making it one of the oldest intentional communities in the world. Since these origins, intentional communities in New Zealand have been established from the top of the North Island to the bottom of the South Island, and these communities parallel the entire spectrum of such communities as they have developed in other countries, from Hippie with open sexuality to lesbian separatist, to monogamous, from secular, to fundamentalist Christian, to Buddhist, to Hindu.

There have been few studies of any of these communities, individually or collectively. Riverside published its own history in 1991 (Rain), and Arnold R. Parr published a study of one aspect of Riverside in 1994. A study of Centrepoint was written by one of its members (Oakes 1986), from a perspective that he has largely recanted (see Oakes 1988 and 1997). There have been a number of theses, mostly from the School of Architecture at the University of Auckland that are invaluable resources (see Brem, Burns, Field, Karlovsky, Slessor, Webb, and Whitehead), Sargent published a research guide in 1997 and a study of the ohu movement in 1999, and a new listing was published as we completed this book (see *Utopianz*). Therefore, this is the first substantial study of intentional communities in New Zealand.

Utopianism and/of the Colonised

If colonies produced utopian literature on the one hand and life in dystopia on the other, where are the eutopias of the Aborigine, First Nations, Inuit, Maori, North American Indians, and other indigenous colonised peoples? The first, and simplest, answer is that no one has done the work to find out. Let us give a parallel example from another colonised people where work is now being done. The only published article on Irish utopianism contends that there is none and gives a number of reasons why it is culturally impossible for Ireland to produce utopias (see O'Farrell). This made no sense to Sargent, so he began to look. So far, he has found over a hundred Irish utopias together with a strong communal tradition and other aspects of Irish utopianism. Similar gaps in the scholarship exist regarding the literature of colonisers, such as New Zealand until Sargent started work. And it is a standard of the scholarship that there is no utopianism from the Iberian Peninsula, and good reasons are given for this gap. But again, no one had looked, and now they are, and the gap is beginning to be filled in.

If we are to apply the 'Closing the Gaps' policy to the eutopias of indigenous peoples, there are still some serious problems. The first problem is where to look. There are already identified utopian streams, so we are not in a complete vacuum. First, there are contemporary indigenous authors writing utopias from within a number of the traditions. Second, there were millennial movements that developed in response to the oppression of the colonisers; but there is very little on the content of these millennial visions. Third, in the tradition we know best (North American Indian), there are quite a few statements that utopianise (romanticise) the past and some that move that past to the future.

But, oppressed peoples do not have access to print in the same way as the dominant group, and there is often an inability or unwillingness to communicate in the language of the oppressor. A simple, familiar example is that there are very few utopias written by actual working people, although many purporting to tell us what is good for them. As a result, we need to look into the indigenous languages and at oral traditions, songs, myths and the like.

The second big problem is, even if we figure out where to look, will we recognise it when we see it? To what extent does one have to be inside a tradition to understand it? To take a personal example, Sargent was quite forcefully told that he should not write or talk about feminist utopianism, even though he was one of the two people who first identified the texts and told others about them. He was told that only women could understand them. The problem is that there is some truth to the argument; outsiders can miss things obvious to insiders. The other side of the coin is, of course, that an outside perspective can also throw new light on a subject.

The utopias of indigenous/oppressed peoples do not generally look like Thomas More's *Utopia* (1516) or H.G. Wells's *A Modern Utopia* (1905). Sometimes they are jeremiads or apocalypses with detailed statements of why the gods are punishing us combined with a brief statement of how good things will be if we shape up. Sometimes they are cockaignes in which abundance is provided (the classic roast pigs running around with a knife and fork in their backs squealing 'eat me'), but only after great trials and tribulations (English wade through manure to your chin for seven years; Dutch eat your way through a mountain of porridge). These are examples out of the Western tradition that have sometimes been excluded from the utopian tradition; we cite them simply to suggest that we should not expect formal, literary utopias.

We are convinced that if people look, from both inside and outside the tradition, with an open mind as to form, utopias will be found. They have been every place anyone has looked so far.

The Problem of Maori Communalism

New Zealand is in the process of becoming a bicultural country and part of that process is the redevelopment of Maori communalism, a process that raises certain problems with our use of the phrase *intentional community*.

Maori communities were originally organised in tribes within which there were definite male leaders with substantial power, but within which there was also real equality on a number of dimensions and a range of questions on which decision-making was communal and consensual. Economically Maori tribalism provided economic security, which is what most theorists mean by economic equality. This communalism was traditional not chosen and was not intentional in the sense that we use it here. What do we do with traditional, tribal communalism?

In the land wars most Maori tribes were destroyed and many of the traditions virtually disappeared, although certain millenarian groups developed that maintained them temporarily. (Such groups are interesting communities themselves.) But today, as the traditional forms are being recreated, the process clearly resembles the creation of intentional communities. Therefore, both Pakeha and Maori New Zealand have traditions of communalism and a present flourishing set of intentional communities.

While our work involves some interviews with Maori people, and the communities that we discuss are not exclusively Pakeha, we do not discuss Maori intentional communities in any great depth. This is not entirely satisfactory, but it is the best we can do. Given the problems of access and the ethical concern about the need for work to be done by insiders, this story is simply not ours to tell.

Methods

This book is a truly collaborative effort based on first-hand fieldwork and hitherto unexplored primary sources. Fieldwork was conducted by Sargisson in 2000 and 2001; and archival research was conducted by Sargent between 1996–2001. Thanks to an initiative by the National Library of New Zealand, a mass of primary material has been preserved in Wellington, and Sargent has used this collection. Intentional communities are encouraged to deposit their archives in the Library, and Sargent has spent months trawling old notebooks, accounts and minute books which tell the story of one aspect of community life. In some cases, these go back over 30 years or more. The fieldwork consisted of one or more pre-arranged visits and in most cases stays of up to a week, during which a variety of methods were used with the aim of gathering as full a picture as was possible in a short space of time. Drawing on previous experience of fieldwork in intentional communities in the UK, Sargisson combined time-limited participant observation with extended semi-structured interviews. Living amongst people in their homes, making an extensive and a detailed audio diary, taking photographs, sketches and notes, and conducting long group or individual interviews afforded her a glimpse into life inside these communities at the time of the visits. Semi-structured interviews can yield material that is rich to interpret and can provide deep insight into personal stories and motives for joining and belonging to these groups. People were extraordinarily cooperative and we owe a debt of thanks to hundreds of people across the country.

Every effort has been made to maintain high standards of ethical practice throughout this research and this extends into the writing process. For the most part, we speak in one voice throughout the text of this book but because of the nature of the fieldwork, Sargisson sometimes speaks as the first person when describing her visits. The 'I' who speaks of community visits, in other words, is Lucy Sargisson.

Intentional communities are fascinating phenomena, and there is much that the outside world can learn from them. However, they are first and foremost people's homes. We have tried to respect them as such and to integrate a respect for their privacy with the demands of academic rigour.

Our system of classification in the chapters that follow is a simple one. Our approach combines chronology, which structures our discussion of The Early Days, and attention to communities' reasons for existing, which structure our discussions of contemporary communities. We have rejected complicated systems that, for instance, distinguish between rural and urban communities, privately and communally owned, because, whilst this information is useful to have, it does not serve well as the basis of a classificatory system. Such an approach does not tell us about the real similarities and differences between and amongst communities. Instead, we have attempted only a minimal classification, which is based on the communities' *raisons d'être*. This has allowed us to compare and contrast different communities that share a similar mission or utopia. We consider these in Chapters 5, 6 and 7, which discuss religious communities, communities seeking a cooperative lifestyle and green communities respectively. This permits maximum flexibility, though we should note that even this loose system of classification has overlaps. Some communities, such as Tui and Earthsong, are committed to both green issues and a cooperative lifestyle. Others have changed over time. Riverside, for instance, started life over 60 years ago as a religious community committed to pacifism and in the 1970s dropped its religious commitments. Where there have been such changes over time we have classified according to their current reason for being. This system has involved both making judgements about communities based on our observation and archival work as well as taking seriously people's understandings of their own choices and lives.

Chapter 2

Contexts: New Zealand as a Utopia

Introduction

In this chapter we consider the role and significance of New Zealand in this story. Certain aspects of the history and culture of this country are particularly utopian. For some, New Zealand is itself a utopia. For early colonisers, New Zealand was a land of opportunity and a perfect location in which to begin a new life.

New Zealand's location and environment contributed to this idea, and still attract people who want to build a new life. Intentional communities across the country contain a mixture of New Zealanders and foreign nationals, most of whom are from North America and Western Europe, but with a growing number from Asia and the Middle East. New Zealand is a beautiful place and its remoteness attracts people who want to withdraw and begin afresh. Its climate is generally benign, which makes self-sufficiency a more realisable goal than it would be in, say, the Scottish Highlands. We shall examine the role of the physical environment in the history of utopian settlement. Disparate groups, including farmers, tourists and people seeking an alternative lifestyle have all been drawn to New Zealand as a place in which to realise their dreams and aspirations. This diversity has created certain tensions. We acknowledge these in brief discussions of the politics of land and the economic ups and downs of a nation reliant on the natural environment.

In the last couple of decades New Zealand has been casting herself as a tourist paradise. For instance, thrill-seekers are encouraged to come and bungie-jump in the deep and stunning South Island gorges or surf or canoe the white water of the fast-running bluer-than-blue rivers. Beach-lovers are encouraged to resorts like Pauanui, and walkers and lovers of wilderness can camp on the remote Coromandel Peninsula. We look at the ways in which the marketing vocabulary for tourism tapped into twentieth century hopes and desires for self-fulfilment and self-discovery and consider this as another part of the story of New Zealand as a utopia.

Colonisation[1]

Colonisation and immigration are almost inevitably two faced. There would be few plans to colonise and even fewer immigrants without the hope that something good will result.[2] And those hopes and desires are often disappointed by the hard reality of the settlement process. So it was in New Zealand.

The earliest settlers were the Maori, whose story has been told by others (see, for example, Belich, chapters 1–4). The first European or Pakeha settlers were individual or small groups of sailors who were shipwrecked, put ashore, or chose to stay after landing. Such people have played a role in the history of utopianism in New Zealand in the first utopia set on its shore, *The Travels of Hildebrand Bowman* (1778) and in Ian Wedde's *Symme's Hole* (1986). The author of *The Travels* was a sailor on one of Cook's voyages, and Wedde writes about such sailors in *Symme's Hole* and other works.

But the establishment of communities of Europeans took place initially in the second quarter of the nineteenth century and continued throughout the rest of the century. These communities were produced both by official policy and individual initiative. Official settlements included both those initiated from Britain and a scheme of 'special settlements' created by the New Zealand government. Settlements created through individual action came from both outside New Zealand and from individuals within the country who hoped to establish a community or communities to fit their aspirations.

The Official Settlement Utopia

Initially the settlement process was thought of as quite radical and utopian. In 1838 *The Times* reported, in an attack on the proposal:

> In short, we are to have a Radical Utopia in the Great Pacific, wherein, in pure honour of Queen Victoria, and in pure spite of home institutions, the doctrines of Jeremy Bentham and Robert Owen are to realise such unheard-of triumphs as shall utterly shame and outstrip the laggard progress of more antiquated nations. (*Times*)

The editorial ends by calling it 'a humbug'.

But as E.R. McCormick wrote, commenting on the *Times* editorial, 'A utopia, perhaps, but surely not a Radical utopia' (307), and there is little that can be identified as Jeremy Bentham. There is, though, one follower of Robert Owen who hoped to establish an Owenite community in New Zealand. In 1854 in London Robert Pemberton published a detailed proposal for an Owenite community in New Zealand. Nothing came of it, and the settlement of New Zealand was designed to be a conservative utopia with a gentry.[3]

The plan outlined by the colonial promoter Edward Gibbon Wakefield (1796–1862) and other early visionaries was designed to produce in New Zealand a Britain without the very rich or the very poor. The pyramid of the class structure was to remain with the top and bottom lopped off. The best known and most thoroughly documented of these settlements is Canterbury, although there were other settlements in Port Nicholson (Wellington), New

Plymouth and Nelson.[4] But the Wakefield scheme was only attempted in Canterbury and even there only briefly.

As early as 1839 the New Zealand Company put out an advertisement that said:

> The aim of the Directors is not confined to mere emigration, but is directed to colonisation in its ancient and systematic form. Their object is to transplant English society with its various gradations in due proportions, carrying out our laws, customs, associations, habits, manners, feelings – everything of England, in short, but the soil. (Qtd. in G.B. *Parliamentary Papers*, 18)

Canterbury was to be a Church of England settlement, complete with a Bishop, which would include a strict hierarchy within those who settled.

And in 1850 the planners said:

> We intend to form a settlement, to be composed entirely of members of our own church, accompanied by an adequate supply of clergy .... (*Canterbury Papers*, 6)

And Lord George William Lyttelton (1817–76), a supporter of the Canterbury settlement, wrote, 'What we wish is ... to plant ... a community ... to include all that is good in our society at home; to exclude, as far as possible, all that is evil' (Qtd. in *Canterbury Settlement*, 6).

What happened is reflected in the words of John Robert Godley (1814-61), the founder of Canterbury:

> When I first adopted and made my own, the idea of this colony, it pictured itself to my mind in the colours of a Utopia. Now that I have been a practical colonizer, and have seen how these things are managed in fact, I often smile when I think of the ideal Canterbury of which our imagination dreamed. Yet I see nothing in the dream to regret or be ashamed of, and I am quite sure that without the enthusiasm, the poetry, the unreality (if you will,) with which our scheme was overlaid, it would never have been accomplished. (Qtd. in 'Farewell Breakfast to Mr. and Mrs. Godley', 9)

Some people believed that this utopia should be like Britain and wrote of the glories of transplanting England to the Pacific. Anthony Trollope (1815–82) described what he saw as the typical situation, saying:

> The New Zealander among John Bulls is the most John-Bullish. He admits the supremacy of England to every place in the world, only he is more English than any Englishman at home. He tells you that he has the same climate, – only somewhat improved; that he grows the same produce, – only with somewhat heavier crops; that he has the same beautiful scenery at his doors, – only somewhat grander in its nature and more diversified in its details; that he follows the same pursuits and after the same fashion, – but with less of misery, less of want, and a more general participation in the gifts which God has given to the country. (2: 457–58)

Or as Charles Hursthouse, an early settler in Canterbury who returned to England, quotes from a letter written back to England from Canterbury:

> It is this fact that for me gives the country such a charm, the charm of our home beauties stealing over the wild grandeur of this favoured land, and heightened by a climate, of which the most lovely of English days can scarcely convey an idea. When Christchurch has grown to a pretty town, when the young oak of England stands by the side of the giant trees indigenous to New Zealand, when the avenues to houses are lined by the graceful and beautiful shrubs, when the green grass of England is sprouting in her meadows, fenced by hawthorn hedges, when daisies and butter-cups flower over the land, when the timid hare springs across the field, and the coveys of partridges break from cover, and the sun of heaven shines brightly through the pure atmosphere, tempered by breezes from the Pacific and the Alpine shore, then there will be but one thing wanting to make New Zealand the Eden of the world – the charm of age, the vestiges of the past, the spot endeared by old associations and traditions. (1: 99)

Of course, the reality of the introduced plants and animals was often extremely destructive and their effects are still being fought today.

The other major early settlement, Otago, was also established as a potential utopia, but Scotch Presbyterian rather than Anglican. In 1847 the Rev. W. Burns wrote that:

> The colony will become ... a centre of high-toned and liberal education for the young – and a refuge, as to sympathy and support, for the evangelical missionary of every denomination. It ought thus to become the centre of an influence which would reach the Asiatic and American continents, embracing the myriads of islands sprinkled upon the bosom of the Pacific, and be instrumental in the furtherance of that final consummation of our world's progress, when 'the earth shall be full of the knowledge of the Lord, as the waters cover the sea'. (Qtd. in Free Church Colony of Otago, 12)

But, as with Canterbury, the reality of Otago was like the reality of most New Zealand settlements, a personal desire for a better life. People came and settled, initially within the confines of the parameters established by the colonisation company, but many concluded that they preferred life outside those restrictions. They either moved outside the settlement geographically or participated in the transformation of the settlement into one that better suited their desires.

These settlements and the ways they changed have rightly been a dominant theme in New Zealand history, but a few settlements were proposed, and even fewer developed, on a different basis, one which attempted to either create or maintain a specific way of life. Generally, but not always, these were based on the desire to live in a community with a particular religious orientation. Specific examples of these and the 'Special Settlements' will be discussed in Chapter 3, which looks at early communal experiments.

The Environment

New Zealand is, surely, one of the most beautiful countries in the world. Its environment and benign climate have acted as magnets for hundreds, possibly thousands of years. It is a land of plenty. Its flora is prolific. An earthly paradise; New Zealand is lush, warm and beautiful. Subtropical local climates in the north means that bananas will grow in your garden. The dry heat in the south is perfect for soft fruits. Little wonder, then that so many people have identified it as a place in which to create their utopia.

Early settlers exploited this to the full. They found massive and ancient Kauri trees towering above thick forests through which ran streams and rivers of fresh water. Massive Moa birds, some over eight feet tall, lived unmolested until the arrival of their human predators. The indigenous wildlife consisted mostly of birds and many were without predators until the Maori introduced rats and dogs. Legends date the first Maori landings to 970 AD, when Kupe is said to have reached the shores of New Zealand. He was said to have been followed by the Great Fleet in 1350. They lived in pas, massive hilltop settlements, which are still evident. These hills were terraced for defence and for the propogation of crops such as kumara (sweet potato). The Maori revered the land and worked it, and it was perfect for their lifestyle. Many Maori were coastal dwellers and the seas were rich in fish and seafood (including pipi, mussels, crayfish and paua). They harvested and processed flax, taro, nikau palms and cabbage trees for food, weaving and thatching.

The full story of early Maori settlement is not ours to tell, but it is important to our account in a number of respects. Firstly, we need to note the nature of the relationship between these people and the land and sea, which was reciprocal and pragmatic. It does not do to lionise the Maori, for instance, the extinction of the Moa is laid at their door, and they burned vast areas of bush. However, they do deeply revere the land. Maori creation stories stem from the land and sea and their spiritual history is deeply entwined with their ecology. All land has spirit for them and special places are sacred.

Wholesale clearance of land came with European settlers, drawn by the potential of this undeveloped place. Often they were attracted by the climate and the good growing conditions. Correspondence from early European settlers is replete with references to abundance that contrasted with the poverty of the homeland (Sargent 2000). Drawn by stories of land and plenty, settlers colonised the hills and valleys of this beautiful country, employing familiar farming techniques and discovering in New Zealand a stark contrast to the deprivations of home. However, life was not easy.

Common motifs in accounts and writings of nineteenth century settlers include awe at the majesty of the natural beauty of New Zealand, and lush and prolific growing conditions. They also convey desperate homesickness, heartache and isolation from family left in 'the old country'. They worked hard, hacking homes out of wild bush, and clearing huge areas of ancient Kauri trees. They introduced non-indigenous fauna and flora, some of which flourished. Loggers and farmers cleared forests, wanting wood and pasture. Miners discovered coal, granite and gold, which they still gouge from the earth. In the 1800s large areas were cleared by bushmen, whose ingenious rolling roads cut swathes through the forest. Diggers and bleeders worked on the Kauri for its precious gum and for years the forests provided work for hundreds of men and their families.

They have left a mixed legacy – a highly self-reliant rural culture and soil erosion and the extinction of the native plant and bird life. New Zealand has proved a problematic utopia.

The Economy

For over a century, the land provided generations of New Zealanders with a good standard of living. In recent decades this has changed and economic decline has led the government to re-cast New Zealand as a different kind of utopia. From pastoral idyll, it is re-emerging as a tourists' paradise.

In 1950, New Zealand was ranked fifth wealthiest amongst OECD countries in terms of GDP per capita. In 2001 it stood at twentieth (OECD Database http://www.economist.com). New Zealand had built much of its wealth on agricultural exports, and the agricultural economy collapsed due largely to external factors. Markets shifted from Britain to Asia and different products were required. The demand for wool and meat changed and producers had to diversify. Government cuts to subsidies also had huge impact on the rural economy (see Kelsey 1995).

The crisis in agriculture has been at the forefront of New Zealand's political agenda for the last ten years. Tourism has entered the field as a significant source of income, and tourism and farming lobbies make different demands, which have tended to produce a 'hands off' attitude to the environment since 1980. The government wants to attract tourist revenue, and New Zealand's pristine environment is a key factor in its success. However, mass tourism threatens pristine environments. Tourists generate rubbish and sewage and they damage the natural habitat. Also, New Zealand is tempted to promote itself as a utopia for agricultural innovation: a land of opportunity for genetic modification, high-tech production and experimentation. And there is a vocal lobby that views New Zealand as a Green utopia, a paradise for organic food production. It is not possible to know which way things will go, and New Zealand stands at a crossroads. On the one hand lies a path which may lead to economic regeneration and internal wealth from external investment by big agriculture. On the other hand lies the path of internal environmental sustainability, which may be unable to address the demands of a modern national economy. Somewhere in between tread the tourists.

Intentional communities often seek to preserve New Zealand's natural environment. They believe that the government has failed to do this. Many have this as their main reason for being, and they are discussed in Chapter

7. Even more have it as a secondary goal and we shall meet many groups in this book who protect a portion of land while they pursue their own vision of utopia.

Tourism in Paradise

In 2002 (before *The Lord of the Rings* became the unofficial source of symbols for New Zealand) the country's 'official' online tourist website had at the head of its homepage a panoramic scenic photograph. In the foreground sat a lone man on a hillside. His face was turned away from us, looking towards a long narrow headland at the tip of which islands peeked from an azure sea. The light is hazy and the picture evokes feelings of solitude, peace and beauty. A message of utopian opportunity is typed over the photograph: 'What are you looking for?' (http://www.purenz.com/indexnz.cfm 20.02.02).

New Zealand draws seekers and searchers. People in intentional communities throughout the country have moved to New Zealand from all over the world. They see it as a land of opportunity, space, peace and distance from the madding crowds. Many came here initially on holiday.

> *Escape into the natural world*
> Rediscover your passion for life in this land of snow-capped peaks, golden beaches, jewel-like lakes and lush green forests …
> This is nature as it was intended: pure, untouched, energising …
> Leave the crowds behind and discover a sense of freedom in one of the least populated countries in the world.
> Embark on a personal odyssey, venturing into high, distant and magical places.
> Enjoy the freedom of travelling independently.
> (http://www.purenz.com/wilderness.cfm 20.02.02)

This is pure romanticism. Come to New Zealand, this page says, and find yourself. Marketing like this further reinforces the idea of New Zealand as a utopia, a place in which you can discover the 'real' you. Some of the people who have been drawn here seek to do this by living together with others in intentional communities.

Land Politics

Everything discussed so far occurs against the backdrop of a long series of disputes and debates about land. Land is probably the most contested political issue in New Zealand today. Some people say that once upon a time things were simpler: the land was once a source of a good standard of living for New Zealanders. It was closely bound to their sense of national identity. Or so the story goes. Actually, the picture was never this simple. Two incompatible conceptions of the land have co-existed in New Zealand since the arrival of the European settlers. Maori and Pakeha ideas about land have always been in conflict.

The Maori people envisage a spiritual relationship between humans and place. They are deeply connected to it in complex ways and it forms a central part of their sense of identity. It is also central to contemporary Maori politcs:

> Land is necessary for spiritual growth and economic survival. It contributes to sustenance, wealth, resource development, tradition; land strengthens whanau [social] and hapu [cultural] solidarity, and adds value to personal and tribal identity as well as the well-being of future generations ... A Maori identity is secured by land; land binds human relationships, and in turn people learn to bond with the land. Loss of land is loss of life .... (Durie 1998, 115)

Cultural beliefs inform collective land claims made against the Crown, which have led to large payments of compensation. The current issue is over control of the foreshore and seabed that is not already in private hands, the Crown, the government in the name of all the people of New Zealand, the local Maori, or some combination of these entities.

A significant number of the people in New Zealand's intentional communities have been influenced by Maori views of land. None of these communities are Maori, though some members are. But many Pakeha speak of a deep connection to the land, a sense of guardianship and an awareness of the people who have lived on it before them.

Conclusion: From Colonisation to Intentional Community

The story told in this chapter is a complicated one that can be clarified by distinguishing between 'top-down' and 'bottom-up' utopianism. We have said that some people have always seen New Zealand as a utopia. It has been seen as a place in which to begin again; a place in which old mistakes need not be repeated. A place in which land is plentiful and there is the space to build a new life. We have sought to identify key historical influences on the utopian communities that exist across New Zealand. We began by looking at the utopianism of official colonisation and we have finished with the impact of land debates. Along the way we have considered various state level initiatives and measures to change the national economy; attempts to attract tourists and income.

All of these debates, schemes and issues contain a utopian aspect and we have tried to make this apparent without overstating its importance. The picture that emerges is one of a small remote country in which people have been devising utopias for centuries. Sometimes these stem from a desire for a better way of life. Sometimes they are attempts to respond creatively to real world events.

Notes

1   Parts of this chapter have been previously published in Sargent (2001b) and are reprinted with the permission of *Utopian Studies*.
2   The vast majority of settlers immigrated and still immigrate to improve their own lives. Sargent has considered the utopian aspects of such immigration in the nineteenth century in Sargent (2000).
3   See Pemberton (1854). McCormick uses Pemberton's title as the title of his article and comments on the proposal. See McCormick, 314–18. A study is Rockey (1981).
4   There is a pamphlet that discusses the Nelson proposal in vaguely utopian terms, mostly through lengthy quotations from William Ellery Channing (1780–1842), a leading US Unitarian. See Ward (1842).

The Early Days: The Nineteenth Century

Introduction

In this chapter we explore the intentional communities founded or proposed in New Zealand in the nineteenth century. These include special settlements, which the governments in Britain and New Zealand encouraged as inducements to settlement; independent settlements that were established or proposed, including the movement for state farms to overcome poverty; and the first community that parallels the later communal movement, Wainoni, or The Federative Home, founded by Alexander Bickerton (1842–1929). Bickerton was a key figure in early New Zealand utopianism. He wrote a utopia, founded a community and proposed many other projects designed to improve the lives of nineteenth century New Zealanders.

While one of the communities discussed in this chapter, Waipu, still exists and traces its roots to the independent settlement discussed here, it no longer reflects the vision of its founders. None of the other projects discussed here lasted more than a few years, but they were still reflective of an impulse to find a better life for their actual or proposed inhabitants and some of them succeeded in doing so for a time.

Special Settlements

We talked in Chapter 2 about early religious communities. In New Zealand, these developed either under government auspices that encouraged what were called 'Special Settlements' or through independent action. The best-known Special Settlement was Albertland. The best-known independent settlement was Waipu. Both of these settlements were religiously based, but there were proposals for secular communities and an attempt to found what today we would call a commune or intentional community.

Albertland was designed to be a non-conformist alternative to Canterbury and Otago. It was to be a settlement by Baptists, independent congregations, and some Wesleyans north of Auckland (National Association). It was: '… based upon the idea that Christian men, united by common sympathies and aspirations, are calculated to found substantial colonies, and lay therein the foundation of future nations: that they can provide by means of this Association instruction for their children, and see them grow up amid all the influences of a preached gospel and practical religion' (*Prospectus*, 1). While the town still exists, the dream was never achieved (on Albertland, see Borrow, and Brett and Hook).

Independent Settlements

Waipu was established by the followers of Norman McLeod (1778/79–1866), who had followed him from Scotland to Nova Scotia in 1817, to Australia for a year in the 1850s and finally to New Zealand. Some dropped off at each stage (studies of and sources regarding Waipu and its history include Harvey; *Idyll of the Shipbuilders*; Gordon Macdonald; McKenzie, McPherson; Molloy; Morrison, and Robinson 1952 and 1997). McLeod was clearly a charismatic leader and spell-binding preacher who led his diminishing flock from the extreme poverty of western Scotland to relative prosperity in New Zealand, at each stage trying to keep the community together through isolation from others and an extremely strict interpretation of Scripture. Many descendants of these settlers still live in the area. Waipu was never communal, but the people shared their religion and the history of the long trek from Scotland.

There was a community called The Rootsites at Halcombe, near Feilding from 1874 into the early 1890s. Here, the followers of Joseph Bridgeman Roots, brother-in-law and follower of Alfred Feist (1835–73), a charismatic Brethren preacher, established the community to practice a very strict version of Brethren life. There was no private property, and the community farmed, ran a sawmill, a sash and door factory and also had a school in Feilding. Roots was a tyrannical leader and his followers gradually left him (Lineham 1977, 42; and 1993).

Proposals

A community proposed by Robert Fluke Cunningham in a series of pamphlets in the early 1870s was to be called Aurelia and based on what Cunningham called the 'Harmonial Philosophy'. Aurelia appears to be the first New Zealand proposal for a commune in that the *Prospectus* says:

> Our design is to purchase and occupy about four square miles, *i.e.*, 2,560 or more acres of agricultural land of the best quality, in one block, adjoining a large area of common or grazing land – say 10,000 acres in all, … the whole to be cultivated and wrought jointly for the benefit of the Members and their families, and on which shall be erected according to plans which are being prepared, dwellings sufficient to accommodate 100 families with central Lyceum buildings, workshops for various trades, storehouses and out-building – site to be chosen, pioneer company organised, and operations to commence when £1,000 of capital is subscribed. (2)

To avoid the problem of dissension, the Association was restricted 'exclusively to individuals imbued with the leading principles of the Harmonial Philosophy' (*Prospectus*, 1). Aurelia would have included women based on full equality, but would have excluded lawyers and religious leaders.

Another proposal was for a settlement, called Britannia, not under the authority of the New Zealand government. It was to include Stewart Island and those parts of the South Island south and west of Otago and Canterbury, and its capital was to be located at Bluff and called Regina. This proposal included detailed provisions for land ownership and laid out a governmental structure (see Gouland). There is no evidence that anything came of the proposal, which appears to have been generated mostly by the failure of the governments of the time to invest in the development of the area.

The Hurworth Community was a community of sorts based around a group of friends in New Plymouth from January 1857 to March 1860. Essentially the community was composed of young settlers, who called themselves 'the mob', cooperating to support themselves as they settled the land. They tried a number of ways of making a living, including a cheese factory (successful), a store (unsuccessful), a postal contract (they lost money), but they managed to build houses, get married, have children and generally get started with their lives in New Zealand. They had not factored in the land wars, and their nascent community was abandoned. The people, though, generally stayed together and became important in early New Zealand intellectual, political and social life (Porter 94–125).[2]

State Farms

A number of proposals for the establishment of state farms were put forward and some were actually founded. The proposals included *Land Ho!!* (1881) by Alexander Joyce (1840/41–1927), which is set in 1933 and notes that no country any longer allows any private property in land. Joyce is unusual in this early period in addressing the question of Maori lands. He solves what he sees as a problem by giving them access to land in the same way as everyone else, and they all happily become farmers on state-owned land. The anonymous *New Zealand's Great Want. Organisation of Labour* (1894) and W.H. Clarke's *A Co-operative State Farm Scheme* (1894) set out detailed schemes for getting labour onto land through cooperative state farms. According to William Pember Reeves approximately 2200 units were allocated in what he calls 'village settlements' after 1886 and half of the people remained on the land 15 years later (1: 313). He notes, in a scenario that recurs almost 100 years later, that in some cases very poor land was made available and that those placed on such land generally failed (ibid). Still, the actual schemes, much less elaborate than those proposed by Joyce and others, appear to have been quite successful in putting a substantial number of unemployed people onto the land and allowing them to stay there.

Near the end of the century, it became clear that from the point of view of the average settler, something had gone wrong. The land that they depended on to allow them to create their better lives was mostly in the hands of a few wealthy men. As a result, one of the major movements to bring about the utopia of the settlers was land nationalisation. This was the fruit of a major campaign in New Zealand to make land more widely available, a movement that produced a number of utopias. Reflecting the fact that New Zealand was participating in an international movement, central figures in this movement were the Americans Edward Bellamy (1850–98) and Henry George (1839–97). In New Zealand Bellamy's *Looking Backward* (1888) sold out in days and numerous pirated editions were published. George's single tax scheme was behind much land nationalisation, even though his specific proposals were not used.

The Clarionites

A group of emigrants, known as the Clarionites because they were recruited through Robert Blatchford's (1851–1943) British paper, *The Clarion*, were led by William Ranstead (1859–1944). They came with the explicit intention of establishing an intentional community, but the community was never established because the New Zealand government refused to grant land to a group as opposed to individual settlers, a position repeated in the second half of the twentieth century with the group known as Philia and the Russian Old Believers. Most of the Clarionites stayed in New Zealand and became involved in economic and political movements on the left, thereby being instrumental in the emergence of new utopias for New Zealand (Roth 1957 and 1959).[3]

Ranstead visited Alexander Bickerton at Wainoni, the first real intentional community founded in New Zealand and wrote an article about in for *The Clarion*. Some of the Clarionites joined the community and others settled initially on the state farm at Levin. Thus, although they did not found a commune, they were part of the movement and of the first one established in the country.

Alexander Bickerton and the Federative Home or Wainoni

While we know quite a lot about what Alexander Bickerton (1842–1929) intended to accomplish in establishing the first commune in New Zealand, we know very little about what actually happened there. This community, known as the Federative Home or Wainoni, was founded in 1896 on the banks of the Avon River in then suburban Christchurch; Wainoni means 'the bend in the water' and the community was built on a horseshoe curve in the Avon. While it is often difficult to date the end of communal experiments with certainty, it appears to have ended as a community in 1903, while continuing as a park and gardens and the centre of Bickerton's activities until he left for England in 1910. Wainoni is now an Eastern suburb of Christchurch, and there is a Bickerton Street that intersects Wainoni Road, which is a major thoroughfare. A park called Wainoni Park, just off Wainoni Road, exists, but it is not same site. Bickerton Street runs through what had been Bickerton's Wainoni Park.

Bickerton's social and political ideas were expressed in his novel *Morganeering* (1895), in the first printing of his *The Romance of the Earth* (1898) and in numerous pamphlets and speeches, some of which survive among his papers, which are held by the Canterbury Museum. The published version of his eutopia, *Morganeering Or, The Triumph of the Trust*, is primarily a satire on capitalism, but the Bickerton Papers contain a manuscript of 245 pages of a continuation of the novel that doubles its length and includes more of the eutopia, which includes a federation of communes and a broad egalitarianism. Since he was writing the novel at the same time as he was developing plans for Wainoni and much of it is set in a fictional Wainoni, it is possible to use the sections on the commune in *Morganeering* to give us an idea of what he had in mind for the Federative Home.

Bickerton was the first Professor at Canterbury College. Although he was hired as a Professor of Chemistry, he appears to have taught all the sciences, including Physics and Astronomy. He was obviously an inspiring teacher and an original thinker, but he was too eccentric in both his methods and theories for Canterbury and he was fired in 1902. Although Wainoni was not specifically referred to in the actions taken against him, it is clear that he was fired for his opinions and his activities as a citizen rather than any problems with his work as a Professor. In a neat touch, his ashes were ultimately interred in a column of Canterbury College.

Bickerton was a socialist and an advocate of eugenics. Although it undoubtedly did not endear him to the business leaders on the Board of the College, there were many socialists in 1890s Christchurch. And even supporting eugenics would have been acceptable if he had not argued that the rejection of marriage and the acceptance of free love was the best way to produce superior children.

In the novel, there is much on the trauma of marriage and the general benefits of the free choice of mates by women, and Bickerton elaborates on this position in most of his political writings. In *The Romance of the Earth* he says, 'The most striking human sex peculiarity, the most unique characteristic of the whole organic world, is the fastidiously selective passionate love of the female', and continues that '… woman, in the satisfaction of her love, is the purest being in existence' (110). It is his position that free love will result in monogamy. And he links this position to his socialism by arguing that if women are economically independent they will make eugenically correct choices.

In *Morganeering*, when the design of the new society is discussed, the first position taken is that 'Of course private ownership of every kind must cease' because 'that is undoubtedly the "primum mobile" of all sin crime and misery' (Alexander Bickerton (1842–1929), 27/57, Folder 17, item 354a manuscript of a novel. Canterbury Museum, Christchurch, New Zealand, Chapter 36, 61). And he says, 'The first duty then, of the state, is to see that all children are fed, clothed, housed, and educated in body, mind, and soul' (ibid., Chapter 32, 38).

Morganeering is a very bad novel, and it is no surprise that it was self-published. The names given to the characters include such gems as the Servile Crawley family, Miss Verdant Willowgreen, Sir Obsolete Courtly, Lord Littlebrain, the Earl of Crumbling Towers, Wondergilt, Sir Sycophant Tuneful's band, the Wealth Hosanna Chorus, Lord Rippling-bard (a poet) and Hautypouty.

The published part of the novel is mostly a dystopia in which one man controls all the world's wealth. In the unpublished continuation, this man, Wondergilt, having died of boredom, wills all his money to those hoping to bring about a better world. Now controlling the world's wealth, they put into practice the ideas they have been discussing, interminably, while also escaping the clutches of their capitalist enemies and their corrupt political followers.

During the period in which capitalism dominated the world, a Dutch federation of communes emerged and was defeated. This federation provides the basis for the new world. Besides getting rid of private property and establishing the freedom of women to choose their partners, the foci of the novel are on the need to educate the world's population so that it does not slip back into the old ways and on social experimentation to determine the best social organisation for the future.

The elite who now have the power through their control of the world's wealth will lead the poor, uneducated workers who are not capable of seeing what is best for them into the new world. As one of the main characters says (Sterling for his virtues):

> Doubtless ... education is important; but when we have commenced their education, we must gradually lessen their hours of labour, and get them to spend their time in social amusements, suitable to their low intellectual state. (Ibid., Chapter 36, 63)

The novel is full of glittering generalities about the power of love and the satisfaction of working for others rather than oneself, but there is little about the practicalities of day-to-day life. In discussing the commune, they note that work is made play so that even potential idlers are attracted to it. Eugenic legislation takes care of any remaining alcoholics, who are isolated and sterilised. Contraception ensures that no unwanted children are born and the free choice of partners means that prostitution is almost unknown. Each commune has at least 500 members and involves both farming and manufacturing, a combination that was carried out at the real Wainoni.

While the novel suggests the principles involved, what little we know of the real Wainoni indicates the successes and failures of Bickerton's attempts to put them into practice. First, it appears that for all of Bickerton's belief in the evils of private property, he kept Wainoni in his own hands. This parallels the novel, where the leaders kept control of the world's economy as they brought about change.

The real Wainoni is a fascinating combination of ingenuity and naïveté; unfortunately, the naïveté proved more important in the end. Still, in his more analytical moments, Bickerton saw Wainoni as 'a school in which to learn what is needed for success' (Bickerton, *A Federative Home*, 3). His biographer says that Bickerton said that 26,000 experiments had been necessary to perfect the light bulb, which was simple in comparison to improving society (Burdon 69). Bickerton was also realistic regarding the possibility of rapid change, saying:

> Our chief motto is Christ's charge: Resist not evil. Hence we do not fight the social evil, the drink evil, or the costly pipe, and we make no attempt to lessen the multifarious ills that scourge mankind; for we believe that when man is in his true environment – when each lives for all – such scourges will be things of the past. (Qtd. in Burdon, 69–70)

Bickerton described Wainoni as follows:

> The park is largely sandhills in which pines flourish luxuriantly, and amongst which many miles of walks are laid out. There is an asphalt path or bicycle track over half a mile long, an asphalt tennis court; the drives, terraces and garden paths are also asphalted. The house and most of the dormitories and other buildings are on well-drained elevations. (ATL Ms-Papers-0259–094)

He went on to stress that all members of the community have access to all the facilities, mentioning a billiard room, library, conservatories, painting studio, photographic dark room and workshop. Boats and carriages were also owned by the community and available for use by the members, and the community kept a house in Christchurch and a cottage by the sea, both of which community members could use. Others have commented on the beauty of the grounds, and when the Federative Home experiment came to an end, Bickerton turned Wainoni into a pleasure garden that attracted hundreds of visitors.[4]

Bickerton wrote that Wainoni was primarily an experiment in cooperative housekeeping but that 'industries are being established to occupy such members as may for the time being be out of employment, also to produce some of the articles required by the members' (ATL Ms-Papers-0259–094).[5] Members, including Bickerton, who worked outside the community paid a regular fee. Those who worked in community businesses or for the community paid less, some paid nothing and some were paid by the community. There were also associate members, who did not live in the community, and who paid a small subscription and had access to all community facilities on the same basis as members. If they used these facilities extensively, they were expected to pay an amount, determined by themselves, over and above the subscription. Any profit was to be divided among community members; any loss was absorbed by Bickerton. E.J. Howard said that 'Money to the Professor was merely metal disks' (Qtd. in Tolerton 30) and Bickerton supported the community financially. As a result, the loss of his professorship undermined the community.

Work at the community was voluntary, and, like so much else about the community, we know little of how well the system functioned. We do know that housing was provided for all the members through an invention of Bickerton's, the paper house. These houses, which the community called 'carbos', cost only a fraction of that of even the cheapest wooden house, could be built quickly and appear to have stood the test of time reasonably well.

With the demise of Wainoni as a social experiment, Bickerton built a lecture room and continued to lecture (Tolerton, 31), established 'The Wainoni Sanitorium for the Treatment of Nerve Breakdowns', set up a publishing company, Wainoni Postal Publishing and the Wainoni Remedy Company that produced 'Professor Bickerton's Marvellous Ointment', which was good for 'eczema, wounds, burns, scalds, chilblains' (as advertised on the back cover of Bickerton, *Mental Healing*). The pleasure gardens were very successful, with the takings for one day as much as £400.

In 1910 Bickerton sailed to England hoping to publicise his astronomical theories with the help of his former student, Sir Ernest Rutherford (1871–1937). Expecting immediate success, he left his family in Christchurch and his wife died in 1919 without seeing him again. Bickerton married again in 1920 at age 79 and lived until 1929, by which time he was being honoured as a neglected genius.

Havelock North: the Havelock Work and Radiant Living

The late nineteenth century saw the rise of a number of esoteric religions, Theosophy being the best known of these. New Zealand produced its variants of these and one or more of the esoteric religions of the period influenced many New Zealanders. The best known was the Havelock Work, named for its location in Havelock North. The Havelock Work ultimately led to the establishment of the Tauhara Retreat Centre near Taupo and continues today in very small groups of the Golden Dawn in the United States. For a short period, the Havelock Work appears to have produced an intentional community in Havelock North, and, for a time, Tauhara considered itself an intentional community.

Also, in Havelock North later in the century, The School of Radiant Living flourished under the leadership of its founder Herbert Sutcliffe (1886–1971) and his successors. It was also an intentional community, although for most of its existence it was closer in form to a retreat centre, which may be non-profit or profit making but is run by employees rather than members.

The Havelock Work was the late and last significant flowering of the Hermetic Order of the Golden Dawn. This was one of the many occult groups that flourished in nineteenth-century Europe.[6] According to Ellwood (1993, 157), its source was the teachings of Alphonse-Louis Constant, known as Eliphas Lévi (1810–75), who developed the 'laws of magic' that the Golden Dawn adopted and to which it added an additional law.

But the Havelock Work predated and prepared the way for the introduction of the Golden Dawn to New Zealand. In the first decade of the twentieth-century Havelock North was the home of a substantial number of educated, creative, well-off people who made the town into a cultural centre for the Hawke Bay region. This aspect of the Havelock Work commenced in 1908 with an initial meeting attended by over 100 people to discuss cultural affairs and was followed up later that year with readings from Shakespeare and Dickens. Over the years this small beginning blossomed into regular meetings in which locals performed, craft and other classes, an Old English Fete, a Shakespeare Pageant and other cultural activities (Ellwood 1993, 168–69).

One of the main vehicles for doing this was a journal called *The Forerunner*, published from May 1909 until December 1914, with a total of 21 issues. *The Forerunner* published a wide range of materials.[7] The first issue, for example, included poetry; various essays, including one on the ideal house and how to keep it that way; and 'Daily Thoughts for Meditation'. The 'Introduction' to this first issue of *The Forerunner* makes it clear that those in the Havelock Work were open to esoteric religions.

> As each proves true to his own special Ray he will speed from his Birth-star in the vast horizon, and revolving in the fire-mist of his own special hue, will unite with the others and form a vortex of glowing whiteness which will be a Beacon-light to attract seekers after love and truth and beauty. (3)

The person who brought Havelock North and the Golden Dawn together was Robert William Felkin (1853–1926), a medical doctor and an adept of the Golden Dawn. Recommended by an Anglican priest as someone who could help the group reach a higher spiritual level, Felkin was invited to Havelock North in 1912. During this stay, Felkin founded the Smaragdum Thalasses Lodge of the Stella Matutina, which was an offshoot of the original Golden Dawn particularly interested in magic (Ellwood 1993, 174). As suggested by Felkin's introduction by an Anglican priest, neither he nor those involved in the Havelock Work saw any conflict between their activities and their Christian beliefs.

Felkin and his family stayed for a few months and then he and his wife Harriot returned to England, leaving his daughter by a prior marriage to lead the Lodge until they returned permanently in 1916. Felkin led the group until his death in 1926, Mrs. Felkin until hers in 1959, and the daughter Ethelwyn until hers in 1962. The Golden Dawn then continued in Havelock North until 1978.

To the extent there was an intentional community as part of the original Havelock Work, it centred on a building, Whare Ra (House of the Sun), designed by the famous architect James Walter Chapman-Taylor (1878–1958). Built about 1915, it was one of the first buildings in New Zealand built of reinforced concrete, and it still stands (for a discussion and some illustrations of the building, see Siers, and, for a note on its current condition, see Shanahan). Whare Ra served as the home of the Felkin family and included a basement temple of about 1,500 square feet. There was a large seven-sided vault within the temple (sort of an inner temple) that was painted in arcane symbols.

Many people from Havelock North were involved in the activities at Whare Ra, which were much the same as found in most secret societies of the time. Whare Ra reportedly attracted the best families of Havelock North, who ensured that no investigation of it got anywhere.

Over time interest dropped away, and in October 1938 Harriot Felkin purchased about 60 acres of land near Lake Taupo intending it to be used as a spiritual study centre. The original land was sold at various times following the war. In 1971 when the last of the original land was sold, land was purchased above Acacia Bay and Tauhara was established. Over the years since then Tauhara has provided a place of retreat for those interested in the spiritual, as well as others. At times it has been listed as an intentional community, but there is no evidence that it ever was (on Tauhara, see Isaac).[8]

Havelock North was also the site of the School of Radiant Living,[9] which was founded and led by Herbert Sutcliffe (1886-1971), who settled in New Zealand in 1941. Ethelwyn Felkin is reported to have suggested where he should look to establish his School when he visited her at Whare Ra in 1940. At one time Sutcliffe had centres in Britain, the USA, Canada, Hong Kong and Australia and his *How to Re-Make Your Life* has been recently republished in the United States.

The School was centred at Peloha (Peace Love Harmony), and focused on psychological, physical and spiritual health. Diet was important, and while they were not vegetarians, meat was rarely eaten. Quite elaborate diets were advocated and used by both those at Peloha and many followers around the world. Also, exercise (both body and eye) and correct breathing were taught. Stace notes that almost everything taught at the School was borrowed, and we should add that almost everything taught there is still taught in various New Age organisations.

Radiant Living was quite influential in New Zealand.[10] Twelve centres were established throughout the country, which Sutcliffe visited regularly, and thousands took Radiant Living courses. Sutcliffe also made wire recordings of his lectures and sent them to the centres around the world.

Peloha was clearly a retreat centre, for most of the people who visited it, for short courses or to recover their health, but there appear to have been others who lived and worked there. Sutcliffe was clearly a charismatic leader and, like others, was accused of running a cult for his own advantage. There is no evidence of this and he compares favourably with most of the New Age gurus.

Conclusion

While none of these communities lasted more than a few years, and, except for Waipu, have left no lasting heritage, they reflect an impulse to utopia that is central to the New Zealand experience and is given lasting expression in the twentieth and twenty-first centuries. And these communities and proposals anticipate most of the themes, both religious and secular, that later communities reflect.

Notes

1 Parts of this chapter have been previously published in Sargent (2001b) and is reprinted with the permission of *Utopian Studies*.
2 Another family, familiar with the Ruskin Community in the United States, in 1898 discussed the possibility of establishing communities in New Zealand (Lovell-Smith, 53).
3 There is material on the Clarionites in the Ranstead Papers at the Alexander Turnbull Library, and they are mentioned in Eric Beardsley's novel *Blackball 08* (1984). Some additional information can be found in Edge, who was the son of a Clarion settler.
4 The Canterbury Museum holds a number of postcards and other illustrations of Wainoni, mostly from the period after the community, which demonstrate that the grounds were well developed and appear quite luxurious.
5 Cooperative housekeeping was very popular in a number of countries at the time of the Wainoni experiment. See Hayden (1984) and Pearson (1988).
6 The history and rituals of the Golden Dawn are beyond the scope of this book. See Ellwood (1993), 156–84 on the background to the Golden Dawn and a discussion of the Havelock Work within the context of New Zealand's alternative religions. See Regardie and Zalewski on the rituals.
7 An essay by Anna Stout (1858–1931) in a later issue of *The Forerunner* was on cooperative housekeeping.
8 There are somewhere between eight and 20 retreat centres in New Zealand at present. They are generally set up as charitable trusts and are not profit making. Some advertise themselves in ways that sound like holiday camps; others, like Tauhara, have extensive programs, with some arranged by the centre and others arranged by outsiders. Most of them suggest some sort of New Age or spiritual purpose.
9 A small collection of materials from the School are in the Beaglehole Room at Victoria University of Wellington Library, and the proceeds from selling Peloha (to Weleda, a manufacturer of herbal remedies and homeopathic medicine) have endowed scholarships at Victoria and at the Hohepa School, one of the many activities of the followers of Rudolf Steiner. So far, the only study of Radiant Living is the research essay by Stace, and we thank her for giving Sargent a copy. While Sargent has read the materials deposited at Victoria, most of what is said here is based on Stace's essay.
10 Stace's interest in Radiant Living came from learning that Sir Edmund Hilary's family had been deeply involved in it and that he saw it as a significant influence in his life.

Chapter 4

The Twentieth Century: Beeville, James K. Baxter and the Ohu Movement

Introduction

This chapter is concerned to tell the story of three key contributors to the history of New Zealand's communal experiments. All are precursors of those we visit in later chapters, but without these experiments, those of today would not exist in the way they do. The first is the now largely forgotten community of Beeville, which was founded sometime in the 1920s or early 1930s and which lasted for over 40 years as a secular community. This extraordinary community has been influential in many ways on New Zealand's communal history. It is the direct forerunner of one of the country's best-known communities, Wilderland, and inspired many others. It also challenges the conventions of much of the scholarship on intentional communities. The second is James K. Baxter, the New Zealand poet who founded three communities and whose work remains an important influence in the communal movement today. The third is the Ohu Movement, in which the national government sponsored the foundation of intentional communities. The story of this extraordinary experiment tells us much about the dreams and reality of 'top-down' utopianism.

Beeville

Beeville was once well known in New Zealand and among radicals in Britain and North America. It was an anarchist commune that survived for forty years in almost constant conflict with the government of New Zealand. Beeville was vegetarian in a country of meat eaters and pacifist in a country with a horrendous record of treating its war objectors. Beeville had an immense impact on the counter culture movement in New Zealand by being visited by most of the people who became important in that movement.

The early history of the community is obscure because it grew out of an extended family and was initially based on a honey business run by one man and his immediate family. The beekeeping business began in 1927, and, although the most commonly used date for its origins as a community is 1933, some members used 1927 as the beginning of the community. The community, then known as Livelle to some of its members, was wound up in 1972 or 1973. Beeville was legally recognised as a community in 1956, when a Trust Deed was signed, but it had already existed as a functioning entity with private rather than communal property for about 20 years.

Although the names and specific issues differ, the history of Beeville seems at times to be a run through of the history of Hippie communalism before it was first thought of. The interest in Eastern religions, the resistance to conscription, the attitudes toward sexuality, and the practice of vegetarianism, all part of the Hippie milieu, were part of Beeville 20 to 30 years before the first Hippie commune.

Beeville was a secular community that managed to survive and flourish for many years without a formal governmental structure. Much of the best known literature on communalism suggests that this is impossible because longevity is supposed to require the two main structures Beeville was missing, religion and government. The closest parallel is a community in the United States called Modern Times that faded out of existence after a substantial life but was never as cohesive as Beeville (see Wunderlich). How Beeville managed to achieve what no other community has achieved is one of our concerns here.

A preliminary hypothesis is possible. Beeville had four factors that helped hold it together: 1) family ties, although these seemed as often divisive as unifying; 2) the involvement of individuals with undoubted charisma; 3) a shared, if vague spirituality; and 4) common political goals. In what follows, we test those hypotheses by examining the history of Beeville, its political, economic and social structures, and its involvement with the outside world, primarily through its extensive history of war resistance.[1]

At times Beeville seems more like the story of one remarkable family than the story of an unusual experiment in communal living, but it is clearly both.

The first great crisis for Beeville was brought about by the publication of a story about Beeville in the July 1948 issue of *Pix* that was reprinted around the world. The emphasis in the story was on 'free love', and the story brought both condemnation and inquiries about joining. Raymond E. Hansen, one of the founders, wrote two pages of corrections to the story, which *Pix* did not print, but most of these corrections were matters of detail rather than substance. The *Pix* article attracted people to the community who did not accept the general live and let live attitude of Beeville, and who brought about deep divisions within the community, some other members of Beeville left when the people recruited through the *Pix* article left.

Beeville members tended to a vague spirituality that derived, in some cases, from an early interest in India, generated by the Indian resistance movement, and Gandhi in particular. In Ray's case, this was generalised and temporarily found expression in support of the Theosophical Society. He resigned in 1935 protesting against growing authoritarian tendencies but remained a defender of Madame Blavatsky (1831–91). He had a more permanent enthusiasm for Krishnamurti (1895–1986), who he saw as enunciating the principles on which Beeville was built (on Theosophy and Krishnamurti in New Zealand, see Ellwood). As Ray wrote in 1957, 'As Krishnamurti sees it, our liberation must come from within, through self-awareness which disposes of authority and involves no interference with or influencing of anyone' (letter dated 26 March 1957. *The Word* [June 1957], 89). But even for Ray the dimension of spirituality remains vague, as can be seen in his poem 'Life and Religion (The Challenge)', which never mentions religion (Raymond E. Hansen Papers, Alexander Turnbull Library, ARC 84–204 Box 2).

Throughout World War II, the war in Korea, and the Vietnam War, members of Beeville were regularly jailed for refusing military service. Although there were exceptions, given the historical treatment of war resistors, they were relatively well treated, mostly being fined or jailed for short periods.

The Beeville resistance can be dated to the early 1930s, when Ray began to contribute letters to the editor of the *Waikato Times* opposing war, conscription, military service and many, many other topics. In 1942, Ray was called up and returned his notice. He was scheduled for a medical examination and refused to attend. He agreed to attend a second medical examination, passed, and was ordered to report to camp. He refused. Of his seven brothers, six were similarly upsetting the authorities by refusing to serve, refusing to do alternative service in lieu of military service, refusing to take up positions assigned outside the military to help the war effort, refusing to pay war taxes and refusing to provide farm produce to the war effort or even farm records to the ministry in charge of food distribution. In addition, they helped one brother escape from the Waikune Prison Camp. They were frequently fined, which they generally refused to pay, and they all spent long or short terms in prison. By 1946, Harold Hansen had been in prison for almost four years and Owen Hansen had been in prison three and a half years, including four months in solitary confinement.

Ray Hansen was ultimately given a deferment because he was the father of a large family, a farmer, the local school bus driver, ran the only grocery store for miles around, ran the major farm contracting service in the area and, as a result, owned the machinery other farmers needed. Both the Master Grocers Association and the Farmers' Union testified, undoubtedly quite reluctantly, that requiring him to serve or sending him to prison would cause serious local problems.

In 1944, Ray Hansen paid his taxes but noted his opposition to the National Security Tax. The Commissioner of Taxes, undoubtedly to Ray's amazement, responded, fine, we'll credit all your taxes to a different account. After that Ray refused to pay at all and later he refused to file a return. Part of the reason for this action was an attempt to get Beeville recognised as a collective entity that would be taxed as such rather than have the individual members pay taxes. As he wrote to the Crown Solicitor in April 1948:

> It has been made clear to the Commissioner [of Taxes] by our Community that I have no individual income, the only income involved being a communal one. (*The Word* [September 1948]: 139)

At times the community filed its taxes in this form.

The Beeville war resistance gained the community a great deal of local notoriety, and since Ray sent long letters and the legal documents to *The Word*, published in Glasgow by Guy Aldred (1886–1963), the community became well known in some radical circles outside New Zealand. The publicity attracted potential members to the community with, as before, mixed results.

Beeville was an interesting combination of individual initiative and community cooperation because the Beeville economy depended for most of its existence on the initiative and hard work of members who developed businesses with community resources and community labour. The bees were the basis of the Beeville economy. The honey operation was a major source of community funds throughout its entire existence. Other farm produce provided food for the Beeville tables and, together with some of the honey, sold at a roadside stand and provided additional seasonal income. At times a store was run, there was a farm contracting business and farm machinery repair. In the early 1950s two members, Lucien and Francis, the eldest sons of Ray, began to produce vibrated, reinforced concrete posts and these became a significant source of income.

The distribution of income was initially based on a common purse, with certain large expenditures, such as cars, being purchased for the community as a whole. At times, though, it became necessary to distribute income on a set basis. Beeville was never rich or poor, but it provided its members with a reasonable standard of living that compared quite well with those of its neighbours. But the Beeville economy clearly depended on the hard work and skills of its members, and, as have other communities, it periodically had 'free rider' problems, members who wanted to consume without contributing. And here, as later at Riverside, there were even members who disparaged those who worked hard while happy to live off that hard work.

The system of making decisions at Beeville is not clear. The assumption is that decisions were consensual, but the frequency of factional infighting makes it clear that this did not always work. It is also clear that to a large extent individuals made their own decisions without reference to the community. But large expenditures of money, the establishment of a school, the construction of new buildings, etc. required community decision-making. And one gets the impression that Beeville was unable to develop an effective system of resolving conflicts. At the same time, Beeville functioned as a community for 40 years, so the infighting and factionalism is obviously only a small part of the story. Conflicts were resolved, but they sometimes threatened the existence of the community before the resolution was achieved.

Any group of anarchists is likely to have problems with sending their children to local schools and being pacifists is unlikely to make it easier. In 1963, one of the Hansen children was harassed by both other pupils and teachers for refusing to take part in cadet training. The community's efforts around that time to establish a primary school undoubtedly reflects both the education their children were receiving and their treatment in the schools.

Anarchist theories of education were among the recognised contributions of anarchism and educational theorists like Paulo Freire (1921–97) and A.S. Neill were already well known (see Freire and Neill).

In January 1964 *The Waikato Times* ran a front-page story headlined '"Freedom" School Is Seeking Recognition, But No Finance' about the attempts by Beeville to establish a school at the community. It was clear that the lack of interest in public finance was a major factor in the generally positive tone of the article.

Dan Hansen wrote an essay entitled 'A Community School' which states that in the winter of 1962 the community tried an experiment to see if they could run a school at the community. He then goes on to illustrate the education they have in mind, an education favoured by anarchists that tries to avoid the distinction between schooling and life.

The plans to apply anarchist theories of education to a specific community rarely gets below the level of generalisation, but a few striking points are made, and some examples of the experiment are given that demonstrate the connection of Beeville to anarchist theories of education and probably caused problems with the authorities.

The document stresses the need children have for security and belonging and notes that the community setting provides them, argues that discipline is not needed if the teacher gains the respect of the students, and emphasises that the school will use what the jargon now calls 'experiential learning' to embed learning in the lived experiences of the child and relate education to the occupations found within the community.

In addition, the school will ensure that the pupils get sufficient exercise; eat well and learn about the need for a good diet (a vegetarian diet is specified); are introduced to the culture available in the area, including Maori culture; learn about sexual love and learn to live peacefully. Many of the points were not designed to win the support of educational bureaucrats, but they did get approval for the school, and it opened 4 February 1964 taking pupils up to age thirteen. Beeville was wound up in 1973, and in the process it became a very different community with decisions made by majority rule, lawyers involved and hurt feelings all around.

But Beeville gave rise to other communities both directly and indirectly. Directly Beeville gave rise to Wilderland, still in existence as we write in 2004, founded by Dan and Edith Hansen. And indirectly Beeville and Wilderland gave rise to the whole New Zealand communal movement of the 1970s; it is hard to identify anyone active in that movement who had not passed through or been influenced by Beeville's successes and failures. The only real exceptions being Riverside, founded in 1938 and Centrepoint, founded in 1978 and coming out of a very different tradition imported from the United States.

Thus, Beeville is a remarkable community whether taken in the New Zealand context or in the context of the worldwide intentional community movement. Beeville's history may raise more questions than it answers, but they are the questions basic to our understanding of the movement. What are the defining parameters of an intentional community? What mechanisms, personal and social, hold a community together and pull it apart? But it does conclusively answer one question in the affirmative that many students of the movement have answered in the negative, an anarchist community can succeed for many years, whatever ones definition of success.

James K. Baxter and Jerusalem

James K. Baxter (1926–72), who became known as Hemi, the Maori form of his first name, was the best known New Zealand poet and was affiliated with a number of short-lived communes, most notably Jerusalem (Hiruharama in Maori). None of the communities, including Jerusalem, were important as communities, but they and Baxter played a unique role symbolically in the development of the New Zealand counter culture.

Baxter was an erratically outstanding poet, a significant social critic, a playwright and literary critic, an iconoclast who much enjoyed upsetting strait-laced New Zealanders, an alcoholic, a convert to Roman Catholicism and a guru to many young people, including, particularly, those in the New Zealand drug culture (see his 'The Ballad of the Junkies and the Fuzz'). He was also a symbol of an emerging freer sexuality in New Zealand. Baxter, the iconoclast, became a cultural icon.

Baxter published his first volumes of poetry at age eighteen and was recognised as a major new talent early in life. His alcoholism also appeared early and for many years he dropped in and out of university and jobs; *The Dictionary of New Zealand Biography* describes him as a 'poet, postman, teacher, dramatist, writer, social critic'.

At times, it seemed that a commune formed around Baxter every time he settled in one place for a few days, but he was most closely associated with three communities. The first community, No. 7 Boyle Crescent, was a short-lived urban community in Auckland and served as a "safe house" for runaway youth and drug addicts. The second and most important was Jerusalem, where Baxter made two attempts to meld Maori values and his Roman Catholicism. The third, 26 MacDonald Crescent in Wellington, another short-lived urban commune, was intended to provide shelter for homeless youth and existed briefly between the two Jerusalems.

All three of the Baxter communities illustrate the strengths and weaknesses of an open community, in which everyone was welcome. The great strength of such communities is that they provide temporary refuge for those in need. The weaknesses include the constant turnover that makes it difficult to finish any project and the fact that they attract, among others, seriously dysfunctional or damaged people. Baxter certainly attracted the latter and was quite happy to do so. But, as a result, it is hardly surprising that the communities were short-lived.

In Baxter's 'Elegy for Boyle Crescent', he notes that the house had been trashed by the police so that it looked like a drug house in the photographs that they took, but he remembered it as a house where 'the junkies loved one another'. He presents Boyle Crescent as a completely open commune where anyone could crash whenever they wanted and would be accepted by the other 'members' of the community. There was not, of course, any formal structure or membership, just whoever happened to be there at any given time. Rent was paid by whoever happened to have the money to pay it when it was due and someone always did. Boyle Crescent lasted about six months in 1969. After the police trashed the house, the site was bulldozed.

26 Macdonald Crescent was a squat and lasted only six weeks in 1971. It was intended as a safe house for homeless youth but included alcoholics, drug addicts and students. The house, which Baxter described as rat infested, is in an area where most houses have been broken up into rooms or flats for students near Victoria University and still stands.

The most important Baxter-related community was Jerusalem, which existed in two phases, from 1969 to 1971 (when it was closed down) and again in 1972. When Baxter died, the heart went out of Jerusalem, and, although the community continued for some time, it was not a functioning community for most of that period.

Jerusalem suited Baxter's desire to combine his Roman Catholicism with Maori values because the site included a Maori settlement with a marae and a church, convent and presbytery. It had been the first mission station of Mother Mary Joseph Aubert (1835–1926), who established the Sisters of Compassion, the first Roman Catholic female religious organisation founded in New Zealand, at Jerusalem.

The reality did not live up to Baxter's hopes, in part because he was an attraction in himself and Jerusalem was flooded with people who wanted to be associated with him but did not necessarily want to participate in a community. In addition, many of the people who came to Jerusalem were insensitive to the values of both the Maori, who owned most of the land and buildings and allowed the community to use them rent-free, and the nuns who allowed Baxter to use a cottage they owned. In addition, the local farmers were unhappy at the idea of having the community in their midst, a problem repeated frequently as the New Zealand communal movement grew. Baxter noted that:

> The County Council are unhappy about our standard of living, our crowded lodgings and the dilapidation of our buildings. How can we be poor, though, and never do without kai [food]? How can we exercise the virtue of manuhiritanga, unlimited hospitality to the guest and stranger, and not be crowded quite often? What is wrong with a broken house, if it can keep the rain out? (*Jerusalem Daybook*, 22)

Mike Minehan, who was a long term member of the community and had a child by Baxter that was conceived at Jerusalem, confirms Baxter's comments about the general balance of the community, but emphasises that the local Maori found the way of life – the lack of elementary cleanliness in particular

– unacceptable (Minehan, 31). Minehan also notes that Baxter misrepresented Jerusalem to the headquarters of the Sisters of Compassion, suggesting that there was little or no drug use or promiscuity (Minehan, 45–47).

Baxter made no real effort to establish a functioning community at Jerusalem. He left frequently, which, since he was the glue that held people together, disrupted whatever communal patterns existed. Baxter contended that he was not the leader of Jerusalem and that decisions were made collectively, but while there was undoubtedly consultation on various issues, Baxter, in a real sense, *was* Jerusalem.

The large number of short stay visitors both irritated the neighbours and those, a core of about 25, who hoped to establish something that would last. As a result, the community was asked to leave. As Baxter put it:

> The main problems of the Jerusalem community are not community problems. To put it bluntly, we get along all right. We eat, drink, work, sleep, play the guitar, pay our bills and don't quarrel. All our main problems come from outside. (*Jerusalem Daybook*, 24)

Baxter went to Wellington to stay with his family and became involved in the MacDonald Crescent project. He returned to Jerusalem under an agreement that limited the size of the community. But, again, he did not stay and was not at Jerusalem when he died.

During the first Jerusalem, Baxter wrote the poems published as *Jerusalem Sonnets*, which generally reflect the period before many people gathered around him. He also wrote *Jerusalem Daybook*, which consists of prose and poetry about Jerusalem. During the second Jerusalem, he wrote those published as *Autumn Testament*, which includes a poem explaining to his wife why he left her to return to Jerusalem, the 48 sonnets of 'Autumn Testament', which reflect on his life at the second Jerusalem and other material. These books have been inspirational to the founders of intentional communities across the country and copies can be found on private bookshelves and in the libraries of many communities today.

Baxter practised voluntary poverty, saying 'Why do I go barefoot? Why do I have long hair and a beard? Why do I wear old clothes till they become unwearable? ... Poverty is the actual answer. All men are required by God to have a spirit of poverty' and went on to say that God had called upon him to be 'visibly poor – to do without everything you can do without ...' (*Jerusalem Daybook*, 16). And the money Baxter earned or was given while at Jerusalem, he contended, was not his but belonged to all of the members of the community. In this, he was following in the tradition of monasticism.

But Baxter also did without needed health care and died young. He is buried at Jerusalem and for some years his grave was a site of pilgrimage for those to whom he had been a guru. At various times local Maori charged to allow anyone to visit the gravesite, although this was apparently the result of individual enterprise rather than policy.

One community grew out of Jerusalem, Reef Point, which continued the policy of absolute openness from 1971 to 1974 at the community near Kaitaia. In 1974, they established a house in Takanini while they waited for approval to establish a community on 240 acres of Crown Land in the Taranaki area under the ohu scheme. It broke up in 1974 (on Reef Point, see Bryan; Tim Jones 45–56; and Robertson). Baxter remains an inspirational figure.

The Ohu Movement[2]

The most important communal movement in New Zealand developed in the third quarter of the twentieth century, and particularly at the end of that period, in the mid-1970s. At that time, influenced by both European and North American communal experiments and by a growing recognition of the long tradition of Maori communalism in New Zealand, many New Zealanders considered the possibility of communal living, and a substantial number joined or formed communities.

And, remarkably, the New Zealand government established a program intended to provide public land to people wanting to form communes. The story of this program is one of enthusiasm and high hopes followed by rapid disillusionment, a story of idealism against bureaucracy, naiveté against political realities, weakness against power. But the idealistic, naive and weak were not easily defeated, and a few communities were established and one lasted over 25 years.

According to an official brochure:

> The first indication that the Government was considering a scheme of this nature came in August 1973, when the Minister of Lands [in the Labour government], Hon. Matiu Rata [1934–97], said he was considering the possibility of allowing young people to lease Crown land so they could try living off the land in a communal organisation away from the noise and pace of the city. (*Ohu: Alternative Lifestyle Communities*, 5)

All published reports suggest that the idea originated with either Prime Minister Norman Kirk (1923-74) or Rata. Kirk made the first statement that led to the establishment of the scheme in an interview with the *Australian Financial Review*, in which he referred to the Israeli kibbutz as a possible model for New Zealand. At this early point, Kirk seems to have a specific vision:

> He says he intends to start off with three kibbutzim into which younger New Zealanders could go for a period as a means of contributing with their own hands and sweat to the building of a nation. (Peter Robinson, 2)

Kirk's vision of these communities as a temporary stage in the lives of young New Zealanders got lost as the idea developed, but it is closer to the reality of most communities than the dream of a permanent membership that was at the base of many of the actual proposals that the idea brought forth.

Young people greeted the announcement with great enthusiasm. A meeting attended by over 100 people was called at Elsdon, Porirua, just north of Wellington, on 13 February 1974; invited to the meeting were all the people who had written to the Prime Minister after his initial announcement and most of the people who attended were already involved in communal experiments somewhere in the country. At the meeting Arthur Faulkner is reported to have said that it was the government's job:

> ... to find ways of helping. We may not agree with the way you want us to help but we don't say no. We say no you can't do that but you can do this. That's the sort of approach that we are making to it. Since I will probably be involved, and my four officials, we will do the very level best we can. On the other hand we must avoid appearing to give you a preference. It is just not on politically, not at all. ('Transcript')

Although people attending do not remember this, a report of the meeting states that it was announced that six to eight sites ranging in size from about 700 to 2,800 acres had already been identified as available (ibid.). Given the later history, this seems unlikely, but, if true, it would have provided a solid basis for the disillusionment when sites turned out to be hard to find.

If those hoping to establish communities had known the actual situation, they might have given up. On 7 March, Margaret Hayward wrote:

> Arthur Faulkner, still Acting Minister of Lands, has announced that the proposed communes will be called 'Ohu' – a Maori word meaning to achieve something 'by means of friendly help and work'. (Hayward, 223)[3]

> But press officer Peter Kelsey, who has transferred from our office to work on the scheme, of which he is an enthusiastic advocate, tells me the Lands and Survey Department has decided that applicants should have only land designated as suitable for nothing else, 'and that's pretty bad land to go on to'. (223)

The Ohu scheme appears to be a classic case of an idea coming from the top levels of government and being almost immediately undermined by the bureaucracy. Although there is evidence that Faulkner and Rata later tried to overcome this situation, at this point, four months after its initial announcement, the Department of Lands and Survey deliberately killed the Ohu scheme.

Still, the enthusiastic people anxious to join the scheme did not know that their hopes had already been rendered virtually impossible, supporters worked hard to make the scheme work, and they met with such enthusiasm and support from the target community that some things happened despite Lands and Surveys. As a result, the bureaucracy went through the motions of supporting policy while making sure that the communities failed, and the fact that one lasted so long is testimony to the strength of the feeling the scheme touched.

One community, Sunburst on the Coromandel Peninsula got started before any rules were laid down. The people who formed the community had been together in a loose group in the Auckland area and then in the Hokianga area where they thought they had found land on which to settle.

The land on which the Sunburst Community was established was:

> ... on the other side of the [Rangihau] river from the road and access [in 1975] is by foot ... A neighbouring farmer cut a bulldozer track across the river and up the hill. He is going to be repaid with labour. There are five gardens laid out (the heavy scrub had to be cleared first) and a temporary dwelling for the family. Everything has had to be carved out of the bush. They have a license to use 80 hectares (200 acres) for a year. (McSporran)

At that time, they were working on improvements and building housing designed to meet the local building code.

Sunburst lasted about six years; as with most such communities, it is difficult to find out either what happened to it or when it happened. All the evidence suggests that like so many others it just faded away. In fact, at one point everyone returned to Auckland and appeared to have abandoned the community; they returned later and restarted their attempts to build it, and they succeeded for a few years more.

The members of Sunburst found their own land but the availability of land under the scheme became an important issue. But when the district land offices were asked to produce lists of available land, virtually none had any. When this was said to be still unacceptable, a few district offices produced short lists. When this was said to be unacceptable and the offices were required to produce lists of all unoccupied public lands in their areas, it turned out that there was land available in all districts. But this resistance by the district offices demonstrates that no one had done the work needed to get support for the scheme from within the bureaucracy. The later requirement that groups looking for land work directly with the district offices that had previously said there was no appropriate land set the stage for obstruction, delay and frustration, which was precisely what happened.

Any dwellings built must satisfy local building codes. While this did not pose a problem for some, it clearly undermined the desire for other groups to establish an alternative life style. According to *Mushroom* (the main New Zealand alternative lifestyles magazine), the government wrote to the Counties Association telling it that Ohu would have '... to meet all existing by-laws and regulations of the local bodies concerned' ('Ohu' 1974). *Mushroom* adds that it is expected the central government would assist the groups in dealing with 'overly severe' applications of the rules. The belief in this intent is regularly repeated and could be mere wishful thinking, but there is some evidence that in the initial stages, some mediation was forthcoming, and Peter Kelsey accompanied some groups to their meetings with local bodies, but that did not last.

The Ohu Advisory Board described the proposals that came in as follows:

> Most groups seek, and offer, an alternative, largely self-reliant, life style on the land. They are interested in organic agricultural methods and the recycling of materials, in alternative technology and the decentralised generation of energy by non-pollutive methods. Groups are interested in the communal sharing of amenities and equipment, and in experimental social relationships. They are concerned about education and the need to look for and explore alternatives in this sphere, and they are interested in the exploration of alternative forms of architecture, uses of materials, forms of construction and methods of design. (*Ohu*, 3)

Reviewing a substantial number of the actual proposals illustrates that this is a fairly accurate overview, but it misses some of the flavour of the times and the diversity of the groups involved.

One constant theme in the proposals is the desire to return to the land and lead a simple life and, if possible, a self-sufficient life. Many of the groups had no explicit desire beyond this; they had no grand scheme, no formal model of how to achieve the good life, because that good life consisted of a simple, self-sufficient life on the land. This desire is very close to that of most of the original colonists. Those colonists would not have thought of their desire as including simplicity, but they wanted land and the ability to live off the land, and so did their descendants a hundred years later.

There were exceptions to this description, exceptions that were mostly based on religion. These groups ranged from the desire of two groups to continue the vision of James K. Baxter at Jerusalem and combine Roman Catholicism with Maori values to westernised Buddhism to a vague New Age spirituality.

Most proposals stressed the desire to create communities that were in harmony with nature. For example, the Papatuanuku Ohu listed as its first principal 'Living in harmony with Nature and each other, on an organic and ecologically sound basis' ('Proposal for Papatuanuku Ohu'). They found land near Greymouth but were never able to settle on it.

Since a number of the names of proposed groups changed throughout the process of approval, it is often difficult to be certain how the groups that got established and the proposals match, but one group that got established on land where we have the original proposal is the Earth Extract Ohu. (The proposal has the best presentation and includes some cartoons.) At the time of the proposal the group was living together in Devonport and included three architects, a chemical engineer, a teacher, an artist, a photographer and an actor. All were under 25. There were also three members who were in the process of opening a restaurant in Christchurch, the largest city on the South Island, and planned to join the Ohu in about a year.

The proposal included a suggestion that the community would use environmental and energy sensitive building techniques (these are spelled out in great detail), organic agriculture for both self-sufficiency and sale, including fruit and nut orchards. They also suggest that they would, in the future, open a school.

Initially Earth Extract, established in the north of the North Island, succeeded through support from members working in Auckland who hoped to be able to later move onto the land. But it ran into financial problems and, in 1979, it asked the Riverside Community for a loan to help it through a crisis. Because Riverside had spent all the money it had set aside for such loans, no loan was forthcoming, but the community was able to survive.

In 1981 a study of communities in New Zealand reported on Earth Extract, 'It is not yet possible to live off the land – it is not very fertile and would require high expenditure to develop. Until the size of the group increases and some income earning project from the land is developed, there is little prospect of being self-sufficient' (*A Guide to Co-ops*, 41). The community was actively involved in the local community and appears to have been accepted by that community. But by 1981 only one of the original members was left on the land and members living in Auckland were still supporting it.

The longest lived commune established under the Ohu scheme was the Ahu Ahu Ohu, on the Ahu Ahu River, a tributary of Wanganui River, in an isolated area on the east of the North Island. At first access involved rowing across the Wanganui River and walking along a bush track for 50 minutes. When it celebrated its 21st year on the land, it was noted that:

> … over the years and with hundreds of hours of hard slog we how have a 2m track capable of taking all three and four wheeled terrain vehicles with small trailers. (Ahu Ahu Ohu, 1992 Information Sheet)

The Ahu Ahu Ohu was created over the years through the expenditure of great effort. Most buildings were constructed from materials obtained by demolishing buildings and having it flown in by helicopter. Given the effort, the tragedy of fire and flood that took buildings and, repeatedly, the track to the Ohu, Ahu Ahu was particularly stressful. As a result, there was significant turnover; the last of the original members left in 1989. And while this community continued for at least another few years it, now appears to be defunct.

Norman Kirk died in 1974, and although the Ohu were never the high priority for him that some Ohu aspirants believed, it was his policy initiative and, without him, it became less important. Even if the Labour Party had won the 1975 election, the Ohu movement would probably have died, but the National Party won. Prior to the election, the National Party announced its support for the Ohu scheme, but after the election it wound up the Advisory Committee, removed Peter Kelsey, and shifted all authority to Lands and Surveys, thus removing any input from people wanting land or already living in communes. Acceptability to the local community was added as one of the criteria for approval, and rather than being set aside for Ohu, any land available had to be publicly advertised and made available to anyone.

In 1974 *Mushroom* published a letter from the Waimea Ohu, one that never got land. It reads in part:

> We have made three applications for sites on the West Coast north of Westport, two of which have been turned down and the third is still in the pipeline (although we don't hold too much hope). It has taken almost 18 months to get this far and as many of you probably know by now it is hard to keep a large group enthusiastic for that length of time when they could be pursuing other ways of getting some land. ('Ohu Where To Now?')

A letter provided by a member of the Papatuanuku Ohu notes that the Grey County Council deliberately delayed their decision until the same day that the Town and Country Planning Appeal Board ended its six month sitting in Greymouth, thus forcing the Ohu to wait another six months before their appeal could be heard (undated letter about the Papatuanuku. Copy held by authors). Although they believed that they could win the appeal, the Ohu did not survive the extra six months.

Delay was clearly a tactic to defeat the scheme. As was noted in the next issue of *Mushroom*:

> ... the Ohu scheme seems to have become much less the great hope that it once was; mainly through the amount of time involved (can be up to 2–3 years), the energy in writing endless letters to bureaucrats and the overall uncertainties as to whether the groups will gain the land they seek anyway. ('Ohu' 1976)

The bureaucrats had won. It had taken only two years to deliberately destroy the dreams of hundreds of well-meaning if naive young people.

Ohu members were not all agreed on what they wanted to achieve, and the failure to resolve these differences in advance brought tension and potential failure. For example, some people were interested in creating viable farms and even communities that would last and provide a basis for a different way of life while others wanted to drop out and live as simply as possible on the land.

The Ohu movement was unusual for its time period. Most governments, including that of New Zealand, were regularly in conflict, often violently, with the young people of the country. The vision of Norman Kirk and Matiu Rata, if indeed they were the scheme's progenitors, was to create a basis of trust and cooperation between people interested in creating a different way of life on the land and government. The Ohu movement failed utterly to achieve that goal because the government that proposed it never gained the support of the bureaucracies that were supposed to make it work. The result was greater not less disillusionment with government.

Conclusion

Each of the figures discussed in this chapter have contributed to New Zealand's history as a utopia. Hundreds of people visited Beeville during its lifetime and these include people who now live in intentional communities, such as Riverside, as well as people who live in the wider society. It was an extraordinary experiment in alternative living. Its values could not have contrasted more strongly with the dominant values of New Zealand society at the time. It was critical of much of what New Zealand then stood for and yet it flourished. This tells us something of both the community's tenacity and of the apparent tolerance of wider New Zealand society.

James Baxter remains, for many, an inspirational figure. His poetry can be found on bedside tables and bookshelves in many of New Zealand's intentional communities today. He is an interesting figure, as idealistic as he was flawed, like many utopians, and his story tells us much about charisma, leaders and followers. People found him inspiring and wanted to follow his path, he identified a gap in their lives and they wanted it filled. Yet he never consistently led – he would not and did not take responsibility for the people who followed him, leaving Jerusalem to fend for itself on more than one occasion as we have seen. He was an interesting and paradoxical leader towards utopia. Rather than provide a blueprint for perfection his poems and writings gestured towards a better way. Rather than leading a community, he founded one and left it.

The Ohu Movement is, quite simply, unique. We use this word with caution and are aware that there have been state funded cooperative experiments in the past, but none like this one. It was secular, pragmatic and aimed to resolve a particular set of problems connected with urban poverty and housing. It seemed to provide an opportunity of a lifetime to those people who wanted to withdraw from society and live differently. As we have seen, it did not work. The land was poor and the scheme seems to have been was sabotaged by those who administered it. However, once again, it helps us to begin to understand something about New Zealand and utopia. This country is, on the whole, socially conservative, and yet the state, for a while, funded the most extraordinary and radical experiment in communal living.

We cannot say quite why this is so, but we have observed something of this attitude, which is perhaps best described as indifferent toleration. During a pilot study for this book, for instance, Sargisson spent a month on the Coromandel Peninsula talking to people who live in intentional communities as well as people who live and work nearby. Attitudes towards the communities were mixed but very few people expressed pure hostility towards them. Conversations with farmers, workers in the local sawmill, café, domestic workers, bus drivers, MPs and fishermen and women all yielded the same kind of response – a shrug and something along the lines of – 'Well, they don't cause any harm and so I suppose they're all right'. Part of this, we think, can be attributed to the relatively low population in New Zealand. There has been sufficient space for people to experiment without encroaching on other people's territory. Also, people are quite likely to know somebody who has lived in an intentional community. Another factor, we think, is the combined effect of all of the historical movements and figures discussed in the last two chapters. People have been trying alternatives in New Zealand for a long time and many have been seen to work without threatening the wider social fabric.

Notes

1   There is one major problem for the student of Beeville. Overwhelmingly the documentary evidence is found in the papers of one man, Raymond Ernest Hansen (these papers are held at the Alexander Turnbull Library, Wellington, New Zealand, ARC 84–204), the original beekeeper or from negative press stories that rarely even pretended to be objective. While the papers include material from other individuals, much of the evidence comes from the perspective of this one man. This is particularly important during the various internal disputes that the community periodically faced, most notably during the final dispute that ended the community.

2   An early version of this essay was published as Lyman Tower Sargent, 'The Ohu Movement', *New Zealand Studies* 6.3 (November 1996), 18–22. A much expanded version was published as Sargent, 'The Ohu Movement in New Zealand: An Experiment in Government Sponsorship of Communal Living in the 1970s', *Communal Societies* 19 (1999), 49–65, and this material is used with the permission of *Communal Societies*. Since then papers from the Ohu Advisory Committee have begun to appear at Archives New Zealand (ABWN 6095 W5021 22/5340), although approximately a third of the recorded papers are still missing. Although the new papers produced no substantive changes, this version takes account of this material.

3   The Maori equivalent found was 'Ohu', but early documents refer to the scheme as 'kibbutz-type settlements' and 'community farms'. According to Brian Easton, a member of the Working Party, the word was chosen by the Working Party. There were no Maori members of the Working Party.

Chapter 5

Religious and Spiritual Communities

Introduction

Like secular utopianism, religious utopianism stems from deep personal beliefs and can be linked to worldwide movements for change. Like secular utopianism, it seeks to transform daily lives in the here-and-now and to confront larger issues, such as the meaning of life. However, its sources of inspiration, authority and support are quite different. Whereas secular utopianism relies on human ingenuity, creativity and malleability for much of its world-changing programme, religious utopianism looks to divine sources of inspiration and evokes supra-human authority for its programme of change. This, as we shall see, has had mixed outcomes. One can be the creation of illegitimate authority within a community, which can lead to a routinisation of abusive practices. Another outcome can be the development of high levels of commitment and stability (Kanter 1972).

New Zealand has historically been a site of great religious diversity (Colless and Donovan 1980; Donovan 1996) and is currently home to over twenty religious or spiritual communities. These cover the range of world religions and faiths, such as Christianity (Roman Catholic, Anglican and conservative non-denominational); Buddhism (Theravaden and Mahayanan); and Hare Krishna. They also include communities that belong to what is loosely called 'alternative spirituality' (Ellwood 1993) and which are, in the loosest possible sense, communities of a new age.

Some sections of New Zealand's society are intensely religious, while others are deeply secular, and they appear to co-exist quite peaceably. Most of the intentional communities involved in this chapter are expressions of intense religiosity; here people feel so strongly about their faith, calling or spirituality that they have chosen to live with others who share it. Other sections of New Zealand's society are not religious at all. One oft-cited indicator of this is low church attendance: 11–16 per cent of the population, compared with 40 per cent in the USA and 20 per cent in Australia (Ellwood 1993, 197).

We are concerned in this chapter to afford a glimpse of life inside these communities and to explore their utopian visions. Discussion stems in most cases from first-hand observation by Sargisson and archive work by Sargent as well as review of secondary sources. In a few instances visits were not possible. Examples include communities that had closed prior to commencement of the fieldwork (such as Centrepoint) and communities that are closed to scholars (such as Gloriavale).

Table 5.1   New Zealand's religious and spiritual communities

Name of community	Location	Religious tradition	Denomination or descriptor	Members' gender
Bodhinyanarama Monastery	Stokes Valley, Wellington	Buddhism	Theravada (Thai Forest Tradition)	Male
Carmelites	Halswell Rd, Christchurch	Christian	Roman Catholic	Female
Friends Settlement	Wanganui	Quaker	Quaker Community	Mixed
Gloriavale	Heaphy Rd, Haupiri	Christian	Conservative non-denominational Charismatic	Mixed
Karma Choeling Monastery	Bodhisattva Rd, Kaukapakapa	Buddhism	Mahayana (Tibetan)	Mixed
Marist Brothers	Communities throughout NZ	Christian	Roman Catholic	Male with exception of 1 mixed community
Motukarara Christian Retreat	Fiddlers Rd, Motukaraka	Christian	Charismatic non-denominational	Mixed
New Varshna	Riverhead Highway, Kumeu	Hare Krishna	Hare Krishna	Male

Table 5.1 (cont'd)

Name of community	Location	Religious tradition	Denomination or descriptor	Members' gender
Orama	Karaka Bay, Great Barrier Island	Christian	Non-denominational	Mixed
Sacred Name – Community of	Barbados St, Christchurch	Christian	Anglican	Female
Sisters of Mercy	Throughout NZ	Christian	Roman Catholic	Female
Sisters of Compassion	Throughout NZ	Christian	Roman Catholic	Female
Sisters of Our Lady of the Missions	Throughout NZ	Christian	Roman Catholic	Female
St Brigid's – Community of	Throughout NZ	Christian	Roman Catholic	Female
St Francis – Community of	Auckland	Christian	Anglican	Female
St Francis Friary	Torbay, Auckland	Christian	Anglican	Male
Sunnataram Monastery	Ararimu Valley Road, Kumeu, Auckland	Buddhism	Theravadin	Male
Thien Thai Vietnamese Monastery	Hillside Drive, Upper Hutt	Buddhism	Mahayana (Thai)	Male
Tikoki	Tauranga	Christian	Anglican holistic	Mixed

Table 5.1 (cont'd)

Name of community	Location	Religious tradition	Denomination or descriptor	Members' gender
Borderline communities				
Dharagyey Buddhist Centre	Dunedin	Buddhism	Tibetan esp. Gaden Tradition	Mixed
Mahamudra Centre for Universal Unity	Colville, Coromandel Peninsula	Buddhism	Tibetan	Mixed
Lamb of God	Throughout NZ	Christian	Ecumenical Charismatic (90% Catholic)	Mixed
Lifeway	Snell's Beach Mahurangi Peninsula	Christian	Charismatic	Mixed
Old Believers	South of South Island	Christian	Russian Orthodox	Mixed
Former communities				
Centrepoint	Albany	Alternative	Charismatic Personal Growth	Mixed
Full Gospel Mission	Waipara	Christian	Millenarian	Mixed
Havelock Work (led to Tauhara Retreat Centre)	Havelock North	Theosophy	Golden Dawn	Mixed

Table 5.1 (cont'd)

Name of community	Location	Religious tradition	Denomination or descriptor	Members' gender
Otahuna (founded 1972)	Christchurch	Christian	Catholic	Mixed – families
Radiant Living	Havelock North	Theosophy	Charismatic	Mixed
Te Piringa (1992–96)	Wellington	Christian	Assembly of God	Mixed

Before moving on to discuss the utopias of New Zealand's religious intentional communities, we need to know something more of their collective intent, vision and aims (see Table 5.2).

Three quite different kinds of religious or spiritual community have emerged from this survey. These focus variously on contemplation, social change and personal growth. These are offered as analytical categories, which have been drawn from empirical evidence and shall be used to structure the discussions that follow. Examples of each type of religious community will be offered and these descriptions form the basis for discussions of different forms of utopianism.

Contemplative Religious Communities

Bodhinyanarama Buddhist Monastery

> Primarily, this is a place of monastic residence, and offers training and guidance for those who are interested in exploring and living a monastic life based on moral discipline and wise reflection. The contemplative atmosphere and discipline allows individuals to recognise, investigate and let go of the many manifestations of selfishness which were identified by the Buddha as the cause for human suffering. Emphasis in the monastery is placed on both individual and community practice and finding the balance between self-reliance and the ability to live and work with others. (Bodhinyanarama Guest Leaflet)

Bodhinyanarama community is a Buddhist Monastery in the Theravadin tradition, founded in 1985. This form of Buddhism has its origins in Thailand and Bodhinyanarama is particularly associated with the teachings of a meditation master, Ajahn Chah, who died in the early 1990s. It is a male community that, at the time of my visit in April 2001, had a membership of seven monks (Sangha), of whom five were Bikkhu (ordained monks) or Semanera (novices) and two were Angarika (supplicants).

The community is situated in a 51 hectare reserve of regenerating bush, covering the steep sides of a deep valley. The word Bodhinyanarama means 'Garden of Enlightened Knowing'. The community is close to the small town of Stokes Valley and yet it feels remote. At the centre of the community is an area containing a courtyard, and a room that is bare of furnishing but for an ornate statue of Buddha. This is the main hall, where the community takes its meals. The room is wooden, light and spacious. Slightly to one side of this main area is the community kitchen, which is in a separate building. The kitchen contains basic cooking facilities but cooked meals are not usually prepared here as Bodhinyanarama belongs to the mendicant tradition and, therefore, relies on donations of food from the wider Thai Buddhist community.

Table 5.2 Aims and activities of religious and spiritual communities

Name of community	Aim/vision	Members' main activities
Bodhinyanarama Monastery	Experiencing 'the truth of the way things are'	Contemplation, meditation, work, teaching and fulfilling the needs of NZ's Thai Buddhist population
Carmelites	Cloistered community: separation from the world for the sake of the world	Prayer, contemplation and work
Friends Settlement	Quaker education and lifestyle	Various: work inside and outside community; education centre; communal worship and meetings
Gloriavale	Complete Christian lifestyle	Various: work and worship in an enclosed Christian community
Karma Choeling Monastery	Seek inner balance	Meditation, teachings from Lamas, yoga
Marist Brothers	Education in Roman Catholic tradition and general learning	Youth work, teaching, outreach
Motukarara Christian Retreat	Christian support and nurture for underprivileged and needy	Work: refurbishing community, worship
New Varshna	Proselytise Krishna's message	Meditation, public chanting, vegetarian food preparation, discussing Krishna

Table 5.2 (cont'd)

Name of community	Aim/vision	Members' main activities
Orama	Christian community offering rest, training and retreat	Running retreat centre, prayer, meditation and work in community. Links with Marist Brothers
Sisters of Compassion	Continue the Mission of Christ: serve and respect the disadvantaged	Care of elderly, infirm, handicapped. Links to Maori community
Sacred Name – Community of	Contemplative community	Prayer, worship, work inside the community
Sisters of Mercy	Continue the mission of Christ through schools and other services	Teaching, social work, empowerment of the marginalised
Sisters of Our Lady of the Missions	Continue work of founder Euphrasie: empowering disadvantaged (women, youth, indigenous people's and refugee)	Social work, refuge support, counselling, teaching, mission work, chaplaincy
St Brigid's – Community of	Follow St Brigid: engage in contemporary issues	Social work and support
St Francis – Community of	Continue work of St Francis	Love, joy and humility
St Francis Friary	Continue work of St Francis	Love, joy and humility

Table 5.2 (cont'd)

Name of community	Aim/vision	Members' main activities
Sunnataram Monastery	Theravadin Temple	Meditation
Thien Thai Vietnamese Monastery	Thai Monastery	Meditation
Titoki	Ecumenical Healing Centre	Healing, alternative therapy, spiritual practice
Borderline communities		
Dhargyey Buddhist Centre	Teaching Centre for Tibetan (esp. Gaden Tradition) Buddhism	Teaching
Mahamudra Centre for Universal Unity	Preservation of Mahayana tradition	Various. Meditation, running centre, teaching
Lamb of God evangelism	Promote ecumenicism in accord with teachings of Catholic church	Various. Teaching, worship, pastoral care,
Lifeway	Spread the word of Jesus	Various. Running college, TV station, training God's 'First Wave Army'
Old Believers	Isolation from the world to live simply	Farming, worship

Table 5.2 (cont'd)

Name of community	Aim/vision	Members' main activities
Former communities		
Centrepoint	Follow teachings of Bert Potter and personal growth	Various therapies and practices, work inside community
Full Gospel Mission	Prepare for second coming	Various with a patriarchal enclosed community
Havelock Work (led to Tauhara Retreat)	Education, peace, love and harmony	Not fully communal, Whare Ra
Otahuna	Live in community as early Christians had done	Community-building, ran a farm and, in later years, outreach work
Radiant Living	Follow teachings of Herbert Sutcliffe	Promote physical and mental health
Te Piringa	Live a more Christ-like life	Work with Church organisations. Helping the needy

Up the hill, at some distance from the hall and kitchen, is the temple. Scattered along the hillside are the monks' private dwelling spaces: each has a small wooden hut in which to sleep. Some of the land has been cultivated to gardens but most of it is wild.

This is a spiritual community with the dual aim of a) spiritual enlightenment of the members and b) service to the wider Thai Buddhist community. This service takes the form of spiritual guidance and leadership and the provision of sanctified space. The relationship between the Sangha and the wider Buddhist community is interesting – lay Buddhists give the monks food and provide material sustenance. To give is a privilege. The Sangha provide ritual, blessings (if requested) and other symbolic forms of religiosity as well as practical guidance and teachings.

The word 'Sangha' means 'truth'. To become a monk it is necessary to be an Angarika for at least a year. Angarika have shaven heads and wear white robes and have made a commitment to the rules of the community. They are bound by the daily regime but have not made this a lifetime bond. Semanera and Bikkhu Sangha all wear saffron robes. They follow a disciplined path of contemplation, meditation and poverty and, to an outsider, their lives appear strictly regulated and austere. Ajahn Sucitto (his name means 'He who is already practised in meditation') has been the senior monk at Bodhinyanarama since 1999. The life of the monks is ordered and regulated in such a way as to afford them maximum freedom for contemplation, meditation and spiritual practice. For example, Bikkhu own no personal possessions and may not handle money. They spoke of this as a form of personal and spiritual freedom. The community relies on gifts for sustenance and benefactors include Buddhists throughout New Zealand. Financial transactions are handled by novices or supplicants. If the Sangha travel beyond the community they take with them only their saffron robe and food bowl. They must beg for meals.

The community takes just one main meal a day, in the late morning, and may not eat after noon. This is in order to leave them free for spiritual matters. The Sangha do not prepare food. The daily meal is supplied by a different donor each day, on a prearranged rota that runs up to a year ahead. Food is vegetarian and rituals of blessing and timing are rigorously observed. At the time of my visit, for instance, a Sri Lankan family had brought the food from two hours away across a mountain range. This was clearly a special occasion for them for which the entire family had taken a day off work and school. They requested that the Sangha bless the food and that the 'goodness' of the gift be passed to the father's dead parents. There were about 20 different dishes of vegetarian food – fruit, biscuits and cakes – of which the monks ate but a fraction. The remainder (now blessed) was taken home by the donors.

Physical life at Bodhinyanarama is quite austere. Members may not sit on furniture and so spend their waking lives sitting on the floor or standing. Food intake is minimal, and life is governed by a series of rules or precepts. Guests are asked to observe the same rules as the novices. This includes close observation of the eight precepts that comprise the monastic code of conduct:

1. Harmlessness – not intentionally taking the life of any living creature.
2. Trustworthiness – not taking anything which is not given.
3. Chastity – refraining from sexual activity.
4. Right speech – avoiding false, abusive and malicious speech.
5. Sobriety – not taking any intoxicating drink or drugs (smoking is discouraged).
6. Renunciation – not eating after midday.
7. Restraint – refraining from attending games and shows and from self-adornment (guests are asked to dress modestly and women are asked not to make eye contact with the monks).
8. Alertness – to refrain from overindulgence in sleep.

It also includes adherence to the following timetable. The day begins at 5.15 am with optional chanting and meditation. At 6.30 am domestic chores are conducted, such as sweeping the hall, and at 7 am the community takes a light breakfast. Between 8 and 10.30 am guests undertake work, which is allocated by one of the Sangha (the work master). The main meal of the day is at 10.30 am. This is usually formally offered by the laity to the Sangha. The monks chant a blessing and guests eat either with the monks or in the kitchen. The afternoon is generally free for individual spiritual practice. At 6 pm the community drinks tea. At 7 pm there is chanting and meditation and the day usually ends soon afterwards.

Carmelite Monastery, Christchurch

The Carmelites are a cloistered community of nuns, dedicated to a life of prayer. Part of the larger Carmelite tradition, founded by St Teresa of Avila in 1562, this community was founded in 1933. The aim of the community is to 'embrace the world' in prayer.

> The Carmelite nun lives with Jesus crucified for the salvation of the world, offering herself to him, sharing in the mystery of His death and resurrection, and so playing her part in His redeeming work. (http://www.karmel.at)

The Sisters set themselves apart from the world in order to intercede for its salvation. They 'sit' with the suffering and ecstasy of Jesus better to do this.

The bulk of each day is spent in silent contemplation or work. Life in this enclosed community is timetabled in such a way as to provide support for the challenges that this brings. Each day revolves around seven Divine Offices, beginning at 6 am with Morning Prayer and ending at 9.30 pm with the Office of Readings. Two hours in each day are scheduled for 'recreation', described variously as a chance to talk, laugh, relax and give and receive support. The community earns income from making altar breads, vestments and religious art. They produce food in their gardens and run a small farm.

Full membership of this community involves massive commitment, which severs all prior relationships. It involves several steps and a number of years. The final commitment is a lifelong vow of poverty, chastity and obedience, which are identified as three aspects of a complete surrender of the self. The first step is that of the Postulant, which usually lasts for up to 18 months, at which stage the Postulant becomes Novice and receives a habit. Following at least two years as Novice, they make 'profession' of the vows (of poverty, chastity and obedience) for three years. The only times the sisters see their families during these stages are at the 'profession' (vow) ceremonies. The final vows are binding for life.

Community of the Sacred Name

Founded in 1893, The Community of the Sacred Name is an Anglican convent. It was founded as a mixed active and contemplative community, and at one time sisters worked with the 'wayward women' of the city of Christchurch. Current numbers are low at nine members, some of whom are quite elderly, and so the community is now largely contemplative. Explanations for this included a general decline in Anglican congregations, especially amongst young people (with the exception of Pacific Islanders); and the wide variety of alternative options now open to women in the Anglican Church. The advent of the ordination of women (over 20 years ago in New Zealand), for instance, saw an immediate decline in the number of supplicants.

The community's core values are prayer, Christian vocation and service. Life at the Sacred Name involves high levels of communal interaction, including shared work, meals and the seven daily 'offices' of prayer. All of the Sisters work according to their ability in the house or gardens. When I arrived, for instance, Reverend Mother Judith was cleaning the bathrooms. Full membership involves a series of formal stages that include being Postulant, Novice and Nun. Women must first express an interest and stay in the community for at least a month. At this stage, they are described as Postulants, 'knocking on the door' of the community. The Postulant may then apply to become a Novice. If the Sisters agree (by two-thirds majority), then the Novice is accepted. The process can take many years and some never proceed to take the full vows. For example, Sister Zoe, who had spent 15 of her years at the community as Reverend Mother, had been a Novice for seven years. Initial vows by Postulants and Novices are quite simple, but become deeper and more complex. Full vows require a lifelong commitment and one's suitability or otherwise for such a step is assessed by the sisters.

Their imposing brick convent is set in beautiful gardens and has recently been refurbished. Inside, rooms are warmer and lighter than they appear from the outside. The convent is located on a major road and yet the (walled) gardens are surprisingly tranquil. The Chapel, kitchen, dining room, television room and library, bathrooms and common room are all shared – Sisters have their own bedrooms. Life is quite simple and is patterned around the offices of prayer.

Meals are taken together in the communal dining room. Space is organised to reflect the hierarchy (in the dining room and Chapel, for instance, the Sisters sit according to seniority). Membership involves a vow of poverty, but the community itself is financially stable. Its income sources are (decreasingly) donations and bequests and (increasingly) the fruits of the nuns' labour. Examples include ecclesiastical embroidery and hand made cards. The sale of cards, I was told, had financed the construction of a new wing (currently guest accommodation and a conference centre), which, in turn, generates income.

Contemplative Religious Communities: Discussion

It is apparent from these brief descriptions that members of contemplative religious communities seek a mixture of things. They want inner emancipation, which they seek through discipline in their physical life. In different ways they aim to intercede, supplicate and to devote their life to a higher cause. Their various utopias envisage salvation or access to a higher truth and contemplation is the route to this. The utopias of these contemplative communities take a threefold form. Firstly, the immediate utopia is a life of religious observance and/or spiritual practice. In order to achieve this they need to create a space in which this is possible. Secondly, is a utopia in process. The immediate utopia of a life of prayer is part of a wider utopian vision and a larger process. This may be personal enlightenment and/or salvation; it may be the enlightenment and/or salvation of humankind. Finally, they seek an ultimate utopia. This is the attainment of perfection, enlightenment and/or salvation.

In terms of what we have called the 'immediate utopia' of everyday life, these communities attain their goals. Life is structured. Social interaction, time management, material goods, relationships – and support networks – are all managed so as to maximise the opportunities for contemplation. Each of these communities is a structural part of a wider tradition and network of religious or spiritual faith and practice. Each views itself as part of a process of enlightenment or salvation, which can be said to be a utopia in process. The third aspect, the 'ultimate' attainment of utopia is perfection. This may be nirvana or salvation, and is, of course, impossible to assess even though it is of central importance to the members.

However, even the attainment of immediate utopia does not come easily. Contemplative communities are often enclosed in order to maximise the opportunity for prayer and meditation and the pursuit of the chosen spiritual practice. Nonetheless, a contemplative lifestyle is frequently disrupted by day-to-day concerns. Intentional communities are organisations that require management and issues of conflict will always arise, even amongst the most peaceable and mindful of people and this is something that we shall return to in Chapter 8.

Religious Communities of Social Change

Motukarara Christian Retreat

This embryonic community was founded in 2000 by a small group of people around a charismatic leader, Carlos Bennett, who is an unregistered pastor. It aims to provide retreat and eventually to become an intentional community for the underprivileged and socially deprived. Its mission focuses on people living in poverty who have experienced mental breakdown. Their publicity material offers these people 'Christian healing'.

The community was, at the time of my visit in February 2001, embryonic, consisting of two resident adults, four children and three further non-resident members. The property is state owned (crown land) and is leased for 40 years by a backing organisation, the Eloi Trust (comprised of Carlos Bennett and family members).

The physical space was formerly a Christian holiday camp and covers approximately two acres, comprising a main house and office and a series of hut-like units minimally furnished with bunk beds. This group took over the property in a state of serious disrepair, rat and cockroach infested, and at the time of my visit in 2001 was cleaning and restoring the buildings to habitable conditions. There is the potential to accommodate approximately a hundred people at Motukarara. Buildings also include communal shower blocks and kitchens as well as a large hall in which worship occurs and on the walls of which is painted: 'The Lord Saves' in a number of languages. Outside the main building are a lectern and a semicircle of chairs for outdoor worship.

This small and deeply committed group expresses a desire to fulfil a Christian mission through a) empowering seriously deprived adults and b) evangelical worship. They aim to enable people to re-evaluate their lives and begin afresh, through either a temporary stay or permanent membership at/of Motukarara. Drug and alcohol addiction, mental breakdown and emotional disturbance are, they believe, symptomatic of a double-edged social malaise of poverty and weak Christian values. This is a pragmatic attempt at realising a wide-ranging vision of social reform, in which a community is created as a space in which people can take a step towards a better life.

The group has genuine commitment and energy. The female members in particular are devoted to the leader, who exercises a charismatic authority. The group is dedicated, hard working and enthusiastic. Such a new community is impossible properly to assess, but we include it in this study as an example of a small scale and local attempt to realise an ambitious transformative vision.

Sisters of Compassion (Daughters of Our Lady of Compassion)

The Daughters of Our Lady of Compassion were a Roman Catholic organisation, founded in 1892 by Suzanne Aubert at Jerusalem, which later became home to James K. Baxter's Jerusalem community. They are now known as the Sisters of Compassion. The early community aimed, in its own words, to 'continue the Mission of Jesus Christ'. They did this by supporting the impoverished Maori community at the settlement of Jerusalem. The Sisters of Compassion retain a commitment to and relationship with the Maori people and three Sisters remain at Jerusalem to keep the memory of their roots alive.

The community today expresses an egalitarian religious philosophy in which each person is created by God and, therefore, has a right to respect, life and honour. From this comes a duty of care. The task of the Sisters is to fulfil this as part of what they identify as the Catholic Church's 'healing and justice seeking Mission'. They aim:

- to be symbols of hope
- to embrace all people without discrimination
- to share our Mission and History to ensure the continuation of the spirit of Suzanne Aubert
- to acknowledge the strong influence of the Maori people in the shaping of our tradition
- to welcome the opportunities of working in partnership with Tangata Whenua [the People of the Land]
- to be open and responsive to the needs of the time within our communities
- to question fearlessly, risk the unknown and challenge the institutions of power
- to use our gifts to empower those with few choices to live with dignity
- to respond to the needs of people in so far as our resources and capabilities allow
- to utilise our resources effectively
- to have our Homes and Services characterised by mutual respect, common goals, effective communication, collaboration, and shared responsibility
- to evaluate regularly, in the search of accountability, our response to our Mission commitment
- to ensure our Co-workers share our Missions and are given the opportunity to foster their personal and professional development. (http://www.hoc.org. nz)

The Sisters are based at a number of centres and homes throughout New Zealand, including St Raphael's home for young disabled people at Carterton, and the Home of Compassion at Island Bay, Wellington, which is a nursing home. Whilst the Sisters comprise a religious community across the country they are borderline in a discussion of intentional communities. The homes and services are not full intentional communities in which all members have chosen to live together for a common purpose but rather centres of care run by the Sisters. Strictly speaking, the Homes of Compassion are homes to providers and recipients of care.

The Friends' Settlement/Quaker Acres

In 1920, the Religious Society of Friends of New Zealand, with the support of the London Yearly Meeting and various New Zealand Friends, established a school in Wanganui. Known as the New Zealand Friends School, it lasted until 1969, when, for financial reasons, it was wound up. The school, renamed the Holdsworth School after one of its founders, was purchased by the government and became a school for emotionally disturbed boys. With the proceeds of the sale, a fund was established that provided key loans to help in financing community buildings and the establishment of an intentional community. Early in the 1970s, part of the site was identified as the possible location of a specifically Quaker intentional community, and, over the next few years, permission was given by the local council and plans developed for the establishment of such a community.

In the early years of the community, records were found that included a proposal to establish a community in conjunction with the school at the time of its founding, but it was only with the winding up of the school that a community actually came into being (see 'Quakers Have Established Model Community', 339 and Buchanan).

As reported in the October 1973 *NZ Friends Newsletter* ('Proposed', 5), the New Zealand Yearly Meeting had given its encouragement to the proposed settlement and a planning committee was being formed. A committee had been established by June 1974 with the intent of bringing a definite proposal 'to create a Quaker Settlement along the lines of an Infant Pendle Hill' (a Quaker community in the United States established in 1930) to the next Yearly Meeting ('NZ Yearly Meeting', 7–8). By July 1975, the local council had given approval for buildings to be erected and a ceremonial planting of 100 trees took place (Smithells 1975, 10).

The first members moved in to the first newly built home in mid-1976, with other members in other homes following shortly thereafter. These first members were four retired couples, which was expected, but it had always been made clear that the community was to be for all ages, and it quickly attracted young Friends as well as older ones (see Smithells, 1976). The initial buildings were built between 1976 and 1979 (the first was a communal workshop to provide a working base for the other buildings), with most of the work done by members of the community and members of the Society of Friends under the direction of Michael Payne, a Quaker architect (see Buchanan for a report in a local newspaper, Slessor on the architecture and Stover for a brief report on volunteering on the site).

As the community first took shape, the *NZ Friends Newsletter* reported:

> The Wanganui Educational Settlement [the then official name of the community] is, in essence, a religious community. The common faith and set of values will be the essential component for providing the cohesion, vision and patience as this experiment in Quaker living unfolds. The settlers have no blueprint for the future

but are sure that the way will be shown to them as they begin to live together in faith. They also need the strength that comes from knowing that the Society as a whole is behind them – or more accurately right beside them. ('Wanganui', 3)

In addition, the community intended 'to develop a new life style, living more simply, in small houses, using the minimum of the world's resources, and sharing expensive capital equipment' ('Quakers Have Established Model Community', 343).

The property is owned by the Wanganui Educational Settlement Trust, which includes representatives of the settlers and a representative of each of the nine Monthly Meetings of New Zealand. Today there are 15 houses which range from a unit designed for one person to a shared-occupancy unit (see Green), which was later divided into two rental units. In addition, there are community facilities that are used by members and made available to groups.

This group makes guests welcome. They may stay in the guest 'flats', close by the new Quiet Room for a small fee and are welcome to participate in daily worship. The site is attractive with architect-designed houses combining visual harmony with individuality. The land includes a small peace garden, paddocks and a wood; and there are communal garden spaces as well as private areas around each home. The overall effect is one of space and intimacy. It is a tranquil settling for a busy community.

As with all intentional communities, levels of participation in community life vary across the group. Those with jobs outside the community or small children may have less time to commit, while others take responsibility for the maintenance, accounts and administration of the Education Centre. For some members the Centre is still the most important part of life at the Friends Settlement. For others, it is living with like-minded peaceable people. The group as a whole combine outreach via education with daily practice of Quaker principles. It is at once a deliberative and dynamic community, being both stable and forward-looking.

Sisters of Mercy

Probably the best known nun in New Zealand in the last years of the twentieth century was Pauline O'Regan (1922–), who grew up in a rural area of the West Coast of the South Island and joined the Sisters of Mercy in 1942 (on her childhood, see O'Regan 1991). In her *A Changing Order* (1986), she traces the changes in the order brought about by Vatican II and in doing so describes the traditional convent she joined at 20 as '… a world complete in itself, a world that felt free to ignore the changing patterns and fashions of the society in which it was so conspicuously set' (65). But she also shows how Vatican II made it impossible for the order and the convent to continue to ignore the world by 1972. The transformation in this one woman by the changes brought about by Vatican II is a striking example of the radical changes that have taken place, particularly in Roman Catholic convents, in the last 30 years (for an autobiography of a nun who left her order, see Graham). Throughout her personal odyssey, O'Regan continues to emphasise the central role of community in her own life and the importance she assigns to community life outside the religious life (for her emphasis on community, see O'Regan and O'Connor).

She notes that when she joined the Sisters of Mercy:

> ... religious life was based on the belief that the world was essentially evil and therefore dangerous to the spiritual life. (*A Changing Order*, 65)

A 'convent language' was used that was clearly separatist in intent. Within the community, dress defined one's role as postulant, novice, nun having made her first vows, and nun having made her final vows. The trip from postulant to final vows took about six years and each stage was clearly marked by the changes in dress as well as clearly defined rights and responsibilities.

Community life was highly structured and each day followed a strict pattern. The virtues to be learned and practised were simplicity, humility and obedience, and she says that during her noviciate:

> ... it was humility and obedience that were to get the most practice. (Ibid., 72)

The vows of poverty and chastity were also central to the religious life.

> Poverty was seen as a detachment from all worldly things, and it meant possessing nothing but the bare essentials. (Ibid., 75)

Even language reinforced this vow with the possessive pronoun never used ('the pen to my use' not 'my pen').

'Particular friendships' within the order were not allowed and were among the faults pointed out at the monthly 'Chapter of Faults,' a process very similar to the criticism sessions that have been a mechanism of social control and social cohesion in many intentional communities (on the well-known practice of 'mutual criticism' at the US Oneida Community, see *Mutual Criticism* and McCarthy). As O'Regan describes it:

> This custom has been practised for centuries in religious orders. In effect it is saying that every Sister, from the oldest to the youngest, from the Reverend Mother to the newest novice, stood in need of the community's forgiveness. (*A Changing Order*, 78)

Meals were, of course, in common, and Thomas More must have taken his description of the common meals in *Utopia* (1516) directly from the practice in religious orders, down to the structured seating and the readings at meals. Of course, the orders did not have to allow for small children and pregnant women, as More did, but beyond that, the parallels between More's *Utopia* and O'Regan's description of the meals in her convent in the mid-twentieth-century are overwhelming. There were also community celebrations and daily periods of recreation, which all helped to bind the community together, as do such activities in secular communities. O'Regan notes that she gradually became aware of the continuity of the community: 'We were part of a family of women, dedicated in a special way to God's work, generation after generation' (ibid., 80).

O'Regan notes a sign of future change that took place within her order in the 1950s. European religious orders generally had a class system built into the order with a distinction between the 'choir' and the 'lay' monks and nuns. The 'lay' were essentially servants who did the cooking, laundry and housekeeping and could never aspire to positions of authority within the order.

> The youngest nun, on the day she was professed, had seniority over lay nuns who might have been professed for fifty years or more. (Ibid., 86)

In 1951, the lay nuns of the Sisters of Mercy revolted and demanded to be integrated into the order. They won acceptance and were give equal status well before the revolution brought about by Vatican II.

O'Regan herself participated in a later revolt in which she and two other nuns left their convent to establish a community of the three sisters in Aranui, a poor Christchurch suburb. Having taught for years in the convent school, she taught at Aranui High School so that the community could be self-supporting. She describes the negotiations to obtain a state house, moving in, and then simply living in the community and meeting others, particularly other women, slowly and gradually, on the street, over the fence and in the shops. The nuns wanted to be accepted as neighbours, not as authority figures, and they appear to have managed to do so. Their goal was to help, and, as they realised how isolated many of the women felt, to facilitate the creation of self-help communities, or in the language of Liberation Theology that she uses, 'basic Christian communities' or 'small Christian cells' (O'Regan and O'Connor, 113. On such communities in Liberation Theology, see Hebblethwaite). Their initial effort was not directed specifically at Roman Catholics or even Christians; they were simply concerned with assisting those needing help. Later, their concern turned more toward Christian community (see the chapter 'An Experience of Christian Community' in O'Regan and O'Connor and the guide to people power within the church, Burns and O'Regan).

Religious Communities of Social Change: Discussion

We can see from these brief introductions that certain threads run through this group of communities. For instance, spiritual and religious communities with a utopia of social reform are generally active and interventionist. In contrast to contemplative religious communities, they seek to realise change in *this* world.

Often, they seek to realise spiritual or religious truth through action. They are service driven, pursuing a mission, and are oriented towards action.

Some of these groups occupy a marginal place in this project because their mission of outreach and social work dominates their sense of community. As a consequence some are barely communities. Most religious communities in New Zealand that dedicate themselves to social reform do not remain in one location and do not establish a stable intentional community. There are two main reasons for this. The first is pragmatic and concerns finite human resources. Living in community is difficult and demanding. So is outreach work. It is generally necessary to focus *either* on establishing and maintaining the community, *or* to focus energy on outreach and social change. To work hard simultaneously at both is almost impossible. The second reason concerns these communities' aims and utopias. Often, their central work is 'out there' where the problems are perceived to lie. This is their priority and this is where they focus.

These communities are essentially practical but like the contemplative communities, they have a threefold utopian vision. The immediate utopia is a life of service and good work. This is how they spend most of their time. The utopia in process moves towards the larger aim of social change in the context of a particular religious or spiritual teaching. And the ultimate utopia is a better world. This world will be a) guided by spiritual and religious values and b) transformed in material terms.

These groups believe that piecemeal, small-scale initiatives can make a difference to the world. The most ambitious reading of this would involve a re-application of what Tom Moylan calls the 'critical utopia' (Moylan 1986). Briefly, in this reading, utopias can be:

> 'Critical' in the Enlightenment sense of *critique* – that is expressions of oppositional thought, unveiling, debunking, of both the genre itself and the historical situation. As well as 'critical' in the nuclear sense of the *critical mass* required to make the necessary explosive reaction. (Moylan 1986, 10)

Moylan does not apply this analysis to utopian communities, but rather focuses on the written utopias of what he calls 'an historic bloc of opposition' which comprises socialism, feminism and environmentalism (ibid.). However, it is possible to apply this view of utopianism to communities. To do so would be to perceive these small-scale local initiatives to represent critical mass of opposition to problems of poverty. However, this would be to overstate their effect. They may help to stem the tide of poverty in urban New Zealand, but they do not prevent it from growing.

So, whilst attainment of the ultimate utopia of is unlikely, these communities do daily participate in a processual utopianism, striving day by day to make a small difference. Often the biggest struggle in these groups is balancing outreach (care for others) with community-building (care for self and each other). Rising poverty and social dislocation lead members to focus increasingly on work outside the community and the community suffers as a result. It is no coincidence that the most 'successful' of these communities in *community* terms, Friends Settlement, is also one of the least active in external outreach. Instead, outreach occurs mostly on-site, within the community space in the Education Centre. In this way it is part of the community, rather than apart from it. This inhibits the development of a dislocated focus and goes some way towards explaining the longevity and stability of this community.

Spiritual Communities of Personal Growth

Centrepoint

The community of Centrepoint no longer exists but it has lasting influence within New Zealand. It was wound up in February 2000, following a protracted series of legal cases. Some former members of Centrepoint have founded a new community on the site called Anahata, and this is discussed in a later chapter. We can learn much from the Centrepoint experience and this is why it is included in this discussion. Centrepoint was, without doubt, a utopian experiment in communal living. It was, in some ways, a very successful community. In others it proved disastrous, and it is for this that Centrepoint remains infamous.

The utopian vision on which Centrepoint was founded and ran for over 20 years aimed primarily at the personal growth of its members. This, it was believed, could be accomplished through spiritual development and social experimentation.

At its peak Centrepoint was home to up to 300 people, and was New Zealand's largest, most influential, and, in some ways, most successful intentional community. It was a spiritual community based on personal and sexual liberation; and was even listed in the New Zealand census as a separate religion. This community was based around the teachings of Bert (Herbert Thomas) Potter (1925–).

In its heyday Centrepoint generated high levels of income from counselling and psychotherapy; it also had a plant nursery, a paper-making press, a pottery and other co-operative enterprises. It was, or appeared to be, financially affluent. The community owned a (now valuable) 30 acre plot of land in Albany, near Auckland, with extensive buildings, and a substantial community house with numerous rooms and good facilities. It had its own well-equipped school. The buildings are impressive and the grounds beautiful. There is a swimming pool and (now neglected) gardens. It attracted new members, right up until the end. Former members speak of many positive aspects of being a part of Centrepoint Community.

Life at Centrepoint was fully communal and this provided members with a real sense of belonging. By 'fully communal' we mean that every aspect of life was shared. Members ate together in the community house, slept together in the open-plan 'longhouses', which were modelled on the traditional Polynesian longhouse and which had no dividing walls, just a series of mattresses on the floor. They shared their possessions and pooled their income. Even the bathrooms provided an opportunity for closeness, with communal toilets and showers. Births were an event to be celebrated and took place generally in what now serves as the lounge of the communal house with the full support and presence of other members.

Bert Potter led the community through charisma and held daily sessions in which he offered guidance. When it worked, Centrepoint made a lot of people happy. They lived alongside each other in a very close community and explored themselves – and others – to the full. His leadership was established right at the start of Centrepoint's history in 1978. He founded the community with 36 followers and the original trust deed states that the community existed to 'receive the teaching of Herbert Thomas Potter' (*New Zealand Herald*, 29 February 2000, 9).

Centrepoint was closed by the courts in the year 2000, following years of high profile allegations of sexual abuse and financial mismanagement. The community had survived a series of trials in which Potter and other prominent members were imprisoned but was eventually closed on a legal technicality. The last court case was in February 2000, which settled payments on Potter and several of his closest followers, on condition that they left the community, and a small group of former members began Anahata community on the site. Anahata is not primarily a spiritual community and is discussed in Chapter Seven.

Potter was convicted on drug charges in 1990 following a police raid on Centrepoint which yielded LSD and Ecstasy, which was apparently being manufactured on site and distributed to members. He was further convicted in 1992 and imprisoned for seven years for indecently assaulting five minors. Six other members were similarly convicted.[1] Potter returned to Centrepoint after his release from prison and did not leave until he was 'bought off' following the above-mentioned court settlement. Centrepoint community had gone badly wrong, and a number of factors including a corrupt leadership, structural problems and increasing isolation yielded a community now remembered for paedophilia and the mental and sexual abuse of its members.

Centrepoint sought personal liberation and emancipation from the 'straightjacket' of conventional religiosity and morality. This was a widely-held aspiration at the time. Potter believed that we could all become God (as he had) and that this was accomplished by breaking down certain defence mechanisms and behavioural patterns (hence psychotherapy), and the exploration of a newly liberated self (hence sexual exploration). The keys to personal growth (and ultimate Godliness), were 'openness' and responsibility. Sexual experimentation was a part of this and aimed to generate energy, and to focus and release tension.

'Openness' and 'responsibility' took a number of forms. In some cases, they were euphemistic for closure and manipulation. Membership of Centrepoint involved routine participation in Potter's 'cures', counselling and confrontational therapies. Much of the counselling at Centrepoint was in 'open session', wherein members told the entire group their problems. The aim was 'No barriers' (Anon, 6 May 2001). In practice, former members say that this generated extreme emotional vulnerability. When combined with submission to Potter's 'cures' (suggested tasks in response to problems identified in group sessions), this yielded a vulnerable population. For instance, one woman who felt herself unattractive to men was tasked, within a given timeframe, to sleep with every man in the community. It should be noted that she has not described this task as abusive.

For many, Centrepoint was, for a time, utopia realised. Former members speak of the exhilaration and liberation that they felt during encounters and of the intense love that they felt from the group. The community was certainly close. As mentioned earlier, most of the toilets were communal, as were most showers, privacy being antithetical to openness. Personal space was minimal and this produced intense interactions and relationships. Former members describe it as exhilarating. Every aspect of life was shared. Of course, this also meant that every aspect of life was 'open' to scrutiny by Potter and his elite. As an increasingly hostile press and public opinion beleaguered the community, a sense of siege grew at Centrepoint. Relations inside the community were under growing strain and eventually spun out of control. It must have been like living inside a pressure cooker.

Even in the days when Centrepoint functioned, adult life was, by all accounts, intensely emotional and absorbing. Children 'ran feral' (Anon, 2 February 2001) and were, to a large extent, unsupervised. Former child members imply that those adults who did pay attention to them were paedophilic, and that their parents were too wrapped up in their own complex relationships and therapy to notice this.

The demise of Centrepoint was unpleasant and painful for those concerned but it was constitutional, legalistic and, on the whole, not physically violent. The experience tells us something of both the dark side of utopia and of the dangers of enclosed intentional communities. Intentional communities, remote from the outside world, can quickly attain peculiar perspectives on 'right' behaviour.

Titoki Healing Centre

Titoki was founded in 1975 and opened in early 1976 by Donald Thomas Ferguson (1930–), then Vicar of the parish of St George of Gate Pa in Tauranga and Archdeacon of the Tauranga Archdeaconry under the auspices of the Anglican Church. It is located outside of Whakatane. Titoki is a small community and retreat centre staffed by an ordained chaplain and a small, unpaid staff who are provided with accommodation, meals and other incidental expenses. Most community members appear to stay for only a few years.

Titoki originated as a healing ministry, inspired in part by a similar but much larger community, Burrswood in Sussex, founded by Dorothy Kerin

(1889–1963). Titoki was based on Ferguson's belief that God had called him to a special ministry to assist the ill. Ferguson retired in 1988, and, since then there have been a number of resident chaplains.

Titoki practices the laying-on of hands and anointing, but it has always been well connected to the medical establishment, with a doctor on call and one or more nurses in residence as members of the community. In practice, Titoki appears to function as a hospice for the terminally ill, as a short-term care facility for those recovering from an illness and needing temporary assistance, and as a retreat centre.

Titoki originated within the Anglican Church and has a number of daily services conducted by the resident chaplain, but these services, while initially Anglican, have for many years been described as 'ecumenical'. Titoki publishes a newsletter, now available on line, called *Open Hand* (available at http://www.titoki.nz.co/Newsletter/html).

As with many other communities, potential members are encouraged to visit first for a few days so that both the potential member and the community can make an initial judgement of suitability. The potential member is then invited for a three month 'noviciate'. If this works out, and it sometimes does not, a formal service is held to recognise and welcome the new member.

Titoki has been in contact with other religious communities in New Zealand such as the Convent of the Sacred Name, an Anglican convent in Christchurch, which was discussed above, Orama on Great Barrier Island and the Glade Christian Community, which used to be in Pauanui.

Religious Communities of Personal Growth: Discussion

This is a disparate group of communities. They nonetheless share certain aims. These include personal growth, spiritual development and self-improvement. They want to fully realise their ideals in practice. They are introspectively inclined and concerned primarily with the interests of their members. Religious communities of personal growth focus primarily on what we earlier called an 'immediate utopia'. This provides a space in which members can live in the company of others doing likewise. Some of these communities are enclosed. Some engage in outreach. Some are New Age. Taken as a group, these communities are different from others because they are primarily places in which people can focus on a lifestyle that fully articulates their beliefs.

These communities seek a religious or spiritual lifestyle. They take a number of different forms, and the full mobilisation of a belief-system into daily life requires a certain amount of isolation and the most extreme form of holistic lifestyle community is the isolationist and purist one. This is, perhaps, the most extreme form of utopian community: the enclosed community in which members live a 'pure', 'untainted' religious or spiritual lifestyle. Because these communities are closed they are also the most difficult to access. One of these is Gloriavale.

Gloriavale

Gloriavale is a major community which is well known among Christian communities but little known otherwise. Previously known as the Christian Church at Springbank and the Cust Community and called The Cooperites by the media,[2] it is a withdrawn, separatist community, which identifies with the theological separatism that gave rise to such major religious/communal movements as the Amish and the Hutterites.

Gloriavale community is difficult to place. It is variously (and wrongly) described within New Zealand as New Age, fundamentalist and a cult. It shares certain structural features with the contemplative religious communities, but is not mainly focused on contemplation. It seeks change in the here-and-now, and could, therefore, perhaps be considered as a community of social change. Seeking to live a life that fully articulates a belief system, it shares some features with personal growth communities. And yet it does not really fit any of the above categories and so we present it separately. Gloriavale is closest in character to communities like the Hutterian Brethren, founded in the sixteenth century and flourishing today particularly in North America. But while Gloriavale clearly learned from exposure and visits to and from such communities and sympathetic people like the Amish and Hutterite scholar John Hostetler (whose papers are the primary unpublished sources for our understanding of the community), it is the twentieth century creation in New Zealand of Hopeful Christian and his followers, and we hope at some future date that a serious study of it will be possible.

Gloriavale is first and foremost a Christian community, and for its members its *raison d'être* is to work and worship together. People marry for life and raise their children in economic security. Thus, there is a complete utopian vision in this life, which they see as also preparing them for the next life.

Founded in 1969 by Neville Barclay Cooper (1928–), an independent preacher with connections with independent Pentecostal churches in Australia and New Zealand who took the name Hopeful Christian, the community was initially established north of Christchurch. In the 1990s it moved to Lake Haupiri in an isolated part of the South Island. The community aims to be self-supporting and has become more and more so over the years. It grows through selective recruitment and its high birth rate.

The group originated as Cooper, clearly a charismatic leader, gathered followers around him and led them into a community with similarities and, at one time, ties to the Hutterian Brethren (on the Hutterian Brethren, see Bennett, Horsch, Hostetler and Peters). According to *What We Believe* (1989) each member of the community makes 'A Declaration of Commitment to Jesus Christ and to the Christian Church and Community at Springbank,' which says:

> I believe that the Bible is in every part the inspired Word of God and that it is the final and absolute authority for every belief and practice in the Christian Life. I

believe that the New Testament has replaced the Old Testament as the covenant by which we live, and that the Old Testament must always be interpreted in terms of the New Testament. (23)

And continues, 'I forsake all that I have to follow Christ, renouncing forever all personal ownership of houses, lands, money and all other possessions' (23). Each member is expected to give all their property to the poor or to the Church at Springbank, as it then was. Within the community, property is held in common and no one can claim return of property once given. Each member also pledges that they will never take legal action regarding the Church at Springbank, and 'I give the leader of the Church at Springbank the absolute and unfettered right to administer and use all the property, assets and money of the Church at Springbank for the benefit of those within or without this Community ...' (24). No one is allowed to borrow or save money and there are no pensions or insurance.

Gender differences are marked by modest dress that differs for men and women, and each member declares that:

I will keep the Christian order of the home in which husbands love wives, wives obey husbands and children obey parents. I will never accept divorce or the 'remarriage' of divorced persons. (26)

Men and women also work separately in traditional gender-defined occupations. Leaders of the community are to be male and future leaders are to be chosen by past leaders.

The Hutterites and Cooper's followers do not reject modern technology but use it for their own ends. For example, the Cust Community, as it was then known, was once recognised in New Zealand as on the forefront of the development of biogas to run farm machinery, trucks and cars. The first vehicle in New Zealand to run on compressed biogas was at Cust (Anderson. See also Caley, Fitzsimons and McArthur).

The next stage in the history of Gloriavale is in dispute. If one believes the media, then sometime in the late 1980s a dramatic change came over Cooper and, as a result, the community and effects on the community were far reaching.[3] When Cooper's wife died, he married the oldest woman in the community, who was 88 at the time. When she died, Cooper married a 17 year old. Various television and radio programmes were devoted to the community, usually stressing scandals and alleging sexual abuse. We do not have inside knowledge of these allegations. It is a fact that Cooper was arrested twice on abuse charges; the first charges did not stand, and while he was convicted on a number of charges that he denied, he spent little time in jail. Ex-members brought all the charges, and we should bear in mind that this is often an unsafe source of information. We saw with the case of Centrepoint that a hostile press can lead a community to introversion, and it is hardly surprising that Gloriavale is suspicious of outsiders.

There were problems in the community. In the late 1980s the Bruderhof were reported to have set up a 'safe house' in Christchurch for members of the community trying to escape. One of Cooper's sons committed suicide after he had left the community and another kidnapped his own wife from the community three times and once took her to a Bruderhof community in the United States. Each time she returned to New Zealand and the community and she remains in the community, as do some of their children.

In 2004 there are over 350 people in the community, 150 of them children. The community runs Gloriavale Community Christian School, which had 113 students in 2002. It is a registered school under New Zealand law and is regularly inspected, and there is also a registered preschool enrolling with about 70 pupils.

They bought the land they now occupy in cash from 11 failing landowners, and there are two large farms. As newcomers to the district they did not want to compete with established economic activities, so they established a business servicing and repairing planes and helicopters as well as other businesses that fit into the economy of the West Coast. It has been estimated that in 2002 Gloriavale put between 300,000 and 350,000 New Zealand dollars into the local economy every month (Madgwick). The community has established a positive reputation in the area by buying as much as possible of what it needs in the area, inviting local residents to concerts (in 2002 over 3,200 people attended the four-week concert season), and generally being a good neighbour. Their businesses in both Christchurch and later on the West Coast have been successful; the people are good workers, do what they say they will, stay to schedules and provide quality products.

Given Cooper's age, the next crisis to face Gloriavale is likely to be his death. While there is a group of men around Cooper and the transition is undoubtedly set, such groups usually have problems when the charismatic founder dies (see Miller, ed).

Conclusion

This chapter has offered a glimpse of life inside New Zealand's religious communities, exploring their utopias and everyday realities. We have looked in some detail at religious communities from a range of traditions and have learned something of life therein. We have considered communities with a range of aims or utopias: contemplation, social reform and the creation of a holistic lifestyle. We have identified three layers of utopianism to be driving these communities: immediate, processual and ultimate.

The first conclusion has to be that realising a utopia in an intentional community is not easy. The first level of utopianism is the most accessible: that of the immediate utopia of lifestyle, which seeks daily to live one's ideals. Even this is difficult. Things go wrong, even in the best planned and organised community. Conflicts occur and things require attending to, and this distracts from the original mission or utopia. Even in the community of Bodhinyanarama, where members do not have to prepare meals and do not work for income, daily matters of management require attention.

The second level of a utopia in process is also attainable, or rather, it can be attempted and practised. Intentional communities are often part of a larger movement for change and daily practice can be part of a larger process of transformation. Communities can be part of a movement towards a given utopia.

The ultimate attainment of utopia is impossible to assess and probably rightly so. This lies in an afterlife about which we cannot know. The ultimate utopia is always just around the corner, just over the horizon and just out of sight. In this way, utopia serves as an aspiration, providing a motivating vision for a better way of life.

Notes

1 Keith McKenzie (aged 71), medical doctor, convicted of indecently assaulting a minor and struck off the medical register. David Mendelssohn (aged 48), convicted of indecently assaulting three minors: four years in prison. Ulrich Schmid (52), convicted of sexually assaulting two minors: one year in prison. Richard Parker (45) convicted of attempted rape of a minor: four years and five months in prison. Henry Stones (51), convicted of indecently assaulting a minor: nine months in prison. And a year later, in 1992, Kenneth Smith (75), convicted of indecently assaulting two minors: damages and community service.

2 While the community has published one book but this book is not available in any library. One of the authors was given a copy of the book published by the community, and this copy will be given to a New Zealand library when this book is published.

3 Unfortunately most of the evidence regarding this period in community life comes from apostates, and it is extremely difficult to judge the quality of such evidence. While the press tends to too readily believe scandals about communities, there is a tendency among scholars to too readily discount them. See Cummings.

Chapter 6

Cooperative Lifestyles

Introduction

In 'Cooperation and Utopianism' Sargent pointed out that cooperation and utopia are closely connected (Sargent 2001). The quest for cooperation touches and transforms every aspect of our lives, from our closest relationships to our financial investments. That is why this cluster of communities is so diffuse.

For instance, many of the communities in this group reject private ownership of property, saying that it yields an atomised social structure. They are also critical of the nuclear family, which is believed to contribute to alienation. This is connected to a view of the public and private spheres. 'Normal' families consist of two parents (a man and a woman) plus children. One parent, historically the father, enters the public sphere of money and work and earns a living and thus spends a significant part of his life outside the home. The other parent, historically the mother, remains in the private sphere of the home and rears the children. The public sphere has traditionally been considered the locus of power and the private sphere requires protection, being the sacrosanct and autonomous space beloved of liberals ever since John Stuart Mill's *On Liberty* (1859).

Intentional communities often seek to widen the structure of the family. Mothers complain of isolation and depression within the nuclear family. Fathers find that they experience alienation from their children and partners. Children, it is argued, become better social beings in larger groups. These communities disrupt the relationship between public and private spheres. The home becomes more of a public space than it has traditionally been. Life inside them is less private than in the mainstream, the home is public showcase for alternatives and the home itself becomes a site of political or ideological opposition (Sargisson 2000).

The quest to live a cooperative lifestyle confronts key institutions, norms and assumptions. Not all of these communities are collectively owned, but many are, and for some this is important. They feel that ownership causes as well as reflects our patterns of behaviour. Whereas private property and the nuclear family breed individualism and competition, these intentional communities attempt to promote collectivism and cooperation. For some, cooperation is sufficient in itself. For others, cooperation is part of a wider ideology or worldview; thus, there are some overlaps between this category and other chapters.

79

In the discussions that follow, we consider the idea and practice of cooperative ownership before discussing samples from a range of cooperative communities. This is a long chapter because there are many different kinds of cooperative communities in New Zealand, and we have structured our discussions in such a way as to maximise accessibility and clarity. The main body of the chapter reflects the connections between different groups. Communities for whom cooperation itself is the main reason for existing are considered together, as are women's communities, anarchist communities and communities that seek to foster cooperation through education. We also devote a section to the discussion of co-housing, a new form of intentional community in New Zealand. Riverside, which is in many ways a unique community, is considered under the sub-heading of 'peace'. This long-standing community practices cooperation in many ways and has seen many changes, but it has promoted peace for over 60 years. This approach allows us to note both similarities across this group of communities and differences between the sub-groups.

Cooperative Ownership

The idea and practice of cooperative ownership in New Zealand had its historical roots in Maori culture and rural pragmatism. As discussed in Chapter 2, Maori conceptions of ownership are collective, use-based and reciprocal and emerge from ideas about identity. Pakeha practices of cooperative ownership grew from the economic needs of isolated rural businesses, which developed trading and producer co-ops. The earliest recorded were in Timaru and Christchurch in 1881, and the New Zealand Cooperatives Association (NZCA) is still dominated by trading co-ops. Established in 1982, this organisation lists as its objectives:

- to encourage, promote and advance New Zealand Co-operatives;
- to act as a representative Association for those engaged as cooperatives;
- to promote discussion and co-operation with decision-makers at all levels of Government designed to further the interests of the cooperative movement;
- to collect, verify, and publish information regarding the cooperative movement;
- to provide services and expertise to those engaged in the cooperative industry to carry out research into all aspects of the movement. (http://www.nzca. org)

It offers training programmes to senior staff within cooperative enterprises and monitors legislation. It lists amongst its members farming, retail, wood, plumbing and courier services. The website contains just one link to an organisation concerned with cooperative housing, McKinley Douglas, a consultancy firm.

Notwithstanding their absence from the NZCA, housing co-ops exist across New Zealand. A housing co-op is a legal entity founded on cooperative principles, in which members (usually residents) control the legal body that owns the housing. They are both tenants and collective owners, but individual portions of ownership have no direct transferable financial value. This is because 'shares' in co-ops usually have a fixed and nominal resale price (for example, one New Zealand dollar). The property belongs to the co-op, to which they all belong and in which they have staked their one dollar. Any mortgages or loans are held in the name of the co-op. Members pay monthly rent, some of which pays the mortgage, if there is one. Remaining monies from the rent are spent on or given to collectively agreed projects and causes. These may be within the community itself, such as a refurbishment, or else in the local, national or international community. Some, for instance, provide free or cheap loans to other co-ops, others give to charities.

New Zealand's structure of (legal) ownership does not make it easy to form a housing cooperative and different rules apply to Maori and non-Maori groups (see Appendix). Some intentional communities form co-ops as tenants-in-common. Legislation regarding tenants-in-common allows ownership of an undivided share of land and buildings. However, this is complicated in practice and most of New Zealand's cooperative intentional communities exist under the umbrella of Trusts. Here, Trustees control the property for the benefit of others. The Trustees Act of 1956 set out the powers of Trustees, which are wide-ranging; and those of Beneficiaries, which are minimal. The legal structure of Trusts is thus autocratic and does not lend itself to an egalitarian social structure. However, most communities negotiate this by making all members both Beneficiaries and Trustees. Most choose to be a Charitable Trust. This, again, is problematic and does not lend itself to their goals. The legislation regarding Charitable Trusts permits them only for religion, education, or the alleviation of poverty. This is severely restrictive and sometimes the Trust Statement of an intentional community does not reflect its true or full aims. This is what finally permitted the High Court to close Centrepoint Community and that action has caused considerable nervousness in intentional communities throughout the country. There is an ever-present threat of closure if a community is found not to reflect statements made in its Trust Deed. This is a recurrent problem – the deeds were often written instrumentally in order to fit the legal requirements. The actual community may have always been different from the description that legally defined it, or it may have evolved and changed over time. Whatever the case, many groups are now nervous. They lack an effective political lobby because housing co-ops are underrepresented by the NZCA, and so the current legislation is unlikely to be changed. It certainly accounts for the similarity of many Trust Deeds across the range of diverse communities. We found that the differences between the communities discussed below was not strongly apparent from the documentation and could only really be appreciated by employing qualitative research in the form of visits, participant observation and interviews.

Table 6.1   New Zealand's cooperative communities

Community	Location	Members	Core values
Aradia	Colville, Coromandel	Women only: 3 adult	Feminist lesbian
Beachcomber	South Brighton	Mixed: 12 adult, 6 children	Sustainability, holism, mutual support, personal growth
Chippenham	Christchurch	Mixed: 15 adult, 4 children	Cooperation, respect, equality
Creekside	Christchurch	Mixed	Cooperation community
Earthsong	Waitakere	Mixed: 32 households	Co-housing environmentalism community sustainability
Earthspirit	Kaitaia	Women only: 3 adult	Feminist lesbian separatist
Graham Downs (Renaissance)	Graham Valley	Mixed: 20–25	Anarchist community
Katajuta	Punakaiki	Mixed: approx. 8 adults	Cooperation equality
Kiriwai	Featherston	Women only: 2 permanent 2 longstay	Lesbian separatism
Mansfield	Christchurch	Mixed: 15	Cooperation
Peterborough	Christchurch	Mixed: approx. 12 adult plus children	Cooperation support poverty cooperative ownership
Riverside	Motueka	Mixed: approx. 23 households	Peace, equality, cooperation
Te Ora	Graham Valley	Mixed: 6 adult 5 children	Education environmentalism cooperation community
Timatanga	Whenapai	Mixed: 12 adult plus children	Education cooperation
Township of Gordon Collective (1981–1994)	Dunedin	Mixed 10 adult 1 child	Cooperation political activism

Pursuit of a Cooperative Lifestyle

Beachcomber/Freebird

Beachcomber was established in 1995 and in 2001 had developed into a community of 12 adults and six children. The property, a former motel, is situated near the beach in South Brighton and is owned by the Housing for Women Trust. Community members are rent paying tenants. This is not a housing co-op because members are Beneficiaries but not Trustees, and this leads to a sense of disempowerment amongst the members, who would like greater autonomy. For instance, the property is not in good repair, and this is something that was often mentioned in interview. Residents have ideas about fund-raising and ways in which to transform the former motel into a functional community space, but the Trust lacks the funds, and, some feel, the will, to respond to their suggestions. The central aim of the Trust is the provision of housing for women in need, in particular victims of domestic violence. Its resources are limited, and there is money available for basic repairs but little else.

This is a loosely connected community, members of which cite spirituality, holistic lifestyle and supportive community as their core values. The following extract from a group interview gives a good idea of the dynamics of this group.

LS: Are there any values that you share as a group?
E: I see us as being open
Group: Oh yes … [general agreement] …
E: And sensitivity. Some of us are ill. Each has their habits. Some of us need sleep during the day, like I generally sleep in the mornings. So, there can be a bit of a tiptoeing past.
K: I think there is a common thread of healing, with a stress on alternatives.
Group: Oh definitely … [general agreement] …
G: … But, while we're on this subject, I wanted to say the word 'consensus'. That's something we've spent an awful lot of time working on: Not compromise but consensus.
E: Yes, and it's important to stick with it because it is a LONG process.
G: And that's why it's important that we see each other and be able to look TRULY at our own perspective and WHY we hold certain views. (Beachcomber, Group Interview, 6 April 2001)

Some members of Beachcomber are suffering long term and debilitating illnesses, such as chronic fatigue syndrome and, for this reason, communal activity tends to be sporadic and unstructured. The group nonetheless provides a supportive environment.

Beachcomber members include nuclear families, single people, lone parents and children. The future of the community has been under question because of the financial insecurity of their arrangement with the Housing Trust for

Women (HTW). Some members want to try to buy the property so as to be autonomous, but this has not proved possible. As a part of this process, a small group established the Freebird Trust in June 2000. The core aim of this Trust is to:

> relieve poverty, advance education, AND carry out other charitable purposes. In particular the Trust will work to create and maintain communities and to provide other support and assistance consistent with this charitable purpose. (Freebird Trust Deed)

Freebird aims to achieve this through work with the wider community, by supporting people with 'physical, emotional and mental difficulties'; alleviating poverty by encouraging the bulk purchase of food; supporting community arts; providing holistic health care education; supporting other groups doing similar work; and living in harmony with the natural environment. Much of this could be achieved, they feel, by living in a showcase intentional community.

At the time of my visit in spring 2001, the buildings were being re-roofed, and people were camping out in the community house. Living space is not usually communal, and personal accommodation comprises one former motel unit (usually three rooms with bathroom and kitchen) and small garden per household. The community has shared gardens created by some members from former car parks. Income at Beachcomber is generated individually either by paid work outside the community or from state (for example, invalidity) benefit.

Chippenham Community

The Chippenham community in Christchurch, founded in 1971, is probably the oldest urban secular intentional community in the world. Urban communities normally have a short life, so that the continued existence of both Chippenham and Creekside (founded only a few years later – see below) is undoubtedly unique. Chippenham's survival is striking because it was founded by political activists and such communities tend to be among the most short-lived.

In 1972 Chippenham added a second house, Mansfield, which abuts the Chippenham garden at a right angle. From the beginning there was interest in having a rural community affiliated with Chippenham and in 1973 a property of 40 acres near Oxford, called Gricklegrass, was added. This community is primarily concerned with environmentalism and is discussed in the next Chapter. From the earliest records, it is clear that it was always the intention to have both an urban and a rural community. When Gricklegrass was founded, income was shared and income came from both livestock and crops and a requirement that each work outside the community ten days in each quarter and give the income to the community (Jones, 106).

The communities were established under the umbrella of Community Assistance, Incorporated and documents suggest that the name should be taken seriously, as would be appropriate for the political activists that formed the initial group. It was then stated that

The objects for which the Association is established are:
(a) to provide benefits, facilities and assistance to the members, their husbands, wives, children or other dependants or to the widowers, widows children or other former dependants of deceased members in such manner as may from time to time be determined by the Association.
(b) to assist such persons or bodies whether incorporated or otherwise as may from time to time be determined by the Association.

Early members of Chippenham were deeply involved in both local and national politics as well as in the alternative movement. Chippenham founded the magazine *New Zealand Environment*; published a newsletter called *Men Against Sexism*, was the address given in the first issues of *Mushroom,* the main journal of the alternatives movement; the first meeting of GreenPeace NZ was held at Chippenham; HART (Halt All Racist Tours) held its planning meetings at Chippenham and the HART newsletter was published there; the first women's refuge originated there; Chippenham residents were involved in the early stages of the gay liberation front in New Zealand; and an alternative school started there.

In 1978 the choice was made to divide the houses along gender lines; men at Mansfield, women at Chippenham. In 1974 the women had become active as a group and were involved with establishing the Women's Refuge Centre. In 1975 the men formed their own consciousness-raising group and published the pamphlet 'Men Against Sexism', which worked to break down role stereotyping. The split was designed to break down emotional stereotyping and create more nurturing among the men ('Lives Apart'). However, it was short-lived.

The early reports on Chippenham indicate that the desire to establish an alternative school and develop a cooperative store were part of the process that brought the people together. In 1972 a two-day-a-week commune crèche was started with parent and non-parent volunteers. One day was at Chippenham and one day was at Mansfield. Chippenham established a bakery, called Vital Foods, which was initially intended to provide on-site jobs for members with children. The bread was initially reported to have been somewhat erratic in quality but improved over time. In order to expand, Chippenham borrowed money from a fund that Riverside Community had established to assist other communities. (Riverside's minute books suggest that the loan was never repaid.)

The desire for an alternative education is almost a constant among intentional communities and many communities try to establish one. The process of doing so is often extremely difficult, not least due to disagreements over what sort of alternative education is wanted. Such questions do not come up in religious communities but are common in secular communities. An undated document entitled 'The Commune School' reads as follows:

We want to:

be a teaching/learning co-operative, not a 'school' in the normal sense of the word.

have *members* not teachers/or pupils.

have *jointly defined* educational goals, subject to constant revision and discussion at regular meetings.

maintain a network of information and resources, and contacts with individuals, groups, and organisations.

Each member should agree to make him or her self available both as teacher and learner according to individual ability and resources.

People's interests or courses of study should be treated as *equally valid*. There is no reason why academic work should be treated as more important than crafts and manual works. (Emphasis in the original)

Other proposals were put forth for both a school for the community and for a school that would serve Christchurch more broadly. There was considerable controversy over the specifics of the proposals, but Chippenham was involved with a school that was finally established. That school, Four Avenues Alternative School, no longer exists.

Chippenham, Mansfield and Gricklegrass communities are now part of what is now called the Te Ngakau o te Rakau Inc, Heartwood Trust (Heartwood). Heartwood was established in 1996, in a period of serious conflict during which Community Assistance Incorporated was wound up by the High Court (see Chapter 8). At the time of Sargisson's first visit in spring 2001 the community was comprised of eight adults and three children. It has since expanded to its capacity size of 14.

Chippenham is unusual in that (most) members live under one roof in the community house. The norm in New Zealand communities is for households to live separately. Members work outside the community, mostly in paid occupations. These vary and include nursing, film making, carpentry, librarianship and university study. Chippenham is relaxed and friendly. It is open to WWOOFers (Willing Workers on Organic Farms) and on each of my visits there were WWOOFers happily ensconced who had come from the UK or Ireland to spend time in New Zealand off the tourist route, participating in daily life and work.

Following a three month trial period, people may join the community and become a member of Heartwood, which has monthly meetings that rotate around the three communities. The communities are fairly autonomous under this structure and may, up to a point, write their own internal rules. Chippenham, for instance, has established statements designed to avoid conflict that new residents must sign. One Chippenham statement is entitled *Information for Guests and New Residents*, and includes the statement/warning that '*Residents are collectively responsible for many tasks normally undertaken by private landlord* – a position of stewardship that offers greater freedom and empowerment but also greater responsibility' (emphasis in the original). New members sign a statement ('Chippenham Household Community Policy'), which stresses the importance of community meetings, in which collective decisions are made, and which emphasises the need to participate in meetings. House meetings deal with membership and can choose to evict people who fail to meet their responsibilities.

Financial matters are the responsibility of the Heartwood Trust, the board of which includes former and current members plus one person from a separate but nearby community (Peterborough). This combination aims to incorporate long- and short-term perspectives on the future of the communities, and to draw on the experience of people with communal backgrounds. Heartwood is in a stable financial position but does not have complete freehold of the properties due to costs incurred during a prolonged legal dispute (see Chapter 8). Members all pay a relatively low cash rent to Heartwood plus a 'sweat rent' to Chippenham, in which they undertake to work for two hours a week for Chippenham (for instance, cleaning, conducting maintenance, decorating, or gardening). As we saw above, one of the aims of the founders of Chippenham was the provision of high quality housing in a cooperative situation for low income earners and this system was developed with that aim in mind.

The house, Chippenham Lodge, was built by George and Francis Goldney in the early 1860s and named after their birthplace in Wiltshire. It is light and spacious with high ceilings and large rooms. Shared space consists of a huge lounge, a kitchen-dining room, laundry, pantry, two bathrooms and well-maintained organic gardens. Bedrooms are private spaces and again are large and light. This community is lively, friendly and welcoming and plays a vital role in the network and history of New Zealand's intentional communities, being not only one of the oldest but also home, since 1995, of the publication *Chip'N'Away*, a Newsletter for intentional communities. *Chip'N'Away* is solely funded by a budget from Heartwood.

Chippenham is unusual in New Zealand on several counts: it is urban, it is a commune and it claims no particular grounding philosophy. High levels of community interaction occur: meals are shared and cooking is done on a voluntary rota. Chippenham, Mansfield and Gricklegrass form one of the most unusual collectives of intentional communities in the world.

Mansfield

Founded in 1972 and part of the Heartwood Trust, this community had just two adult members and one child in March 2001. Mansfield has the capacity to house 15 people but had been experiencing problems and was, at the time of Sargisson's visits, unable to retain new members. Subsequently a further five adults and two children have joined and in 2003 numbers had stabilised at seven/three. Mansfield is an urban commune, with a shared house and outbuildings, set in a large garden, which is shared with Chippenham.

Mansfield is a large and slightly shabby single story wooden structure. Heartwood recently funded the provision of a new roof, and the next project is internal decoration. Members have their own rooms, which are private and shared space includes the bathroom, kitchen, lounge and a sunny dining room. The veranda provides further social space as the house has a no-smoking policy. It is an attractive house, and Heartwood is funding an ongoing programme of refurbishment. Outbuildings include a sleepout and sheds. The garden is beautifully kept on organic principles.

Members pay a cash rent to Heartwood and a sweat rent to Mansfield. Heartwood owns the property with a small mortgage and is responsible for maintaining the building. The community is responsible for interior decoration.

Mansfield Community was at a lull at the time of my stay in 2001. In communal terms it could be described as a low period, or a quiet time. Intentional communities often experience periods like this, especially those which are co-ops. These tend to have higher turnover than communities which require a buy-in. Leaving an intentional community is always difficult but leaving one in which you have capital invested is even harder. Mansfield had particular local circumstances that account for some of their problems in recruiting new members and these are discussed in Chapter Eight. However, the community plays an important historic role in New Zealand, being part of the CAI and latterly Heartwood. Moreover, it has revived since 2001 and is now beginning to flourish once again.

Creekside

In 1973, a group of friends bought property as tenants in common in St. Albans, Christchurch intending to build a small community something on the order of what became the co-housing movement (see below). The community, which still exists, illustrates the advantages and disadvantages of building a community around a group of friends.

The community, called Creekside because it was build along the edge of Dudley Creek, grew out of discussions in the 1960s among a group of friends at Canterbury University who became interested in the various experiments in communal living that were becoming known at the time. Most were members of the Student Christian Movement who became involved in the restoration of an old house that had been donated to the SCM. According to members of the community, this work provides part of the background to their decision to make the bold step of forming a community themselves.[1] Working together, they formed bonds that led them to believe that they could fulfil their earlier dreams of living together.

They bought the land, which had one house on it, and hired an architect to design buildings for the community. The two buildings that the community built symbolise the desire for both privacy and community that inspired the early members. Each building was two stories high and was comprised of two separate dwellings that opened into each other in their lounges.

Thus, the families were both separate and together. Initially (and typically) they had trouble getting approval and financing for this design, but ultimately (and untypically) they were able to get all the necessary approvals and the financing.

The initial group was composed of five young couples, although two contiguous properties were purchased later by other couples and joined to the community. One of those properties remains part of the community; the members living in the other property withdrew from the community in 1988. Thus, Creekside has always been small and, particularly at the beginning, the interactions within the community were close.

Given the relative youth of the founders, children were regularly added to the community and, by all reports, Creekside was a remarkably good place to grow up (see 'Creekside Kids'). It was also, because of the internal support system, said to be an excellent place to raise children, although there are reports of disagreements over child rearing practices that became at least temporarily divisive. Creekside is structured so that the area roads are outside the community; as a result, it provided a safe and private place for children to play. Also, as the children turned into teenagers, Creekside is an urban community with easy access to the city.

Childcare could be shared, particularly in the buildings with the shared lounges. Each child's bedroom had a baby alarm intercom system that could be connected to the other side of the building and, as a result, there was always some familiar adult available to respond.

Quite a few things were shared, such as laundries, a freezer, workshop, television and garden. Vehicles and bicycles were shared to some extent and, in one instance, two families bought a car together. Initially, there were as many as four meals in common each week with a formal community meeting about every two weeks.

As with many other communities founded around the world at this time, the intent was to combine privacy and community, particularly breaking down the relative isolation of the nuclear family by providing adults and children others with whom to interact. Some early members report that there was pressure to interact within the community rather than with friends and colleagues outside it.

The most traumatic event, apparently unexpected, was when one of the original couples left the community. Initially this couple took study leave outside the country and someone else lived in their unit for a year. The couple returned and stayed in Creekside for over two years but then chose to leave the community. Given that the five couples were young professionals, it would have been very surprising if people had not left, but this couple leaving to remain, at least for a time, in the Christchurch area, suggested that there was something not quite working about the community. But since others of the original group remained in the community for 20 years, it obviously worked for some, even if not for all.

Over the years, privacy became more important, particularly as children became teenagers. The combined lounges were walled up, and there are fewer common meals. But Creekside has survived as a small urban community and most of the people who lived there look back on their lives there with pleasure.[2]

Katajuta

Katajuta Farm became an intentional community in 1971, when a group of friends from Christchurch decided to find somewhere to live a cooperative and anarchist lifestyle. They had been flatting with a car pool and some shared . resources and wanted to increase their interdependence, collective autonomy and quality of life in a communal setting. Having searched New Zealand for a suitable location they eventually bought land on the remote (and stunning) West Coast of the South Island. The land consists of sea-facing bush and required clearing by hand before vehicles could bring in building materials. The current six to eight adult members have all been at Katajuta for many years and the community is relaxed and stable. This is a mature community. I attended their thirtieth anniversary celebration.

Freedom and autonomy have remained important. Defying conventional wisdom on intentional communities, Katajuta has survived for an extraordinary length of time without a governing doctrine or set of values beyond a shared desire for cooperation and the space in which to 'do their own thing'. (See, in contrast, Kanter's 1973 thesis on commitment.)

The land is owned by Kataujuta Farm Co., the board of which consists of all members. Members have built their own homes on the land and pay a low monthly rent, which includes $15 'privvies' for the privilege of being at Katajuta. They live in individual households scattered through the bush and hills overlooking the sea and almost invisible from the nearby road. Tucked into the bush is a community house, currently home to one member. Other buildings include a geodesic dome, a converted housetruck and wooden buildings. Income is generated individually and some members work as skilled artists and craftspeople as well as offering accommodation to backpackers. Some belong to a craft cooperative, which runs a successful gallery shop in nearby Punakiaki.

This community is well organised, being governed by a set of minimal rules (Community Agreements), which function effectively. This has not always been the case and periods of Katajuta's past have been turbulent. At one time Katajuta was infamous for wild behaviour, drug abuse and even violence. Learning from bad experiences, Katajuta refined its Community Agreements and amended its practices. Several other communities in New Zealand have subsequently borrowed the Agreements. As such, it is an important document, worth looking at in some detail:

Katajuta Community Agreements
1.   The ideal of the group is TO LIVE IN HARMONY WITH THE LAND AND THE PEOPLE LIVING ON THE LAND (emphasis in original).

This states the primary objective of the community and is the governing principle. The legal structure is fully explained in the Constitution but the Agreements summarise it thus:

> 2.   Every member is granted a sharehold in Katajuta Farm Ltd. This shareholding is non-transferrable.

The third agreement aims to ensure compliance over time, and/or regularly to remind members of their commitments to each other.

> 3.   Members must take responsibility for their own membership. Annually on our anniversary all residential members must reaffirm their support for the company by signing Katajuta Community Agreements.

The fourth agreement explains 'privies'. The fifth aims to avoid conflict over use of the natural environment and to implement the first principle:

> 5.   All members are required to bring building, fencing, tree removal, water access, access, burning off and earthworks proposals to the group for approval.

One of the remaining agreements is a commitment to consensus decision making in all cases and the rest (three more) are about what happens when people join and leave the community. I was surprised that this otherwise concise document should go into so much detail on this last matter but members explained to me that they had experienced serious problems in the past with new members. At one time they were extremely relaxed about who could come to live at Katajuta and had encountered problems with new members both behaving inappropriately and refusing to leave. The full set of agreements is included in the Appendix.

The key to the success of these agreements is their adherence to the governing ideal of the group. Members explained with delight that they had only one 'real' rule and that they considered themselves anarchists. Their system works (nowadays). This one rule is the governing principle of harmonious living with the land and people, and decisions are made by consensus so that process reflects principle. This group has lived together for years, and they are able to operate with minimal rules. Other groups, with different internal dynamics prefer a more tightly structured approach to self-governance, at least in their early years (see, for instance, the card system which is used at Earthsong, Otamatea and Anahata and which is considered in the final chapter).

Peterborough Street

Peterborough Street Community was established in 1982. The community occupies four adjacent houses in the city centre. The properties are owned by the Otakaro Land Trust, the primary objective of which is:

to relieve poverty among the economically disadvantaged and poor of Christchurch
... by establishing an equitable and empowering social structure which does not
create a class of poor and economically disadvantaged. (Otakaro Land Trust Deed:
Peterborough Charter)

The foundation of this structure is described as

- common ownership of land
- cooperative control of profit and not-for-profit enterprises
- the creation and promotion of working examples which are
  - locally based
  - democratic
  - sustainable
  - cooperative ....

*The Peterborough Trust Trustees Group aims to attain the primary objectives by
creating, running and promoting a housing cooperative.* (Otakaro Land Trust Deed:
emphasis in original)

Peterborough is an urban cooperative housing scheme which, in the past,
has operated at high levels of communality and which has an important place
in the history of the New Zealand cooperative movement. The community has
historic connections to a cooperative bakery and organic food store as well as
Prometheus, New Zealand's cooperative bank. At the time of my visit in 2001,
collective activity was lower than in the past, consisting of a weekly pot-luck
meal and working bees on the buildings and gardens.

The homes are owned freehold and without mortgage by the Otakaro Land
Trust. (The original mortgage was fully repaid some years ago.) Members pay
rent and make a labour commitment to the community. This is usually 'paid'
in regular working bees. The community retains a stable mixture of single
people and families, who live in different houses, in household units. Several
singles share a unit, whereas families have their own space. Each house has a
private garden and access to communal gardens and buildings at the back of
the properties, including a laundry, office and a large building (formerly home
to community businesses and currently used for storage).

This community is relatively affluent and has been in the position to recently
make a substantial interest-free loan to another local intentional community.
Members are all in paid employment and many are in professional employment.
One offers training in consensus decision making, a skill that he says he gained
directly from living here (see Swain, 1996).

As part of a commitment to reflection and continuation of their community's
raison d'être, Peterborough Street Community recently took part in a social
audit, in which the 12 current members and 54 former members were asked
to complete a lengthy questionnaire. The results are interesting, showing the
social profile of members, such as age upon joining (largest groups, comprising

almost 50 per cent were between 25–29, closely followed by people between 30–34); ethnicity (68 per cent Pakeha); income band and employment status while in the community (the largest groups for both past and current members being 'part time employed', followed closely by 'self-employed' and 'full time employed'). Participants were also asked about their reasons for joining and leaving the community and about internal process and structures. The overall picture that emerges from this survey is one of a self-critical group, most of whom are committed to the Community and its aims. Former members felt overwhelmingly that they had learned a lot from the experience of living here and this is a recurrent theme to which we shall return in the last chapter.

Co-Housing

Co-housing has its origins in Denmark. Saettedammen and Skraplanet were established in the late 1960s, followed by Trudeslund (1972) and Nonbo Hede (1976). These were known as *bofoe llesskaber*, 'living communities'. By 1990 there were 140 *bofoe llesskaber* in Denmark. They range in size from six to forty households and most are home to 15 to 30 households (McCamant, Durrett and Hertzman 1994, 16). Key figures in the early development of Danish co-housing were Jan Gudmand-Hoyer and Bodil Graae. They wrote and spoke of dissatisfaction with contemporary life and sought values that appeared to be disintegrating. Living in a city, they felt, led to isolation and alienation and they identified city housing to be a cause of this. Seeking something more like a village community within an urban context, they sought to live near the city in order to continue in professional employment. Working with a group of friends, they purchased land and planned a housing development at Hareskov, outside Copenhagen, in 1964.

Hareskov was short-lived due to local opposition, but an article by Gudmand-Hoyer around these experiences proved an inspiration to people across Denmark. Entitled 'The Missing Link Between Utopia and the Dated One-Family House', this short article was published in the national press and is said to have sown the 'seeds of inspiration' for co-housing in Denmark (ibid., 137).

Co-housing communities have been established all over the world. They are especially successful in mainland Western Europe. In 1977 Hilversum was set up and by the end of the century there were approximately 40 co-housing communities underway in the Netherlands. In Sweden, large communities (of 50 households or more) are popular and there has been some success re-developing existing (dysfunctional) high-rise units into co-housing schemes. Development in Norway, Germany, France and Britain has occurred later and is still at earlier stages. The Cohousing Association of the United States claims that over fifty co-housing neighbourhoods have been established in Canada and America since the 1980s (http://www.cohousing.org).

Advocates of co-housing stress the inadequacy of 'normal' housing arrangements. Traditional housing arrangements have not, they suggest, accommodated the needs produced by economic and demographic change. Traditional housing caters for the nuclear family in which one parent works and the other looks after the children. However, families arranged like this are a declining phenomenon. Nobody caters, in planning terms, for the needs of the adults and children in sole parent households; for two-parent households in which both parents work; for single adults; or for adults whose children have left home. Add rising housing costs and an increasingly mobile population, they say, and the result is modern cities and suburbs which lack a sense of community and people who lack a sense of belonging.

Similar criticisms are made by the members of many other intentional communities, but co-housing claims to be distinct from that of other groups. The difference, they claim, is that co-housing is non-ideological, non-hierarchical and pragmatic. Our discussions in this book show this distinction to be of little value as many intentional communities are non-ideological, non-hierarchical and socially heterogeneous. There is an identifiable core to co-housing that was first articulated by McCamant and Durrett in their 1984 book, *Cohousing, a Contemporary Approach to Housing Ourselves*, which has become the cohousing 'bible' and contains practical discussions of 'how to' establish and maintain communities as well as some historical and philosophical discussion. They identify the key principles of co-housing as a commitment to participatory processes in which residents are part of community planning, design and management, a strong emphasis on design for neighbourhood and common facilities (McCamant, Durrett and Hertzman 1994, 38–42).

Two further core principles are a commitment to a non-hierarchical structure and 'separate income sources', in which households are responsible for their own income and finances (http://www.cohousing.pl.net).

We can see from this that co-housing communities are designed (usually from scratch) by their founders and further that they are designed to foster community whilst preserving privacy. For instance, they contain a mixture of common and private space: homes are private but there is a 'common house', which contains shared facilities that vary from community to community. These may include, as at Trusdesland (Denmark), a laundry, dark room, television room, walk-in freezer, guest room, music room and a computer room. Others have children's playrooms, libraries and rooms specifically designated for use by teenagers. Outdoor shared facilities might include a play area for children and common orchards or gardens. Often parking is prohibited beyond a certain point and pathways are designed in such a way as to facilitate chance meetings, winding between the houses instead of in straight lines through the settlement. Intentional design to facilitate all of this is a feature of co-housing. Most co-housing communities also attempt to facilitate social diversity by combining a mixture of privately owned and rented houses and flats.

Earthsong Eco-Neighbourhood

This co-housing project began life at the planning stage in 1995. It is New Zealand's only up-and-running co-housing scheme. Building began in 2000 and in 2003 has reached the second stage of building what will be a neighbourhood of 32 homes. Whilst some suggest that co-housing belongs on the borderlines of a survey of intentional communities, we include it because of its strong community ethic and, further, because it marks a new development in the search for a cooperative lifestyle. In this case, that lifestyle is city based and ecologically sustainable.

Earthsong is a showcase for community design and the group, which has met for years to plan the community, has considered each aspect of community development (such as, ethics, physical design, decision making and induction). This group combines pragmatic planning with utopian desire – the desire for a better way of being (Levitas, 1990).

> We are a group of people currently living in regular nuclear households, but with a vision of how a different way of living could be more sustaining of us individually, collectively, and globally. Our vision includes building a cohousing community ... while also caring for the earth that sustains us. (Earthsong: http://www.cohousing. pl.net/infobook/principles.html)

The site covers four acres and will soon contain 32 semi-detached homes. Earthsong has incorporated the principles of both co-housing, and permaculture into its design. Permaculture aims to maximise natural efficiency and minimise human effort in the maintenance of local ecological systems (see Mollison 1999). In line with this, building methods employ low impact techniques and use readily available local materials. Rammed earth is used for external supporting walls; it is warm in winter and cool in summer. Upper stories are built of untreated and chemical-free wood from plantation Poplar, Macrocarpa and Lawson Cypress trees. Solar heating provides most of the hot water. Building materials are chosen with care and regard to their energy content, toxicity, environmental impact, durability and suitability for recycling. The design of the site has taken into account an existing orchard and makes best use of the lie of the land.

Whilst in-going costs are relatively high,[3] running costs should be low once the infrastructure is complete. Earthsong combines mixed ownership, with some private ownership (some unit titles are still for sale) and some rented accommodation. Purchasers sign up to the community's ethics and principles, which are explained by one of the group's founders, Robyn Allison:

> The three links that support our vision statement are, to be socially sustainable, to be environmentally sustainable and to be a model to demonstrate to others how it is possible to live more sustainably, really. So the environmental sustainability is obvious, really – it's all in place: water systems, solar power and that sort of thing.

> Social sustainability is really about the whole nature of cohousing, which to me is about having that balance between individual autonomy and group cooperation and it is a balance of the key words for me. Looking out for each other, being part of a wider group, everybody has different skills and different time availability and things like that. There are older children who don't have other children in their lives, who would really love to spend some time with young children, for instance. And there are young adults with babies who often struggle to get some space. It's a compilation of different people's circumstances, it's just amazing ... The other thing about social sustainability is the cooperation over all sorts of things – minimising our use of resources – it means that we can have a really rich, full life without everybody having to own this, that, and the other thing and everybody having to manage on their own. (Robyn, Earthsong, 14 April 2001)

The group takes collective responsibility for all decisions that effect its future and decisions are made by consensus. They meet once a month and have planned each stage of the community's design together with an architect.

Whilst this does not form an explicit part of their vision statement or public account of themselves, the founders of Earthsong have also put thought into the financial sustainability of the settlement. It is located within easy travelling distance of Auckland on a road with a bus route to enable people to travel easily to work. (Many rural communities in New Zealand have faced financial crises, as employment is scarce in remote locations.) A later stage of building concerns the establishment of on-site road front businesses in two large units, all of which will be consistent with the community's ethics (for example, green retail outlets).

> We're not trying to be a rural community. We're just close to everything because we're not trying to be fully self-sustainable. There's a really strong intention to keep integrated with the wider community so that we can be available to them; they can actually come out and see what we're doing and see what can be achieved on an urban site, and take ideas away, and the city is available to us for work, schools, – that's really important. (Ibid.)

Getting this dream off the ground has been difficult and the group has experienced some problems. For example, their building contractor went bankrupt and subsequent quotations for remaining work were significantly higher than the one in the original budget. As a consequence, they have borrowed from the Prometheus Bank. It has required massive amounts of energy and commitment on the part of its members to establish this community, and this has not been without personal cost or difficulty.

But Earthsong is a pioneer community in New Zealand, being the first co-housing scheme in the country. Its members are committed to their dream of a more sustainable lifestyle and are working pragmatically to create a space in which this is possible and systems and processes that will enable it to become a reality. The group consists of a mixture of families, including single parent households, dual parent households, couples and single people. A women's house has recently been purchased. The site has been designed to promote the social sustainability that Robyn describes. At the front of the property, near the road and the site for new businesses, is a car park and the remainder of the property is car-free. Footpaths wind from the car park past houses to the community house, which lies at the centre of the site. This is so that people will encounter each other as they come and go to and from work, school or other activities outside the eco-neighbourhood. Shared space will include the community house, orchards and gardens.

Feminist Communities

I visited and/or interviewed members of three women's communities in New Zealand, Earthspirt, Kiriwai and Aradia. These are all separatist feminist groups who seek a cooperative life amongst women.

Earthspirit

In 1985 two women who sought to create a separatist lesbian feminist community founded Earthspirit. Membership has risen and fallen over the years and the property is currently owned by three members.

Earthspirit is a rural community not far from the town of Kaitaia. Physical space includes eight acres of land: paddocks and gardens. The main house was on the property when it was acquired by Earthspirit and contains shared space including laundry and bathrooms. Other structures have been built by members of the community. New Zealand's restrictive planning law makes expansion difficult, as they cannot build additional homes. Nonetheless the community has historically consisted of larger numbers, who have lived in temporary structures or housebuses.

Earthspirit is a friendly community and members speak openly and reflectively about the challenges of community life, dynamics and relationships; the community has been through many changes over the years. The two founding members still live there but other women have come and gone. There have been changes in living arrangements; currently, each woman has her own separate home, but earlier life was more communal. One thing that has remained a constant at Earthspirit is the commitment to cooperation and to creating a feminist life amongst lesbian women.

Earthspirit was founded on feminist principles as a politicised lifestyle choice, which has taken various forms through time. It currently involves separatism in a woman-only living space. At one stage, they felt that it would be appropriate to try to live out the principle of non-possessive love between women. Here, the lover is not a possession or an extension of the self, is not owned and not controlled. This is incredibly difficult to live with and these women has struggled through difficult times and, through some painful experiences, explored their own limits and capacities. However, their commitment to lesbian separatism is unshaken. Asked about shared values, members responded thus:

> Minerva: We want to live together as lesbian women. (Minerva, Earthspirit, 11 April 2001)

> Nut: It has changed a bit over twenty years, but men not being here is one value that we've always shared. And I guess that working out relationships and talking about them, not just relationships, but things that go on – working them out, talking them out. I think talking things out. What else? Sharing things, having our own houses, having something to ourselves, we want that. (Nut, Earthspirit, 12 April 2001)

> Arafelle: I guess the main one is living with lesbians only and basically being separatist. We did consider ourselves separatist in the beginning and I think we are still living that way, more or less. We have cooperative relationships with men, our neighbours and others, but we hardly ever have men come here at all and we don't have them as social contacts or anything like that, and that was the basis from the start, and to do as much as we can for ourselves, to be as self sufficient as possible in all sorts of ways whether it's the gardens, the orchards, building our own houses and learning all the skills that women normally rely on men for as much as possible. Then there are the values of taking care of the earth and being organic as much as possible, not using poisons on the land. (Arafelle, Earthspirit, 12 April 2001)

The women of Earthspirit have great integrity. They spoke of their experiments without hiding the fact that this has been a long hard process. Living your ideals can be difficult, especially when these involve re-forming close personal relationships.

Educational Communities

Members of this group of communities are all focussed around a school, which is either the community's *raison d'être* or else is of significant importance to a substantial number of community members. These schools aim to provide an alternative education, focused on values of cooperation, respect and responsibility. Some have been incorporated into the state educational system, while some remain independent and self-funding.

Te Ora

Te Ora, a 30-acre former tobacco farm, was purchased in 1981 by a group of friends who sought a rural cooperative lifestyle. One original member remains and, at the time of my visit in 2001, membership stood at three households, six adults and five children.

Unlike the nearby community of Graham Downs (also called 'Renaissance'), Te Ora has been unable to develop in size. From its early days, the community has been unable to expand, blocked by the local authority's refusal to grant permission to build dwellings for multiple occupancy. Consequently there is just one central house, currently home to one household, with temporary and mobile accommodation in the gardens and orchards. The land has been tenderly nurtured from its tobacco-growing state to the current mixed grassland, organic gardens and orchards. The original 72 shares of Te Ora were, at the time of my visit in March 2001, split between two members and this was the occasion of protracted conflict, which has now been resolved.

Since its inception, Te Ora has been involved with (and home to the Head Teacher of) an alternative school, Mountain Valley School. This serves the local neighbourhood as well as the nearby community of Graham Downs. Mountain Valley takes children of nursery (pre-school) age as well as primary school age. The nursery is in a separate building, allowing the smaller children to play and learn free from the rough and tumble of larger children. The primary school is in a light and airy building, which has separate spaces dedicated to different activities, such as reading, mathematics, cookery and woodwork. The children have a large amount of choice over their education in a system inspired by the Montessori schools. The mechanism for choice involves going to the designated space for that activity. An adult helper or the teacher comes to them and finds them work appropriate to their level. The Head explained that the children generally choose a balanced education without hesitation and compare well with pupils of state primary schools when they come together for secondary education.

Timatanga

This semi-rural community was established on the site of a former chicken farm in the 1970s, with a view to creating an alternative lifestyle and education for their children. They turned much of the four and a half acre site into communal gardens, converted the chicken sheds and farm buildings into houses and they founded a school.

This is an attractive community, with homes clustered around a central green space at the head of which is the school, which is still operating and now state registered. At the time of my visit in April 2001 levels of community interaction were minimal. The seven current households occupy separate living space, and there is no community house at the moment. At the far end of the property are the gardens, in which some members cultivate plots, and there are shared orchards of avocado and other fruit trees. Five households own the property and two are tenants, who are families with young children. The other households are all long-time members, most of whom have been at Timatanga since its inception.

> Elaine: We are a community that is strongly connected to the school that we run and the school is an important part of why we are here and an important part of why quite a few of us originally made a commitment to being here. We are a community

that has gone through a whole lot of different stages, through from quite an insular community that was more like an extended family, predominantly concerned with giving our children a good background and good opportunities, to now when we are more like a village of seven families.

We wanted to give our children an extensive education, we wanted to give them an education that would give them the opportunity to expand into their potential without pressuring them, so we wanted to give them a lot of freedom but we also wanted to give them a lot of resources and support to facilitate them growing into whole healthy people really. That was a really important part of why we were together initially. (Elaine, Timatanga, 24 April 2001)

Bronwyn: Timatanga was formed, in my opinion, because of the school, and that everybody that was involved with the community was involved in the school. Over the years, that has changed, and not everyone here now is involved with the school or even feels strongly about the school, and I think that is an oversight in terms of actually running the community, having a vision for the community. It may have also been something that worked to the advantage of the community in some ways. In the last few years, it has coasted along; there has been no sort of direction or even common meeting ground because there have been some people who have fallen out here, but at the moment, it is a great place to live, I feel. It is happy, it's a nice environment, and the people who are here, who want to be involved in the school, are involved in it. (Bronwyn, Timatanga, 24 April 2001)

Bronwyn grew up at Timatanga and has returned here as an adult. She was training to be a teacher at the time of my visit. Elaine had been at Timatanga for 24 years, had taught at the school in the past, and had recently started doing so again. Her adult son, who lives at Timatanga, talked of his education there. So for these people, the school is still important. Other families, whose children have grown up and left the community, now have very little contact with it.

These statements give a good idea of how the community has changed over the years. It was formed around the school and for some members this is still important. However, as with all communities that survive for a long time, there have been changes and, at the time of my visit, the group was in a phase of low communal activity and households were tending focus on their own concerns.

Anarchist Communities

Many groups have described themselves as anarchist over the years. Generally speaking this means that they are non-hierarchical and egalitarian, have no ruler and few rules. The community of Graham Downs is different, being anarchic not only in its internal arrangements but also its ownership.

Graham Downs (aka Renaissance)

This mature community was founded in 1978 and survives with a membership of between 20 and 25 adults and children. Its longevity is remarkable as this community breaks all the rules of conventional wisdom regarding intentional communities. It has no core values, doctrine or belief system; currently no management structure, meetings or processes; and no rules for membership. The land is owned in Trust by Renaissance Trust for the people of New Zealand and all New Zealanders have a right to come and live at Graham Downs.

Graham Downs was founded as an anarchist commune, committed to free and open membership. At times membership numbers have been higher, and membership is in continual flux. Unlike nearby Te Ora, Graham Downs was successful in its early applications for planning permission and gained the right to build eight houses. However, numbers exceed this and so most people live in temporary or mobile dwellings, such as housebuses or caravans. The land is extensive and beautiful, being approximately 60 acres of mixed undulating farmland and wood, and houses are scattered around the property. Communal buildings include barns, sheds, dairy and a beautiful but currently neglected community building.

Levels of collective activity were low at the time of my visit in March 2001. Communication amongst members was low, to the extent that eliciting a response to letters proved impossible, and my visit was hosted by one household rather than the whole community. Reasons given for the current situation included a culture of high alcohol use by some members, poor interpersonal relations between some members and bitterness following a prolonged community dispute. In the past Graham Downs has flourished as farming community with collective work and high levels of cooperation. It may do so again. My host explained that the physical infrastructure remains and expressed hopes that things will change.

Cooperation and Peace

Riverside

Riverside Community[4] is over 60 years old and still going strong. As a long established community, Riverside has survived against long odds and withstood both internal crises and the fundamental changes in New Zealand society. Riverside is similar to Beeville in that its roots are in the pacifist movement in New Zealand but differs in that Riverside was founded explicitly as a Christian community. The slow abandonment, after some 30 years, of its Christian character produced Riverside's most fundamental crisis and changed the nature of the community, presumably forever.

Some Quakers had tried and failed to establish a community for war resisters outside Auckland in 1916 (Grant, 244), and, of course, Beeville was founded in the early 1930s and was a centre for non-religious war resisters. Although solid documentation is hard to come by, it is generally agreed that discussion of a community of some sort was underway in the late 1930s and early 1940s among some New Zealand war resisters. During this time, Alexander C. Barrington (1906–86), who later joined Riverside, and Ormond Burton (1893–1974) discussed the establishment of a community outside Wellington where derelicts might be helped to recover by working on the land (Grant, 244). This model had been developed in the late nineteenth and early twentieth centuries by General William Booth (1829–1912) of the Salvation Army as part of his scheme to help alcoholics and others to gradually move from the city to the country and then to the colonies (see Booth for his scheme. On Salvation Army communities, see Murdoch and Spence.) In addition, in the United States, Peter Maurin (1887–1949) and Dorothy Day (1897–1980) established a number of Catholic Worker Farms, some of which still exist, with the same intent. Both these experiments were likely to have been known by Burton and Barrington, but whether they were directly influenced by the earlier examples is unknown. Since Riverside has always taken in some people with serious problems in an attempt to provide them with the basis for a new start, it may have been influenced by the discussions taking place in Wellington. And, as noted, Barrington joined Riverside. Burton, who served extended periods in prison and was expelled by the Methodist Church for his war resistance, flirted with the community a number of times but never joined and is reported to have never visited it even though he apparently once suggested that he become its 'spiritual director' (Grant, 246).

   In the early 1940s, there were three attempts to establish pacifist communities in New Zealand, one in the Waikato, one in Otorohanga, south of Hamilton and Riverside, outside Nelson. Riverside was the only one to survive the difficult start up. Although there is disagreement on the precise dates, 1941 is the most commonly accepted date for the founding of Riverside. It was established on a farm owned by Hubert Holdaway (1896–1963) and largely at his instigation. He brought together a number of mostly local Methodists who shared his views about war, and who were willing to commit themselves to an experiment in Christian community. In one article Barrington claims that he and Burton originated Riverside, but he appears to be confusing the idea for a community they had discussed with Riverside, which Barrington did not join until 1946 (Barrington 1956, 7). It is likely that they knew of Holdaway and his plans (they were all Methodists and pacifists), but there is no evidence of their direct involvement.

   About a dozen people were part of this first community, with some leaving as early as 1944. A meeting of members on 4 May 1944, shows the situation, with five attending, three in detention camp and one in jail. In 1946, an influx of those imprisoned far beyond the duration of the war joined the community, and it was re-established on a firmer footing, initially as a partnership (see Parr for details of the early history of the community).

   Riverside was founded as a Christian community and for about the first quarter of a century members had to belong to a denomination recognized by the World Council of Churches. Most were in fact Methodists, and a Methodist Church was built on the property. Members were also expected to be pacifists and members of the New Zealand Christian Pacifist Society.

The early community was centred on family groups and had difficulty incorporating single men (it is not at all clear that single women would have been acceptable) and divorced people were not acceptable. Within the community, women were primarily defined first as wives and mothers and only secondarily as community members. Holdaway, for example, opposed women working for pay, even within the community, although some did. And in the initial distribution of shares, women were given 50 and men were given 75.

There was, though, a women's meeting that dealt with issues deemed to fall within their purview. Such matters were either referred by one of the general meetings or originated from the women themselves. It is also clear that women community members were involved in the larger community outside Riverside through all the activities through which women traditionally interacted with their communities. In addition, community women took in 'state children' and young women on probation. And some community women were actively involved politically and, for example, traveled throughout New Zealand as part of Riverside's anti-war effort. Thus, the apparently simple picture of community women as wives and mothers in a patriarchal setting was, while true, much more complex. From its origins, Riverside women were active well beyond their traditional roles, and it is also worth remembering that at the very beginning many of the men were imprisoned for long periods and the survival of the community depended on the women.

The Community grew slowly but steadily until the 1970s, and while there were some problems, Riverside was composed of members who were so united in their beliefs and goals that they managed to deal with most issues without serious trauma. But in the 1960s and 1970s Riverside, as a well-established and successful commune, attracted people from both within New Zealand and overseas who were looking for a commune to join. Riverside wanted to grow and the core membership was aging, so they may not have looked as carefully at these new recruits as they might once have.

The issue that these new members brought was the single most important issue in Riverside's history, and changed it forever, was religious belief and practice. Riverside was a Christian community and initially held daily devotions before the start of work. These early morning meetings were also places where work could be planned and any matters arising could be discussed, but they were primarily brief worship services and were symbolic of the role of religion in the community.

The people who joined in the 1960s and 1970s did not hold the same religious beliefs as the founders and gradually took over the community, eliminating the Christian character of the community. In the process, founding and early members either left the community altogether or were marginalised within it. From being an explicitly Christian community, Riverside became one with, at most, a vague spirituality. The other central part of Riverside's founding, nonviolence, survived the upheaval and remains a central tenant of Riverside practice, although not as central as it was at its founding. Few, if any, of those who brought about the revolution in Riverside remain in the community today.

One basis for Riverside's longevity is the existence of a solid economic base in a successful farm. The initial role of Hubert Holdaway, whose farm it was originally, in directing the community work force and years of sheer hard work by the members created a flourishing economic enterprise that has provided a stable context for the difficulties Riverside has faced internally and externally.

The first economic base was an apple orchard, and, unlike most agriculturally based communities, for much of its existence Riverside produced primarily for sale rather than internal consumption. Fruit, vegetables, eggs and so forth were distributed within the community as available, but at times food that could have been grown on the farm was purchased because labour could not be spared for gardening. And, even so, Riverside has often depended on what many believe a practice deadly to communities, hired labour. This is in part because apple growing is both seasonal and labour intensive. The practice also requires the ability to provide housing for some of the hired workers and to be able to pay wages before the major income-producing sale of fruit. Riverside was fortunate in managing to develop a good working relationship with its bank, because it regularly had a large overdraft, often well beyond its agreed limits. But the local bank treated Riverside like other farms that would clear their debts once a year. Of course, for the banks charging interest on the overdrafts, this was good business, but many communities dealt with less sympathetic lenders.

The economic base of the community produced two long-term disagreements within the community. These concerned firstly diversification (both in crops and away from agriculture) and secondly organic farming. The first was more easily settled than the second.

Riverside did diversify its agricultural economy, adding new crops, a dairy and other products as labour, knowledge and interest became available. Its attempts to add non-agricultural areas to its economy had mixed results because these generally depended on one individual with particular skills and interests who frequently needed substantial community investment and involvement to get started and who then might leave at any time. Some members worked off the farm and brought their wages to it, but Riverside is located in a rural area, which for most of Riverside's history, had relatively few opportunities for white collar or professional employment.

The organic dispute lasted for many years with the older members obviously worried about changing a system that provided the bulk of the community's income. Younger members, who were less committed to the community and more committed to the principle of organic food production, continuously pushed for change. For many years, the New Zealand Apple and Pear Board's policies supported the anti-organic side, but as evidence grew regarding the health and environmental effects of the chemicals used, the community slowly changed its practices.

The internal economy is based on common property. When someone becomes a full member, they give all their property, excluding personal property, to the community. There has been debate from time to time about the nature of personal property; for example, is a car personal property? And this rule has prevented some people from becoming full members, even though the rule has at times been applied with considerable flexibility so as, for example, to allow people to set aside capital to support elderly relatives.

Once a person is a full member, they receive an allowance (in the earliest days there was a common purse) based on family needs, mostly determined by size, a place to live, access to community vehicles, education for their children and medical care, as needed, for the rest of their lives. For much of the history of Riverside, New Zealand had an excellent and far-reaching welfare system; since this has been largely dismantled, costs have risen for the community. When state-provided family benefit was cancelled, for instance, Riverside created its own.

Riverside tried hard to accommodate the work interests of all its members. The community regularly invested its money to establish an enterprise that would use the skills of a single member of the community. While most such investments produced a profit over the years, in some cases the member chose to leave and the community lost its investment. Some had produced enough return to justify the investment in economic terms; others did not. But for a community profit and loss is only one of the appropriate measures; the satisfaction of a member in her/his ability to use and develop skills has to be taken into account.

One of the ways that Riverside fulfilled its goal of reaching out beyond the community was through donations to groups throughout the world that were undertaking activities of which some Riverside members approved. At its meetings, the community as a whole approved such donations. In 2001 they gave to thirty nine organisations, grouped under the headings Peace, Anti-Racism, Conservation, Overseas Relief, Social Concerns and Justice and International Organisations. These included international organisations like the Red Cross and Oxfam, and national and local groups such as Movement for Alternatives to Prison and Motueka Support Link.

Another such activity was the establishment of a loan fund to assist other New Zealand communes. This program had mixed results because few communities had the resources to repay the loans on any regular schedule or at all. And without repayment, loans could not be made to other communities in need. Many loans were repaid, often late or only partially; others never were.

Decision-making in the community is consensual. Although there have been a number of strong individuals among the members, Riverside has never had a leader, but individuals have had major responsibility in specific areas, particularly in the early years.

Consensual decision-making has the advantage that once a decision is made, everyone can support it. The disadvantage is that it tends to be a slow and sometimes tedious process, and a minority, or even one person, can block change. For this reason Riverside does not accept veto by one person. An odd effect of consensual decision-making is that a process generally thought of as extremely radical is often in practice very conservative because change can be slow and hard to achieve. Consensual decision-making requires people who are committed to the good of the community and many meetings. It helps if many questions are left to individual discretion so that community decisions are unnecessary. In general, Riverside did not follow this practice but made collective decisions about many matters that other communities left to individuals to decide.

As a result, Riverside needed meetings. Early on, the day began with daily devotions, and these were followed by a discussion of the day's work. In addition, there was a monthly business meeting, which in 1957 became fortnightly and later weekly. More frequent meetings were needed, first, due to erratic attendance at morning devotions and, later, the gradual disappearance of these devotions meant the daily meeting lost its effectiveness. In addition to these meetings, there was a formal AGM (Annual General Meeting).

While Riverside has never had a leader, one of the common results of consensual decision-making is the development of an oligarchy, or rule by a few, and that appears to have occurred at periods in Riverside's history. Consensual decision-making requires people willing to speak up, express ideas and carry out decisions, and there are always people more and less willing to put themselves forward. Communities like Riverside are always looking for ways to make consensual decision-making more effective by involving more people. A common approach is to go around the room and ask everyone in the meeting for their opinion on an issue. While this achieves the end of getting more input from the less talkative, records of such exercises generally produce names that are rarely or never recorded at other times.

An interesting case at Riverside is that of A.C. 'Barry' Barrington, who clearly had a strong personality and was never shy of speaking his mind. This caused no problems while the community was agreed upon fundamental principles, but as the community changed, Barrington became a dissenter. He was committed to the community and was not about to leave, as some others did, but his presence in meetings made it difficult to come to agreements. Ultimately, he recognized that he was the problem and chose to withdraw from the meetings while remaining a member of the community. A couple of years later, a proposal was made to invite him back to the meetings and was voted down. As a trained accountant, throughout this period and for some years to come, he kept the community accounts. It is hard to see how the community could have functioned effectively under consensual decision-making if he had not withdrawn, but the situation illustrates a difficulty.

Over the years, Riverside went through a number of attempts to understand how its current members viewed the community, its future and its principles.

Sometimes this examination was stimulated by a crisis, but more often it came about from a perception that the community was drifting, which is a very common experience among communities. The results are interesting because, while the language used changed with the times, the goals and principles did not, although it is not clear that the members recognised this. Most striking is that the goals set out by the earliest members tend to be repeated throughout Riverside's history, even though the explicit religious language disappeared and was replaced with either secular language of ideals or a vague spirituality.

As with other communities, the correct balance between the community and the individual was elusive and had to be regularly re-found. At the beginning, the stresses drove out a few and created unity among those who stayed. And, given its explicit religious and political positions, the balance appears to have been easier to maintain in these early days than it became later.

Particularly in the 1970s, when communal living was something that many people tried, Riverside faced a problem, the free-rider problem, faced by many other communities. Many people joined communities with no real knowledge of what was involved and no commitment to the community. Perhaps they initially intended to participate fully in community life, but, finding that they could slack off and still be supported, they did. Some at Riverside even argued that the community should live off the hard work of its founders and have no thought for the future. In New Zealand, Beeville faced precisely this problem at the same time, and this issue appears to have helped bring about its demise.

The people of Riverside managed to survive a number of such episodes, and, as at most communities, the balance shifted over the years. But, again as with most other communities, Riverside members have had to regularly remind themselves that they belong to a community. Probably the single most common refrain heard in communities was repeated at Riverside, 'clean up after yourself, don't leave it for others to do'. Rules about vehicle use; reminders to return tools; all the issues families face, communities face on a larger scale.

From its earliest days, Riverside included a substantial number of children; in fact, at times there were more children than adults. Initially Riverside was very unpopular in the area because of its antiwar activities, and some of the children, who attended the local schools, bore the brunt of this unpopularity, ranging from jeers to physical attack. This is a common experience of children whose parents choose unconventional lifestyles. The longevity of Riverside and, at times, the sheer number of children from Riverside in the local schools seems to have mitigated such treatment. In 2001 most of the children attached to the community were at local schools.

Over the years, the community has regularly struggled with what to do with and about its children within the community. One recurring concern has been how much additional allowance a family should get for a child and how that amount should increase as the child aged. The current system is quite complicated but appears to work well. In 2001 an adult allowance was $154.10. Teenagers receive 80 per cent of this and children receive proportionately less, at birth they are entitled to 30 per cent of an adult allowance, at one year 32 per cent and so on. Another issue was what provision should be made within the community for the interests of children, such as purchasing books, access and rules regarding television and so forth. Access to community vehicles was a regular issue for adults, and the refusal to give teenagers access to them proved an area of long-term tension between the older children and the community.

Riverside, like many other communities, considered establishing an alternative school for its children and for other children in the area, but they never established one (see *Community Comments* [5 February and 1 July 1977]). The community has subsidised certain types of education, such as music, which is not available through the local schools, and it provided grants for both boys and girls at university or in vocational training.

And Riverside has also faced a question faced by every other community that has lasted long enough to raise the issue, why don't our children stay in the community as adults? As with other communities, there is no single answer. Some children hate life in community; others love it but like children raised in other settings, they feel the need to strike out on their own. Some community children return to community or join a different one after a long or short time outside it. A few stay. There is one family, the Coles, which has several generations of members at Riverside and one of Riverside's key members today, who manages the farm, is a second generation member of this family.

Riverside was often short of appropriate housing but found it very difficult to agree on investing the resources to add housing, on where to put the new house, and on the appropriate design for the house. It also had long discussions lasting for many meetings on whether to sell property, sometimes property that included housing but was not close to the centre of the community. And as it debated these sales, it also debated what to do with the money they might or might not get. At different times in its history, Riverside has tried various experiments in communal living and it currently favours the most common arrangement in New Zealand intentional communities: one household per flat or house.

One long-term issue, which reflects the desire to help community members to fulfill their own goals, was the proposal made by four members of the community to help them establish a new community on land owned by Riverside. Some communities have established a satellite community when membership reached a point where it was felt to be both desirable and possible, but Riverside was not at that point. The debate was lengthy and had reached the stage of agreeing to sell a house to provide the financing and getting approval from the local authorities when two of the proponents suddenly left the community to follow other interests.

Alcohol and drugs have also been a problem. Riverside prohibited drugs but at one point found that one was being grown on community property by a community member. For a long time alcohol was prohibited altogether, and, over the years, Riverside took in many alcoholics from the surrounding area to attempt to assist them in drying out. This activity reflects Riverside's commitment to assist non-community members, a practice that goes back to the founding. But such assistance has also regularly caused problems; the people being helped often appear to have had no great desire to quit drinking or to fulfill whatever promises they made to the community, and a number were personally disruptive. One such case brought about a particularly traumatic incident when a community member, believing he was protecting his wife, attacked a man physically. The community reaffirmed its belief in non-violence, but it went through a lengthy dispute before the healing process could take place.

Some disputes were particularly divisive or difficult to solve. Marriage breakup within a community is always difficult, even more so than outside. Riverside has faced some quite traumatic breakups and spent much meeting time on how to respond as a community to these situations, with particular concern with the effect on the children.

Riverside was actively involved in meetings with other New Zealand communes, both nationally and locally, and a number of such meetings and communal festivals were held at Riverside. As a result, it became both a model for other communities and attracted members from other communities, either after they broke up or, sometimes, while they were still in existence. Movement among communities is a common phenomenon, and Riverside, as an obviously successful community, has been something of a beacon for those interested in communal living, both from New Zealand and overseas.

In its 60 plus years, Riverside has faced and met many challenges that were often not met by other communities. There are few other intentional communities in the world with the life span of Riverside. Some Israeli kibbutzim are older; there are a few little-known communities in the United States that have recently celebrated as much as 75 years; and there may well be others that have deliberately escaped attention. But Riverside is perhaps unique in having managed to survive while changing one of the two most fundamental principles of its founding, its religious base, while holding on to the other, its commitment to non-violence.

Conclusion: Cooperative Lifestyles

Intentional communities often have a serious aim to which all members are committed. This might be saving the environment, achieving a religious utopia, or promoting world peace. However, this does not mean that all members spend every day in the community earnestly pursuing the group's mission. They have other needs to meet: relationships to establish and maintain and personal goals to meet. Sometimes living in community aids this and sometimes it makes these things more difficult to manage.

It is particularly important in this group of communities that these personal needs are met. This is because these communities are often loosely bound. They are more than just groups of friends who share a house, but they often lack the glue that binds many of the other kinds of communities discussed in this book. They defy the conventional wisdom that for a community to 'succeed' (that is, to achieve historical longevity), its members must share a commitment to a higher cause, the most binding of these being a religious commitment (Kanter 1973).

Members of this group of communities often just want to live cooperatively. For some, this is part of a wider or deeper ideological commitment, but for many it is an end in itself. Because these communities often have no wider religious or ideological bond, the communities themselves *are* the glue that binds their members. They must, therefore, meet the needs of their members.

The community with one of the loosest ideological bonds is Chippenham, and here this can be clearly observed. Members gave a variety of reasons for being a part of this group. Some joined because they felt lonely and wanted a sense of belonging, some sought an alternative environment in which to bring up their children. Others liked the structures, which are efficient. Some joined for political reasons. All valued the social environment.

> LS: I'd like you to begin by describing Chippenham Community for me.
> Fiona: Well, I'd say Chippenham is a fairly vibrant community at the moment. I think of it as a microcosm of society as a whole ... we've got such a diverse group of people, diverse ages, and it brings in all the social interactions you have in a wider society, so I think it is wonderful. It's really good. It's a high-energy place. I'm sure you've picked up on that.
> LS: Yes.
> Fiona: We've got a good group, which makes a difference. I actually think the community functions well if you take into account all the aspects of human nature and throw this many people together, living in one house; I think we function pretty well as a group, we've got a pretty good group of people. I think it is working for us now.

Asked about shared values in the group, she says the following:

> Fiona: Well, I think respect is probably the first one, respecting other people's opinions and respecting that people do things sometimes in different ways, and that is not in the basic household chores, but just to respect people as individuals. There is no one living here that actually has a genuinely horrible nature, who likes being mean to people and likes to cause trouble or be vindictive in a deliberate way, and I think that is the basic moral thing. The ethical thing as well – I'm probably the worst with that because I think community living is an environmental thing as well ... the people here do think about those things. They think about the world and the political situation in various parts of the country and the world. People talk about those things and have a standard at which something isn't acceptable, some kind of treatment of a race or a culture is not an acceptable thing. Basically it is a more relaxed attitude to the differences in people, that's what it is really, being more accepting of anyone because you can have anyone come and live here. There's a guy that we're considering for membership at the moment – he suffers from autism [Asperger's Syndrome]. (Fiona, Chippenham, 16 March 2001)

For Fiona then, Chippenham is a community based on the core value of respect. This encompasses respect of difference (age differences, racial, religious and cultural diversity); respectful day-to-day encounters with people, as well as (for her) a duty of care towards the environment. It is linked to egalitarianism and elsewhere in the interview, she spoke of the respectful attitude of adult members towards the children as an example of this. Other members used the terms 'equality' and 'cooperation' to describe the core values of the group, but all described similar phenomena. All felt that there was a common feeling of regard for others and a collective commitment to uphold this.

This permits them to function well as a diverse group under one roof. The community is, as Fiona says, lively and full of conversation. For her as a sole parent this is invaluable and other members described the value of sharing life with such a mixed group of people. Members of Chippenham range in age from toddlers to mature adults, the oldest in 2001 was probably in his late forties. Some members are single without children, some are sole parents, some are couples with children and some are couples without children. Charlotte, who is in her early twenties, particularly enjoyed the availability of older members and the presence of children. Her partner, Whare, had rejoined after leaving as a teenager and was pleased to find Dave still there. Dave has been at Chippenham the longest and has seen it through all the conflicts discussed in Chapter 8. And so they comprise a mixture of experienced and new members.

The core values at Chippenham may be loosely defined but they generate a community in which diversity flourishes and is respected. Utopias are sometimes reviled for their homogeneity, and intentional communities are sometimes assumed to be tightly defined by an in-group of people who are ethnically or socially the same. Chippenham shows that it need not be like this. Members are expected to contribute to collective activities both formal (sweat rent) and informal (shared meals) and in return are part of a supportive group. This mutually sustaining relationship between individuals and the community may not work for every member all of the time (there are always ups and downs), but it is nonetheless a mark of a successful community. This is important for all intentional communities, but particularly so of this group, which lacks the ties that bind many of the others discussed in this book.

Notes

1 The story of the house and its rebuilding can be found in Roberts and Roberts.
2 See Carter for the history of the community from personal reminiscences, detailing both the joys and conflicts and particularly strong on the impacts of people leaving and joining.
3 Earthsong houses are offered at over $200,000.
4 This discussion is based on reading widely in the published and unpublished materials from and on Riverside, an interview with someone who grew up in Riverside, and visits to and interviews with current members. The papers of Riverside and those of a long-term member, A.C. Barrington, are at the Alexander Turnbull Library. In addition, interviews with A.C. Barrington and recordings of some of his speeches and sermons are in the Oral

History Collection at the Alexander Turnbull Library. We have also used material from a file of newspaper clippings at Nelson Provincial Museum, and the few papers regarding Riverside that are in the Macmillan Brown Library at Canterbury University. In addition, Riverside published *Riverside News*, nos 1–7 (December 1953–September 1959); *The Bridge*, nos 1–7 (September 1970–June 1973; *Community Comments* (1976–79); and participated in publishing three issues of a local communal newsletter, *Sunflowers and Blue Suede Shoes* ([1978]), *Sunflowers and Sunday Punk* (Spring 1978), and *Sunflowers* (1979). Riverside also published the following about itself: Rain, *Riverside Community,* and *Why Christian Community.* For other material, see Sargent, 1997. Since the publication of this guide, Riverside has celebrated its sixtieth anniversary, which received considerable press coverage.

Chapter 7

Environmentalist Communities

Introduction

As I evolve in my own understandings of land and land ownership, as I integrate the things I learn about the ancient knowledge of the Maori with my own knowledge and the highly dominant European culture here, I do think that they're 'onto it' in relation to the guardianship of the land and the understanding of conservation and the preservation of resources. In my own history, my family leaves the UK, comes here, and gains freedom by standing on someone else's freedom ... I think as a New Zealander I have to come to terms with my responsibility and accountability in this. It has forged my idea of how I feel about the land, and to continue treating the land as a commodity, as something that can be used and traded and exchanged, is actually leading to the complete desecration of the planet and that at some point, something more real and that is more respectful of the bounty of the land and the cycles of nature, has to be accommodated. ... I learn more all the time as I refine my own ideas, my own more radical Green eco politics with the edge of Maori understandings. (Chrissie, Te Ora, 2 February 2001)

Our survey identified over 20 'green' intentional communities in New Zealand today. These people have chosen to live together because they share a concern about environmental issues and/or ethics. They want to live in a way that expresses this concern and to protect, conserve and live closely with the non-human world. Many communities in New Zealand are shades of green. What marks this group as distinct is that ecology is their main reason for being. The group includes eco-villages, rural communes and communal organic farms as well as communities who develop the spiritual aspect of ecologism, deep ecology.

Green communities comprise the fastest growing group in the country. In some ways, this growth is consistent with recent developments worldwide. In the UK, for instance, Sargisson visited over a dozen communities in 1997/8, each of which had some affiliation to environmental politics or ecological preservation (Sargisson 2000). A few, like the Findhorn Foundation (founded 1962), were mature, but most were under ten years old. The United States has a long history of rural ecological communalism and is home to such long established communities as Twin Oaks (founded 1967) and here too, there has been a flourishing of new groups, committed to living sustainably with their environment. Other groups, such The Farm, have come to focus increasingly on environmentalism.

Background Influences

> That relationship with the bush and the sea is instinctive, because when one opens
> one's eyes for the first time and sees the sea and the bush – I think that goes far
> beyond the mind – and that same goes for the land. I guess it's what you open your
> eyes to. It forms a bond, and you don't want to leave this place. You're a part of it
> and you have to look after it. (Philip Ward, 27 March 2000)

The voice speaking here belongs to a traditional farmer, not to a deep ecologist,
a hippie or a communard. Three generations of this family farm or have farmed
the tip of the Coromandel Peninsula and here Philip speaks of his relationship
to the place. He is a cattle and sheep farmer of wild and remote hill country,
widely respected in the local community as a successful livestock breeder and
spoken of warmly by people in nearby intentional communities. He speaks of
the bond that many people feel with the land of New Zealand.[1]

New Zealand inspires people and so environmental awareness runs deep,
generating a predisposition to conservation. Pioneer life was harsh and
resources had to be saved and this still forms a significant memory, particularly
in rural districts. Notwithstanding this, a recent report shocked the nation by
finding that the average New Zealander produces more trash than the average
American. Many New Zealanders are proud of their beautiful country and
seek to preserve her special habitat. This all forms an important part of the
background to our story.

Another important set of background influences come from Maori
worldviews about the relationship between people and the world they live in.
'The influence of the Maori cannot be over-estimated' (Brian, Mamaki, 21
March 2001). Maori communities are organised around hapu, or tribes, an elder
of which is Chief. Access to these people is difficult but Sargisson was able to
talk with two Chiefs in different districts. One of them, Paki Harrison, agreed
to be interviewed. Asked to explain Maori views of land and conservation,
he began like this:

> The ancient Maori religion was environmental; they didn't have a supreme God
> or entity but they believed in a supreme presence or a supreme power. Everything
> emanated from the Universe and everything would go back to it. This is an argument
> that early missionaries tried to refute. The land, sea and sky – our people, in their
> genealogies, relate to them. They find a common ancestor to the sea. Church people
> and Christians taught us to use the term God to describe this. The sea, to us is a
> God itself. (Paki Harrison, 20 March 2000)

The Maori creation story spiritually links people, place and godhead. In
this account, each created thing has and is a spiritual guardian. Humans and
their environment are divinely connected. Further layers are added to this
relationship by Maori traditions of whakapapa, or genealogy. The result is
a complex sense of interdependence between people and place, sentient and
non-sentient life. So, the Moehau Mountain on the Coromandel peninsula,

for instance, is the resting-place of Tame Te Kapu, captain of the Arawa, one of the first canoes to land in this area. The full name of the Moehau is 'Moengahau A Tama Te Kapua', which translates as 'the windy sleeping place of Tama Te Kapua'. He and his kin are the progenitors of the hapu Ngati Hei, Ngati Huarere and Ngati Hako. And so, place, human ancestors and spiritual (elemental) ancestors all form important parts of tribal whakapapa, which, in turn, inform individual identities.

This is all assumed knowledge in New Zealand and forms the backdrop for Maori and Pakeha societies. These two peoples live side by side and many New Zealanders are of mixed ancestry. It is commonplace in New Zealand to hear a person speak of spiritual beings as familiar, familial, traceable, reachable and touchable. This stems in part from the Maori practice of naming their ancestors (whakapapa). The word 'whakapapa' indicates both the idea of genealogy and the act of naming, remembering, affirming and re-inscribing one's ancestry. To recite whakapapa is to build one's history layer by layer and to affirm it. It connects the person to all of their ancestors, human, spatial and spiritual.

This contributes to a particular view of self as well as a particular conception of land. Maori 'own' land collectively. They refer to themselves as 'people of the land'. They are part of it – as it is part of them. As was the case in North America and Australia, European settlers encountered a people who did not have a conception of transferable permanent ownership.

> The very first instances of land as a commodity was when the settlers began to arrive and they wanted title. Our people didn't understand the idea of purchasing it. They thought if they gave title for their piece of land, then they were allowed to use it for such a time as they were finished with it, and then they would give it back. (Paki Harrison, 20 March 2000)

Maori conceptions of tenure were incompatible with that of the incoming settlers and made no sense within European law. For the Maori, land was held ancestrally (*take tipu*); could be acquired by conquest and occupation (*take raupatu*); could be passed on by a dying chief (*take ohaki*); gifted (*take tuku*); or discovered (*take taunaha*). Tenure was conditional on use and occupation. Maori land has always been (and is still) held collectively. Maori lands (and other significant possessions) belong to the tribe and not to individuals. Some people in green communities would like to return to this view of land ownership.

Land is a huge political issue in New Zealand today. The state is making compensation for the alienation of Maori land but the latest dispute concerns the foreshore and seabed. The Government says it wants to protect for all New Zealanders – the Maori say that this takes away their ancestral fishing rights. In addition to the more visible debates over injustices and expropriation of land, but of equal importance, is the impact of Maori beliefs about ownership on the Pakeha population.

Of course, the Maori, like the other settlers on this land, did cut and burn down trees, and did extinguish certain unique species, such as the Moa, a giant flightless bird of up to eight feet high. Nonetheless, their perspective on land is significant and influential, particularly on this group of communities.

These background factors mean that the wider environmentalist movement finds a natural home in New Zealand. Not all New Zealanders are 'green', by any means, but this backdrop of pre-existing beliefs is significant. It means that ideas from the (relatively new) green movement seem quite familiar. Two of these imports emerged from interviews as particularly important. These are permaculture and The Findhorn Foundation.

The term 'permaculture' was coined by Australian Bill Mollison and his books by that title can be seen alongside the poems of James K. Baxter in many community libraries (Mollison 1978, 1979, and 1992). Permaculture is a pragmatic and holistic approach to organic farming, involving design for life – the careful design of living space and relationships. It offers a practical blueprint for food production, building design and economic and social relationships as well as an implicit ethical code.

> Permaculture involves ethics of earth care because the sustainable use of land cannot be separated from life-styles and philosophical issues. The ethical basis of permaculture rests upon care of the earth-maintaining a system in which all life can thrive. This includes human access to resources and provisions, but not the accumulation of wealth, power, or land beyond their needs. (http://www.conserve. org.nz/evens/otamatea.html)

The term combines 'permanent agriculture' and 'permanent culture'. Permaculture is about designing sustainable ecological human habitats and food production systems. These systems should be, as far as possible, self-sustaining. It seeks to integrate people, human dwellings, microclimate, annual and perennial plants, animals, soils and water into stable and productive communities, developing virtuous and sustaining relationships between these elements by placing them correctly in the landscape. It encourages synergies by mimicking patterns found in nature.

A second set of green 'imports' comes from the lifestyle and beliefs of the Findhorn Foundation in Scotland. In interview, people across the land spoke of personal visits to Findhorn Foundation communities, and/or having read their literature and found it compelling. The Foundation is an umbrella organisation covering two intentional communities and a myriad of satellite associations and businesses. It is probably best described as New Age, fostering eclectic spiritual beliefs, pioneering a spiritual communal lifestyle and, latterly, establishing an eco-village (see Sargisson 2000, and Metcalf 1996).

New Zealand's Green Communities

Some of the communities discussed in this chapter are survivors of an explosion in communes in the 1970s (Sargent 1997). Others are new ecovillages. Some are secular, pragmatic, and aim mostly at conservation. Some are spiritual, and aim mostly to build closer relationships between humans and their environment. Some combine these concerns. All seek to realise a dream. For some, this is a pristine habitat in which native species are re-introduced and treasured. For some, this is a life closer to nature, in which humankind guards rather than exploits nature. For others, this is a world of sustainable economics, non-polemical politics and limits to growth. Others seek bliss and unity through a deep connection with other forms of life. They cover the light-dark spectrum of green concerns.

From this plethora of intentional communities with a 'green' *raison d'être* it is possible to identify four dominant categories. These will be discussed below and are the older rural communes (of the 1970s), cooperative organic farms, green spiritual communities and ecovillages.

1970s Rural Communes: The Older Generation

The communities in this group were all established as communes in or soon after the 1970s. Some, such as Karuna Falls, have recently re-cast themselves as ecovillages. Others still identify themselves as communes. Their founders were groups of friends who sought an unmaterialistic life closer to nature. Often these people were highly educated. Many came from the hippie movement of the 1970s, seeking freedom and an opportunity to 'do their own thing'.

They sought cheap land in beautiful places in which to opt out and live a simpler life. They located their utopian communities in remote backwaters, up mountains, in steep valleys, or on the shorelines of wild coastal districts. The land they bought was usually uncultivated, often uncultivatable and unsuitable for farming. These idealists hacked tracks into their piece of bush and built themselves homes from timber or else hauled caravans up valley sides as temporary (become permanent) homes. The communities are based on shared land, which is collectively owned, and members live in homes that were often built without the proper planning consents (Julie Sargisson 1990). There is always a 'community building' for meetings and shared meals (often now disused). They have changed over time and have all been through more and less cohesive and more or less happy times.

A life close to nature, for these people, meant the rejection of modern conveniences such as mains water and electricity, telephones and washing machines. They lived in shacks, huts, or vans in the bush, remote from roads, shops, schools and medical care. Children were home-educated, and some communes ran their own schools. They had to generate high levels of material and emotional self-sufficiency. This was challenging. In interview people from these communities spoke of both the hardship and of the sense of awe they had felt when living this 'close to nature'.

Table 7.1   New Zealand's green communities

Name Founding date (where known)	Location	Membership and ownership	Aims: key terms (self descriptors)	Description and main activities
Anahata Retreat Centre 1996	Birds Clearing, Golden Bay, South Island	Permanent: 5 adults, 1 child Part time: 2 adults Shared ownership (members)	Holistic lifestyle, spirituality, ecology, education	Remote rural. Communal space = one house plus yurt. Own homes Alternative energy/ sewage disposal Permaculture garden Educational and retreat facilities
Anahata 2000	Albany (old Centrepoint premises) North Island	25 adults 23 children Rent paying Owned by Trust	Cooperation Ecology Sometimes self-describe as an eco-village	High levels of communal living. Founded by former Centrepoint members. Semi-rural
Autumn Farm 1970s	Takaka, South Island	4 households shared ownership	Artisan lifestyle	Small organic farm, shared ownership, collective work
Awaawaroa Bay Ecovillage 1995	Waiheke Island, North Island	15 households Members are equal shareholders in Awaawaroa Co. This gives 999-yr lease	Sustainable lifestyle Organic farming, biodiversity, co-operation, consensus	Rural hill country pasture of 420 acres Building own homes Monthly meetings Ecovillage

Table 7.1 (cont'd)

Name Founding date (where known)	Location	Membership and ownership	Aims: key terms (self descriptors)	Description and main activities
Bree 1970s	Colville, North Island	Unknown	Cooperative lifestyle back to nature	Rural commune
Clearwater 1970s	Kaitaia, North Island	4 households	Alternative lifestyle	Isolated rural farm commune. Own homes. Limited communal activity
Earthsong Eco-Neighbourhood 1995	Waitakere City, North Island	32 homes as yet unfinished. 1 person in residence Freehold	Sustainable co-housing	Urban co-housing project. Rammed earth buildings, ecologically sensitive design. Building in progress
Gentle World 1970	Kaitia, Northland and Big Island Hawaii	19 young adults 2 leaders Freehold	Vegan non-possessive lifestyle	Peripatetic, vegan lifestyle and diet. Free love. Follow leaders 'Sun' and 'Light'
Gricklegrass 1970	Oxford, South Island	5 adults Owned (with small mortgage) by Heartwood Trust. Members pay rent and 'sweat rent'	Ecologically sustainable organic communal lifestyle	Rural farm of 40 acres. High levels of communal commitment and energy. Farm generates rent and small income that is re-invested. Young membership

Table 7.1 (cont'd)

Name Founding date (where known)	Location	Membership and ownership	Aims: key terms (self descriptors)	Description and main activities
Happisam 1970 approx.	Takaka, South Island	Unknown	Alternative lifestyle	Rural river valley commune
Karuna Falls 1976	Waikawau Bay, North Island	20 adults approx. Own homes, shared ownership of valley	Alternative lifestyle, permaculture	Rural commune in valley, now reviewing aims and describing self as ecovillage
Katajuta 1971	Punakaiki, South Island	6/8 adults Owned by Katajuta Farm Co.	Live in harmony with land and people. Anarchist and cooperative	Rural, coastal mature commune on West Coast. Recreation, art and low-impact lifestyle
Kohatu Toa EcoVillage 1996	Kaipara North Island	4 households 7 adults, 4 children – expanding	Establish sustainable ecological community	Rural farm in valley. New ecovillage. Organic gardening and farming, permaculture and indigenous species preservation
Mamaki Farm Village 1984	North Island	12 adults	Cooperative and ecologically sustainable lifestyle. Good communication	Rural ecovillage in coastal valley. Mature and established. Currently no animals and low levels of collective activity

Table 7.1 (cont'd)

Name Founding date (where known)	Location	Membership and ownership	Aims: key terms (self descriptors)	Description and main activities
Moehau 1974	Port Charles, North Island	10 adults (4 resident) 2 children. Owned by Moheau Co. Ltd. Members either shareholders or tenants	Alternative lifestyle, conservation and guardianship of land	Remote rural commune. Own homes. 198 hectares bush and hill country. 1980s created a conservation reserve. Music and craft workshops
Opuhi 1973	Colville, North Island	1 resident adult, 8 members. Owned collectively by members	Alternative natural lifestyle	Rural isolated commune with just one person still in residence. Community house and own homes. Remote. Regular meetings
Otamatea 1997	Kaipara North Island	11 households 17 adults, 6 children Each unit has freehold of 5 acres plus common ownership of 176 acres (Otamatea Ltd Co) – expanding	Establishment of an ecovillage: permaculture, cooperation, support, respect	Rural coastal peninsula. Young community. Separate homes, weekly meetings and regular working bees. Building own homes, work together on communal land (biodynamic). Some animals (cattle)

Table 7.1 (cont'd)

Name Founding date (where known)	Location	Membership and ownership	Aims: key terms (self descriptors)	Description and main activities
Rainbow Valley Community 1974	Takaka, South Island	16 adults, 11 children Some tenants, some shareholders in limited company	Alternative lifestyle, ecology, education	Rural river valley commune, community house and own homes. Weekly meals, working bees. Stable
Tui 1984	Wainui Bay South Island	17 adults, 0 children Owned by Tui Land Trust	Holistic (ecological spiritual) lifestyle	Rural. Highly organised. Individualistic
Valley Farm Ecovillage 1999	Paeroa, North Island	3 households 5 adults, 1 child Freehold mortgaged	Establish (socially, economically, environmentally) sustainable ecovillage	Rural farm in valley. Aspiring community in need of financial backing. Permaculture ecovillage
Wilderland 1965	Whitianga, North Island	Constantly changing membership. Land recently put into (family) trust by owners. Lots of WWOOFers	Alternative lifestyle, organic food production, self-sufficiency	Rural. Currently undergoing change from privately owned to Trust. No longer self describe as a community

Karuna Falls

This community was established as a rural commune at the head of a valley on the Coromandel Peninsula in 1976. It now describes itself as an ecovillage. Food is grown organically and the community expresses a commitment to the principles of permaculture (Mollison 1978, 1979) and has become a national centre for the dissemination of permaculture practices. This is a mature and established community. It is stable, and its 20 members are long-standing residents.

Karuna Falls is set in a beautiful location, lying at the end of a long winding track, surrounded by bush and farmland on the Coromandel Peninsula. It aims to integrate low impact horticulture, agriculture and lifestyle, and members are committed to conserve the land whilst gaining sustenance from it. Karuna's land is steep sided and dense bush. It is well supplied with water by streams and waterfalls. The native bush is slowly regenerating and consists mostly of manuka (New Zealand Tee Tree). Across the ford (weather permitting) the track winds uphill and the bush gives way to a grassy hollow, containing a stage and children's play area, where the community hosts parties and fetes, such as the annual Fig Festival. Seven hundred acres of this land are a dedicated reserve and the remaining 50 acres support the community with homes, nut and fruit orchards, gardens and paddocks and they grow much of their own food. The community was originally permitted to build on the land as a 'farm'. The land is classified as 'Rural A', planning restrictions are severe and they cannot expand.

The central track leads up the steep valley sides and arteries link to members' homes, clustered at the valley head. Membership involves a $3,000.00 fee, which buys the right to build a house. It is possible to 'sell' one's house to another member but not at a market price and this had only happened twice in 25 years. Communal buildings include central community building and workshops but levels of communication and collective activity were low at the time of my visit in 2001.

Moehau

Moehau Community lies in a remote valley on the Coromandel Peninsula. It currently has ten adult members, of whom just four are resident, and two resident children. Moehau was founded in 1974 as a rural commune aimed at an alternative lifestyle and conservation of the beautiful local environment.

They see themselves as guardians of the Moehau Mountain, and intend that an 800 acre reserve on their land should remain forever untouched. This mountain has particular spiritual significance to the Maori people, for whom it is a sacred place and most of it is Maori owned or Department of Conservation land. Access is restricted and pathways often run to nowhere or are blocked. Moehau community owns 1,100 acres of bush and hill country in this region and in the 1980s they created the conservation reserve. The remaining land is used as a farm, orchards and paddocks. The farm provides the community with meat and dairy products and some members a small income. Like Karuna, Moehau is registered as a farm and this restricts building and expansion of the community.

The property is owned by Moehau Company Ltd, which has 45 shareholders, most of whom no longer live there. They have recently welcomed tenants as original members have left and numbers have depleted. Life here is fairly remote although the wider community of Colville can be reached by car. Some members are craftspeople and there are workshops for working with clay, leather, wool and fabrics. There is also a recording studio.

Communal Organic Farms

These communities are small and quite intense. Members generally aim to be self-sufficient in food, and this occupies much of their time. Surplus is sold, bartered, or given away. They are deeply committed to organic food production and this goes beyond a simple concern with dietary well-being. The organic production of food, for many, is part of a shifting relationship with the land in which people integrate with existing systems rather than eradicating them. Instead of feeding soil industrially produced chemical additives, such as nitrogen, these farmers rotate crops to maintain the balance of nutrients in the soil. And instead of feeding cattle antibiotics to treat disease, such as redwater, they grow mixed herb pastureland, which contains such plants as mint and other natural prophylactics. The science of organic food production takes into account the botany of plants, the weather systems of a biosphere, the seasons and sometimes the phase of the moon. It is process that demands time, planning and deep commitment.

Gricklegrass

Gricklegrass was founded in 1973, and is regenerating following a period of disorganisation. Current members are all young, being in their 20s, and in 2001 none had been a member for longer than three years. Gricklegrass, named after a place in a Dr Suess book, is a friendly and well functioning rural community, focused around a 40 acre organic farm.

The farmland is mixed arable and pastoral. Buildings include a range of slightly dilapidated sheds, grain stores and pigstyes, complete with pigs. There are plans to rebuild the sheds. Gardens are expanding, with vegetable plots, herb gardens and a nursery. Members live together communally in the large 'U' shaped farmhouse with courtyard garden. Each has their own bedroom within the house but all share other space, including the kitchen, office, living room, bathrooms and television room. Day-to-day life is more interactive and collective than in many other communities discussed in this chapter. Members of Gricklegrass live communally, eat together and work together on the farm.

Gricklegrass property is owned (with a small mortgage) by the Heartwood Trust, which also owns the urban communities Chippenham and Mansfield. Members pay a fairly low cash rent and also a 'sweat rent', which involves a commitment to work for four hours a week on the property. Most exceed this commitment. Commitment and energy are high and members work hard for the community. At the time of my visit in 2001, for instance, two members, Gus and Andrew, were were working on an ambitious fencing project. Heartwood had allocated funds for this and to keep costs down they had elected to provide the labour themselves. It was slow and hard work. Income from the farm generates their rent and a small income, most of which is re-invested back in the farm. Gricklegrass people are friendly and relaxed, and the community is working hard to combat a bad local reputation gained by some former members who were heavy drug users.

Wilderland

In 1965, Dan and Edith Hansen left Beeville Community to found another anarchist, vegetarian community. Wilderland, on 250 acres overlooking Whitianga Harbour, still exists, although Dan Hansen now refers to it as an organic farm, which, in a sense, it always has been (see Scholes). In 2001 Wilderland was undergoing changes and Hansen did not describe them as a community. But he has since deeded the land to a trust, and there are still a small number of permanent residents, so it is correct to say that Wilderland remains an intentional community.

Wilderland grew around the remarkable personality of this man, Dan Hansen, who, as a result of an accident at Beeville, has been in a wheelchair since 1940. He is often described as charismatic. Hansen is a mechanic and inventor who for years travelled New Zealand in a truck that he had adapted to run on coal gas. Like his brother Ray, Dan was influenced by Krishnamurit (1895–1986), who he first heard speak in Auckland in 1934.

Wilderland has been an influential force in the growth of ecologism in New Zealand. According to Dan, some 4000 people had passed through the community by 2001. At its peak there were 40 to 50 people living there at any one time. In recent years, there have been ten plus WWOOFers from all over the world.

When *A Hard Won Freedom* was published in 1975, Wilderland was an open community with no rules. Each person was expected to provide for themselves and to help out in the gardens and shop and around the grounds. Dan said that in practice 30 per cent of the people did 90 per cent of the work.

Soon afterwards, the 'Wilderland Manifesto' was posted on the wall at the entrance to the community. It read as follows:

To Visitors
We extend our welcome to you and trust that your time here will be interesting and pleasant. Please contact Dan and/or Edith as soon as practicable after arrival.

To Persons Wishing to Stay for a Period or Indefinitely at Wilderland
This should be a matter for serious consideration before any decisions are made. It is necessary that a proposal is put forward and some definite understanding reached. ... It is felt to be important that each person here be concerned to see his or her life as it actually is. This is seen as the basis of true learning and growth free from illusion. ... Much dissatisfaction with present day society exists and there is a widespread feeling that a new society must be created. But we will see this coming about only through vitality, energy, constant awareness and initiative in the individual. Anything which creates a dependence, binds him to a pattern of life and so perpetuates the society he seeks to break away from. ...

The manifesto is a clearly utopian statement. It expresses dissatisfaction with the 'now' and a desire to create something better. It describes Wilderland as 'this field of human exploration' and gestures towards a better way of being, which involves living healthily in body and independently of the values of the present. It explains that organic food production occurs at Wilderland and that this is more labour intensive than conventional methods of agriculture. It offers people the opportunity to participate in and learn of best practices in healthy food production. It identifies factors that inhibit the free development of the individual, and these are things that shackle us to the values and practices of the present. Dependence on drugs is one example:

> If you are to remain dependent on them, i.e. drugs, please stay with it [the outside world]. *This is not what Wilderland is about.* (emphasis in the original)

In 1984, partially in response to attentions from the police, Dan instituted a policy of no drugs, alcohol, or tobacco at Wilderland. Up to that point they had been tolerated, but some people were growing marijuana commercially.

In about 1990, Dan was quoted as saying,

> People have come to live together here simply because they recognise that they have work and interests in common – growing, providing and consuming organic food, protection of the environment, care and education of children (and adults), self-responsibility in labour and relationship, minimising demands on the earth's resources and enjoyment of rural space. (Qtd. in J Sargisson, 45)

Over the years there have been a number of controversies at Wilderland, with the one over drugs getting the most attention. Another involved the 'free-rider' problem, which most communities face sooner or later. In his unpublished discussion of Wilderland, Werner Droescher (1911?–78) called them 'tourists' and said that the community tolerated them because they added to the social life. Droescher also noted a controversy over machinery. Some wanted to limit the use of machinery to reduce dependence on the outside world. Dan, who was a genius with machines, opposed the change. Those favouring less machine use left Wilderland and formed an unnamed community nearby. Droescher said that they became almost self-sufficient within a year (167–68).

Communities that focus on a charismatic founder can face difficulties when this person dies. At present Dan is alive and well but steps have been taken that make Wilderland likely to survive him. The establishment of the trust secures the land and some current members have plans to expand beyond the organic farm to an arts and crafts settlement (National Radio *Country Life* Programme, 27 January 2001).

Green Spiritual Communities

This cluster of communities combines practical environmentalism with a spiritual outlook. This marks a continuation of an existing trend in New Zealand's green intentional communities. The older rural communes, for instance, were often founded by people who sought to develop a spiritual (as well as a physical) connection with nature. Moehau and Ophui are examples of this. The communities discussed in this section have developed this and seek to live in spiritual harmony with the land as well as to preserve it. Often they disseminate their beliefs and have an educational focus, devoting time and space to outreach or training. Often the spiritual beliefs are drawn from Maori culture. Sometimes this is integrated into the vocabulary of deep ecology (Naess 1973).

Anahata Retreat Centre

Founded in 1996, Anahata Retreat Centre is not to be confused with the newer community of Anahata. Anahata Retreat lies on a mountain top, overlooking the sea in Pohara Bay, at the end of a steep five mile track, which winds its way up the mountain from Birds Clearing. It is a stunning location, high above the cloud line and home to Kias (mountain parrots). There were just five permanent adult members and one child resident in 2001. It was founded by members of an extended family and as such occupies a somewhat marginal position in this study, although it aspires to become a larger community. Having decided to come together and live collectively and having found and bought the land, the group was trying to establish collective aims and devising a constitution when I visited in 2001. Core values were emerging around a desire to develop this beautiful location as a centre for spiritual practice.

However, the individual members all had quite diverse – even divergent – reasons for wanting to be here and this may prove an unresolvable tension. One couple was concerned to practice yoga (as guru and student), whilst other members were concerned with practical ecology, or nature spirits. They do not share a belief system and this can make things difficult. Nonetheless, they were committed to developing a community and Anahata Retreat is as a base for both yoga retreat and environmental education. At the time of my stay, there were some thirty guests camping in the grounds, all of whom were participating in a course organised from Tui Community by Robina McCurdy.[2] This course,

'Design for Sustainable Community' ran for four weeks in four consecutive locations. The first week, which focused on cultural sustainability and covered such topics as 'Self-Nourishment and Earth Attunement', 'Group Process Skills', and 'Design for Social Ecology', was hosted by Anahata Retreat.[3]

The group was developing and designing the physical space along permaculture lines following three central guidelines – 1. Let nature do the work, 2. Use integrated functions, 3. Plan physical space. And so the small permaculture garden is close to the house, which minimises the carrying distance for tools and crops and the garden is seen everyday as members walk along the paths to and from their own homes; checking pests and the progress of crops thus becomes easy. Water-hungry plants are clustered together, to minimise irrigation. In addition to yielding eggs, chickens are used to fertilise the soil in a mobile chicken 'tractor', a mesh hut on wheels that can be moved around as required. They thus keep down the weeds as well as fertilising the soil. The sewage disposal system at Anahata Retreat includes two worm farms and specially designed toilets direct liquids in one direction and solids in another, to be processed by worms into useable compost.

The members of this community own the land together and each household has a separate home. Most nestle in the bush and one is perched on stilts overlooking the bay below. Communal buildings comprise a community house (with kitchen, office, lounge and bedroom) plus a sanctuary. The sanctuary is a round building, built from adobe lined strawbale, with a wooden floor. It is offered as an educational facility. Some of the houses are similarly built in the form of yurts, while others are wooden, straw-lined for insulation.

Gentle World

Gentle World is unusual in a number of respects. Firstly, it is a peripatetic community, which spends half of the year at 'Shangri-La', Kaitia, New Zealand and half of the year on Big Island, Hawaii. Secondly, they are vegan; and, thirdly, they advocate and practice free love. Membership varies but in June 2001 there were 19 adults in the two locations. Members follow two charismatic leaders known as Light (a woman) and Sun (a man). Most followers are in their late teens and 20s.

Gentle World was founded in 1970 and bought its first property in Brookside, Florida, in 1973. In 1983 it bought 100 acres with houses in Umatilla, Florida. The North Island New Zealand and Big Island Hawaii properties were both purchased in 1999. Members are evangelical vegans and this involves diet, lifestyle and spirituality.

> The vegan concept is not a fad that will pass with time, it is a necessary shift in thinking that will lead to a heightened empathy for others. It is the expansion of compassion, which is the single most important step in the next evolution of humankind. (Light, at http://www.planet-hawaii.com/gentleworld/VEGAN/vegan. html)

They describe themselves like this:

[We are a] non-profit educational organisation and Vegan Community dedicated to the prevention of human and animal suffering, specifically by educating the public as to practical ways to live spiritual ideals, with an emphasis on the vegan diet and lifestyle. (http://www.gentleworld.org)

Members identify with aspects of the natural world and take names from 'nature', such as 'Flowers' and 'Butterflies'. They are deeply committed to 'living and being' connected to their environment. They aim for what they call a 'more evolved' self. 'We have been so disconnected from nature that we have forgotten our true Nature' (Flowers, Gentle World, 28 April 2001).

Members cite positive aspects of Gentle World as 'the love'; 'learning about veganism'; 'the power of truth'; 'the support of sharing a common goal'; 'living and appreciating nature's beauty'; and 'expanding our integrity' (Email Flowers, Gentle World, 30 April 2001). All are deeply committed to veganism, which, for most, was the thing that drew them to this charismatic group. The most difficult thing about being a part of Gentle World, they agreed, was 'learning how to rise above our individual egos for the common benefit of all' (ibid.). A former member was explicit about this and said that free love was difficult to live with.

Gentle World publishes books on nutrition and has written vegan cookery books and pamphlets. Their website combines recipes, aphorisms and 'inspirational' spiritual information advocating a vegan lifestyle.

Veganism was (and is) first and foremost, the cornerstone of the foundation of our new code of ethics. We longed to live in a whole new paradigm, and it became clear at the start, that the most crucial ingredient needed was compassion – and that veganism expands our level of compassion to a degree of safety that we felt was essential for a truly new world – hence, the name 'Gentle World', and ensuing mission; the spreading of the vegan message. (Light, http://gentleworld.org)

Tui Community

Tui is a spiritual and educational charitable trust, dedicated to environmentalism, but it was hard to place it in this typology. It is one of the most stable and best organised intentional communities in New Zealand and yet its current *raison d'etre* is difficult to identify. For some members this seems to be cooperation, for others ecology and yet others spirituality. Given its importance in the history of New Zealand's green movement, we place it here.

Tui was founded in 1984 by a group of friends who met at a Green festival. They wanted to live together sustainably and holistically. The Tui 'Spiritual and Educational Trust Deed' cites eight primary objects for the group. These include the promotion of a holistic approach to education, which includes attention to vocational training, the principles of community and cooperation,

environmental education and spiritual well being. They offer training, host
educational events and try to lead by example:

> [We aim to] promote education within New Zealand on the role and function of
> sustainable communities by establishing a living, working example of an intentional
> community that combines the essential principles of spiritual awareness, earthcare,
> connection with nature and appropriate lifestyle, where residents and visitors can
> participate in a variety of educational and spiritual practices. (Tui Spiritual and
> Educational Trust Deed)

Tui has drawn people from all over the world and is a sustainable community
in action.

Most members are professional people, working hard at occupations such
as company director, social worker and health practitioner. Some specialise
in interpersonal training and are psychotherapists or counsellors. One, Robina
McCurdy, works as an 'environmental educator' and is the driving force for
Earthcare Education Aotearoa, which operates out of Tui. Robina has worked
throughout New Zealand and in Africa helping communities to design for a
sustainable future. I observed her working with Valley Farm EcoVillage in
2000 building plans for a community that took into account every aspect of
the environment, ranging from water type, amount and frequency of rainfall
and routes of watercourses, to the spiritual nature of the land and its history.

Tui lies in two valleys overlooking the bay. The land runs down to the sea
to a beach and includes paddocks, which are rented out to a dairy farmer. Near
the water is the 'tree field', which has been developed into the most beautiful
campsite. The field once formed part of an anaerobic sewage disposal system
(which is still used but has been rerouted). The trees were planted as a cash
crop and to form part of the dispersal system in the sewage works. The area
is now a campsite with outdoor bathrooms, cooking areas and 'classrooms'.
The bathrooms are built from adobe lined straw and are ornate and fun. Open
air communal showers, toilets and baths are available, as are enclosed ones
for those who prefer to wash in private. One bathtub is designed to hold two
people and the hot tub has been known to hold forty. Building all this proved
a major project.

The land runs up the two valleys, and it is here that most of the homes are
located. These vary widely – most are beautifully built from wood and have
decorative glass, pottery and wooden carvings. Some are small and modest; one
is a housebus. There are two significant community buildings. One is located
near the carpark and contains Tui's dining hall and community kitchen as well
as rooms for leisure (television, snooker), as well as rooms for storage and
resources (food stores, library). This community house has private space for
the use of telephones and computers. The other communal building is recent.
It lies at the top of the property, up the steep slope of the valley. This was
intended to host the weekly meetings and contains another kitchen, a round
sanctuary with a domed ceiling, meeting space and chill-out rooms. There is

a wooden deck from which one can see the sea below. Its location is fabulous. This building was not in regular use at the time of my visit in 2001 because a member had requested that meetings be held in the old building, which lies closer to her home, for the sake of easier childcare.

The community takes lunch together every day and hold weekly meetings. One week this will be a 'heart meeting', sharing feelings, and the next week this will be a business meeting. These are efficiently and effectively run. At the time of my visit no collective projects were in hand, which was a cause of regret to some members but others were focusing on their own businesses and employment. Tui is a relatively affluent community. It owns a 'bee balm' business, producing natural creams and insect repellent and providing paid employment to some members. Membership is stable and most members have been at Tui for a long time. Some of the founders remain and the newest member in 2001 had been there for three years.

Eco-villages

This is the fastest growing type of community in New Zealand today and most are less than five years old. Most ecovillages are meticulously designed. Discussion groups often exist for years before land is found and 'the community' begins to live together. Many never get beyond this stage. Their founders are small groups of people who are deeply committed to a more sustainable environmentally sensitive way of life. They are often founded by people in their late 30s or 40s who have had a successful professional or working life and now seek a life more meaningful. Like the early communards, they want a simpler life closer to nature. However, unlike the founders of the older communes, they do not, generally, want to opt out, or to go all the way back to nature, or to live in the bush with no electricity or contact with the wider world. They have often visited older communes and gleaned knowledge of the pitfalls and problems that these communities have faced.

An influential figure in the history of ecovillages is Robert Gilman:

> An eco-village is a human scale, full-featured settlement which integrates human activities harmlessly into the natural environment, supports healthy human development, and can be continued into the indefinite future. (Gilman 1991, 10)

Most ecovillages quote him in their publicity material. Some add useful riders. For instance:

> Achieving such a truly sustainable community implies:
> Conscious awareness of the inter-relatedness of all life and the cyclic sustainable systems of nature. Understanding and supporting cultural, social and spiritual values of this awareness and how humans can live ecologically balanced lives
> Viable technologies that do not harm, but rather help to heal the planet. (Otamatea EcoVillage Booklet, 2–3)

In a full-featured settlement, all the major functions of normal living – residence, food provision, manufacture, leisure, social life, and commerce – are plainly present and in balanced proportions. (Valley Farm EcoVillage Website: http:// www.ecovillage.co.nz)

Ecovillages are based around shared land, which members are committed to conserve. Homes are generally clustered so as to cut down on roads and to make it easier to provide services such as electricity. Many use permaculture for community design. Building materials are sustainably sourced, and alternative sources of energy are used to the full. Some have shared sources of income but most do not. None are income pooling. Unlike many of the older communities, they are set within easy reach of a town or city.

Anahata

When I visited in May 2001 Anahata had just celebrated its first birthday. It is not, strictly speaking, an ecovillage, but aspires to become one and is often described as such (for instance, by New Zealand's ecovillage online network). It was not designed as an ecovillage but rather as a fully communal living space for Centrepoint Community, discussed in Chapter 5. Anahata consists of thirty acres of neglected garden and bush, and a number of buildings including the main community house and the 'longhouses', modelled after traditional Polynesian villages. Inside each longhouse, in Centrepoint's day, was a single room in which people slept together. In 2001, all but one had been subdivided into bedrooms. The main house is large and is home to an office, a community kitchen and a dining room, where all meals are shared, bathrooms, television rooms, meeting rooms, guest rooms and several 'treatment' rooms (now disused), where psychotherapy and counselling were once offered. The community has a library, a swimming pool and several large though neglected craft rooms, including a pottery.

This is an unusual group and it will be interesting to see how it develops. Anahata is located on the site of the former (now infamous) Centrepoint Community. There is some dispute over the name – the older group at the Anahata Retreat Centre in the South Island somewhat regret this community's choice of the same name. The word 'Anahata' refers to the heart chakra, an energy point in the centre of the chest. The name 'Centrepoint' had similar meaning. The heart is said to be the central point of the chakras. Anahata is a peculiar choice for this group, so keen to disassociate itself from Centrepoint.

Anahata Community consists of three very different cohorts who did not, at the time of my visit, have a shared value base. Firstly, there are its founders. These once belonged to Centrepoint but in later years opposed its leader, Bert Potter, and formed the core of opposition that led to the winding up that community. Chris Perkins, one of these people, recalls those times. Increasingly concerned about the viability of the community under Potter's leadership, he consulted one of Centrepoint's Trustees. He was advised to form a legal body with other discontents and to draw up proposals for change to put to the Trustees. There began a period of meetings and canvassing that was clearly difficult:

> It was right out in the open. I copped quite a bit of flak for it. They [the old guard] had this cute trick of screaming at you – this close [places his hand directly in front of his face]. (Chris, Anahata, 18 May 2001)

Chris and about seven others founded Anahata. They are experienced in communal living and share a commitment to living this way.

The second group consists of new members, who have come from outside within the last 12 months. They are mostly families or single parents, inexperienced in communal living. Many were attracted by an article in the national press, which hailed Anahata as a new green community. Some spoke of a desire to minimise waste by living collectively. Others spoke of an intuitive connection to the land. They liked the fact that there is no need to buy-in to this community. Anahata is a rent-paying community, being tenant of the Trust that now oversees the former Centrepoint land. Rents have been set at a deliberately low level (at the time of my visit, $130 per week per adult, $75 per week per teenager and between $35 and $55 per child, depending on age). This rent is fully inclusive, covering all costs including food. Most of these people express a desire to develop Anahata as an ecovillage. This is by far the largest of the three groups and these people seemed enthusiastic about their new way of life.

The third group consists of former Centrepoint children – people in their teens or early 20s who spent some of their childhood at Centrepoint. Anahata is constitutionally bound to offer help to people who were damaged by Centrepoint and this group was a silent presence when I visited. They kept very much to themselves and lived together in the only remaining 'open plan' longhouse. It is hard to imagine them fully integrating with the other two groups.

Some concern exists about this community amongst former members of Centrepoint who now live in the wider community. It is hard to assess this group or to predict its future because the group was still forming at the time of my visit. Before it can become a viable ecovillage, Anahata will need to build shared ecological values. Before it can become a viable community *per se* it will need to sever links with its past. At the moment, Anahata lives very much in the shadow of its predecessor.

Otamatea Ecovillage

Otamatea was founded by two people in 1997. They sought an environmentally sustainable lifestyle, and found this piece of land at Kaipara Harbour which was large enough to sustain several households whilst being accessible from

Kaipara. Two sides of the property border creeks and a third abuts a bush reserve, owned by Edward Goldsmith (editor of the *Ecologist*). Otamatea is thus protected from contamination by drifting sprays from neighbouring farmland. At the time of my visit in 2001 this evolving eco-village consisted of 11 households, comprising 17 adults and six children.

The land is divided into 15 household units and common land. Each unit has freehold of a five-acre plot plus common ownership of 176 acres. The common land is collectively held by Otamatea Ltd Co. Title to the whole 215 acres is held by this company and the land is administered through unit titles. The units have resource consent and planning permission and are provided with road access and power. Homes are in various stages of completion and vary widely in design, some architect designed and some designed and built by the owners. The result is mixed and interesting.

Community interaction and activity is quite extensive. The community has fortnightly meetings and working bees, and once a week they share a 'pot luck' meal in the community building. The common land is 'biodynamically' farmed. This draws on the work of Rudolf Steiner (1861–1925) and involves attention to anthrosophical beliefs about nature and spirituality (see http://www.anth.org.uk). Biodynamic practices include stirring energy and 'spirit' into fertiliser; and planting according to cycles of the moon. Binding values at Otamatea are drawn from permaculture, and key values are cooperation, support and respect:

> Otamatea Vision Statement:
> Otamatea will practise Permaculture in a spirit of co-operation, mutual support and respect for one another and the land
> * Will preserve and enhance the native ecosystems on the land and sea around us
> * Will create fertile, holistically integrated agricultural systems, and a village culture, that abundantly provides for healthy living at all levels: physical, social, emotional, and spiritual
> * Will do this sustainably, ethically, and with beauty and creative variety
> * Will be a positive part of the wider New Zealand society, especially as a model of sustainability and bio-diversity
> * Will be a part of the wider global cultural evolution, giving and receiving knowledge, wisdom, inspiration, and love. (Otamatea website: http://www.conserve.org.nz/evens/otamatea.html)

Conclusions: Green Communities in New Zealand

Each community is different and all communities change over time, we have offered a snapshot of these groups close to the turn of the century. The older communes are the most remote and life is hard for that reason, leaving many with depleted membership. Isolation causes a number of problems. Life is physically tough – imagine, for instance, childbirth without access to medical care. It also raises social problems. Arguments and disagreements can become more intense in small communities and particularly so in isolated ones. Relationships are put under strain. Isolation can also cause financial hardship. It is difficult to generate an income in remote districts. Changes to state benefit laws in the 1980s and 1990s hit them hard. The founders of some of these communes, such as Ophui, found that after a time they no longer wanted to live in this way and as a result some older groups have few residents. Members retain a commitment to the community but no longer want to live there. The older communes that still thrive have learned how to deal with isolation and with the comings and goings of members.

Because they want something different, the newer ecovillages are generally less remote than the older communes and organic farms. Their utopia is perhaps less romantic and they are less interested in getting back to nature in the raw. They are more human-centred, seeking to create sustainable developments that are in balance with their surroundings. Like the early communards, they seek to preserve and conserve and often have tree planting and culling projects underway, in which foreign plant species are removed and native species re-introduced.

All these communities are concerned with their physical environment. Two key features emerge from observation of these green lives on the land – practical environmentalism and ecological world-views, which are often indivisible.

They employ practical conservation and design or evolve low impact lifestyles. We cannot make special claims for them here – rural homesteads have traditionally been self-reliant for energy and waste disposal and a plethora of pressure groups and campaigns exist in New Zealand around green issues. These communities are, however, special. They are places where people have chosen to come together to live, everyday, a more sustainable lifestyle. They do not use alternative energy because they have to but rather because it fits their worldview. All have developed systems for generating power and disposing of waste and sewage. Most of these communities have (anaerobic or aerobic) composting toilets. Often visitors are asked to urinate in the bush and to use the toilet only for more serious business (this avoids overwetting the compost and prohibiting the anaerobic process or drowning the worms!) Wind turbines and solar panels are commonplace, and some use water powered generators. Brett, at Anahata Retreat had made an outdoor solar shower of black alcathene pipe, in which water lay warming in the sun, ready for (careful) use in the evening. In the South Island, water is scarce during the summer months and both farms and communities develop ingenious schemes for collecting and conserving rainwater. At Tui, for instance, members have built a large structure – approx. 40 feet by 20 – in which to catch rainwater. It lies high on the hillside where most rain falls and its surface is corrugated so the rain runs into channels, down the slope, and into collection tanks, connected by pipes to the houses below. All of this hard-won energy and water is rigorously conserved. Some communities have rules about flushing water toilets, others switch on electrically powered equipment (lights or computers) only during specified times.

These initiatives stem from a deep knowledge of place, an intimacy gained by living closely with the natural environment. Their everyday lives involve a connection to the natural world, which many of them would describe as spiritual and is apparent when visiting these communities. People speak unaffectedly of an intimate relationship to the non-human world. This extract comes from Veronica Black's book about her time in Ophui Community on the Coromandel.[4]

> Before I started this book, I lived for 9 years with [my husband] Heath and my children as they arrived at [Ophui Community] Colville. Heath and I came to the peninsula in 1970 and loved the grandeur and beauty of the high country, the gulf and its islands. Te Moehau across the bay – it stirred something of the Gael in us both; we felt at home among the rocks of the dry headland; it took us in. It gave me a sense of source. I needed to live close to the earth. I wanted to learn something of the land I was born into but barely knew, so I sank into a world of natural forms, of winds and tides, trees and rocks, manuka, flowers, gardens. I claimed the opportunity to 'drop out', to pause, to take time to live like a simple creature on the earth, to be free for a while of the overbearing social and cultural order, de-prescribed ways. (Black 1985, 7)

An awareness of place comes quite quickly in these locations – bathing out of doors or using an outdoor lavatory provoke a different sensibility. Biodymanic and other organic farming practices soon attune one to the phases of the moon and other natural cycles.

> Within the forest is a different world. Detail comes alive; the mystery of generation and decay surrounds you. Tree ferns drop rack after rack of dried orange red branches which were once the lightest youngest green. Wade through the living wet worlds of ferns, haul up the side of a steep valley, struggle for the ridge, swim in a foliage of smells, patterns, leaves and light, and then pause by an old log passing its last years colonised by hundreds of plants. How did such diversity come about, such detail? These really are unknown worlds, captured tight in phyllums, named and classified by the botanists, worlds within worlds, pause to understand, to become conscious, if not of names then of being able to see, to see inside of the 'view' from the kitchen window and through the gap in the hedge. (Ibid., 20–21)

Here, Veronica Black articulates the total-field image evoked by Arne Naess as lying at the heart of deep ecology (Naess 1973; Naess 1979). The self is perceived as part of something larger and consciousness expands in an awareness of life. This is living deep ecology, not drawn from a textbook but rather from first hand intimacy with place.

Of course, not all of the intentional communities discussed in this chapter achieve or desire such a connection. Some are concerned with the pragmatic project of achieving a balance with their environment, conserving what is good for future generations. These people want to work together to preserve this beautiful country. Many species of indigenous birds and plants are extinct, but they are determined to preserve what remains.

Green activism in New Zealand faces serious challenges. Considerable pressure is put on government to go the 'other way' of mass-agribusiness. Powerful lobbies view New Zealand as the perfect place for trialing new advances in genetic engineering. Its remote location and benign climate make this land ideal for such trials. At government level environmental issues yield perpetual frustration and compromise. The Green Party in New Zealand has seats in Parliament and has been in a unique position to exercise influence from inside government. However its coalition partners, Labour, did not share their commitment to conservation, hence perpetual compromises on policy. However, at grass roots level these small communities do seem to make a difference. They have a direct impact on vast areas of native bush, regenerating under their watch, and native seed stocks are conserved by their endeavours. They particiapte in local campaigns such as 'Coromandel No Mining', protesting against gold mining on the peninsula, 'Kauri 2000' a campaign to replant the ancient Kauri forests; and 'Project Crimson', which seeks to replant brilliant red Pohutawa trees. They are part of a wider scene of environmental activism. They also have an indirect impact on the wider population. Many people visit intentional communities and more are aware of them. Some visit for a day or stay for a short time, some buy their fruit and vegetables from community stalls. Many have lived in one or more communities. We met Members of Parliament, academics, lawyers and media broadcasters who had once lived in one of these communities.

The growth of green communities is also connected, albeit unquantfiably, to a resurgence in Maori politics of self-determination and cultural revival. Most of the people interviewed for this work are Pakeha, although some have Maori ancestry, which they seek to explore. Historically Maori have owned land collectively, and we have explored something of the origins of this practice, which lie in Maori spiritual beliefs. These are pre-Christian and have been incorporated into Maori Christianity. Here, ownership is use-derived and temporary. It involves responsibility and guardianship. Some land is of special spiritual significance, but all land is part of a universal divine spirit. The people in these communities seek to use and own land in these ways, which, they feel, are more authentic and more appropriate to them as New Zealanders.

I feel blessed on a daily basis. I think [this place] is visually beautiful, if not stunning, but what that does is bring a sense of responsibility. You have to look very carefully, because such emotion might be difficult to stop or undo, and you have to get on and build structures and the like. (Udaya, Valley Farm Ecovillage, 1 April 2000)

The best thing about being involved with this piece of land and its comings and goings is the absolute affirmation of the cycle of life. That's the best thing, and the ability to give ground for my children to understand that if they can put a seed into the ground and it will feed them a corncob, and if they work real hard they can do the wheat and grain thing if they need to. (Chrissie, Te Ora, 2 February 2001)

The first time I set foot on this land I felt connected to it in a way that puzzles me because I've never felt anything like that before. (Selma, Tui, 4 April 2001)

Notes

1 Thanks to Anthea, Clare and Philip Ward for their support during the pilot stage of this project and in particular for helping Sargisson to meet former members of communities and providing introductions to Maori Chiefs.
2 Organised and facilitated by Earthcare Aorotora Ltd: contact: Robina McCurdy, Tui Community, Golden Bay.
3 The next week was to be spent at Rainbow Valley Community, where participants were to learn about physical sustainability, building with (rather than against) ecosystems. Week three was located at Tui Community and focused on design for sustainable settlements (which included nature 'attunements', as well as sessions on community law, money and businesses). The final week was spent doing supervised practical work and was hosted by the Maori community at Onetahua Marae.
4 Veronica Black was killed in a car accident with her children. I'd like to extend my personal thanks to Heath Black for talking to me about his time at Ophui LS.

Chapter 8[1]

Conflict and Longevity

Introduction

We began this study because we share an interest in utopias and a love of New Zealand. Nobody had ever systematically studied the utopias or intentional communities of this country and we felt this should be done. Intentional communities are a space in which people practice utopianism and have sometimes been called practical utopias. We wanted to learn more about this. Emerging from discontent with the present and seeking something better, intentional communities can be viewed as living utopian experiments. As such they can tell us much about how it feels to try to realise a dream. But of course, they are not only this. They are also people's homes and workplaces. As such, some of what we learned was less to do with utopianism and more to do with the gritty and messy business of everyday life. One of the things that recurred in interview – and in participant observation – was the disturbing effect of conflict within these groups. This chapter will explore this, in part because it is interesting to learn of the murky reality in intentional communities, and in part because our findings seemed to run contrary to the received wisdom about communities and conflict. Also, we learned of ways in which these groups manage conflict. This offers transferable lessons both to people in other such groups and those of us who live in the wider community.

The conventional wisdom about conflict inside intentional communities is that is it endangers cohesion and is a destructive force. Kanter's seminal study of intentional communities establishes conflict as a major source of what she terms the 'failure' of many utopian communities in nineteenth century America (Kanter 1972). However, whilst conflict exists within New Zealand's intentional communities, and whilst this often causes damage to group cohesion, many of these communities are extraordinarily long lived.

This, in itself, is remarkable. Even more remarkable, is the longevity of New Zealand's secular communities. Religious communities tend to outlast secular ones and this is variously accounted for by higher levels of internal discipline and/or commitment (Kanter 1972). However, a significant number of New Zealand's secular communities (such as Chippenham, Katajuta and Rainbow Valley) have survived for over 30 years. Riverside has been around for more than 60 years. Why is this? Is the literature wrong?

In thinking about this puzzle we turned at first to the literature on intentional communities – surely this would help us to understand the role of conflict in these groups? It did not and, somewhat disappointed, we looked next at the vast literature about the nature and function of conflict. This, we found, went some way towards helping us to understand what was going on. We consulted a range disciplines, including social psychology, political theory and sociology. Only by combining lessons drawn from each of these fields, we found, could we begin to frame answers to these questions.

Conflict and Intentional Communities

The literature on intentional communities tends to be theoretically light and to assume that conflict is dangerous and should therefore be avoided. In what is probably the most influential study of intentional communities, Kanter identifies conflict as a major problem. What keeps a community going, she says, is commitment and conflict threatens this. According to her logic most of the New Zealand communities should have 'failed' long ago. They are full of conflict. And yet they survive. We find Kanter's work unhelpful in two areas, namely, her understanding of what a 'utopian community' is, and of what makes a successful one.

The essential characteristics of what she calls a 'utopian community' are 'perfectibility, order, fraternity, harmony (of values and ideas as well as of matters spiritual and physical' (Kanter 1972, 49); experimentation, group coherence and what she calls 'idealisation' (idealism) (ibid., 32–57). This is bizarre – no community of real people is perfectible, even if some nineteenth century ones believed otherwise. Rather they are evolving, dynamic bodies that grow and change over time. One of the problems with Kanter's approach is that she under-theorises utopia, assuming it simply to be a perfect world. Work in the field of utopian studies has been challenging this assumption for decades and most now accept that utopias are expressions of a better way of being (Levitas 1990), social dreaming (Sargent 1994) and not the realisation of perfection. They are not, in other words, the full stop to human progress (Sargisson 2000).

Another problem is that she equates success with longevity and this leads her to neglect conflict as a topic for serious consideration. In her appendix she lists 'successful communities' and 'unsuccessful communities' in America in the nineteenth century (246–47). So-called successful ones are long-lived and unsuccessful ones are not. Simple. Kanter sees conflict as straightforwardly dysfunctional. Key factors, for her, are 'continuance, cohesion and control' (67). The glue that binds, for Kanter, and the factor that accounts for a community's 'success' or 'failure', is commitment. She insists that conflict is destabilising and looks no further into the subject, focusing instead on factors that enhance commitment because commitment equals longevity equals success. Our measure of success is not simply longevity but takes into account the extent to which the community satisfies its members, even for a time.

It is true that conflict is destabilising and that commitment can help people to ride a period of upheaval, but we noticed other functions to conflict as well.

We found that if a community is to survive over time it needs to find ways to manage conflict (see, for example, Abrams and McCulloch 1976). Unrestrained conflict is socially unsustainable in an intentional community, and such groups need to be socially sustainable. Conflict can prevent or inhibit the achievement of goals (Hardy 1979). It can cause pain, resentment and lasting damage to relationships, which is hard to manage in a small tightly knit group. Research in other forms of communal groups supports this (see, for instance, Manning [1980] and Roberts [1980] on conflict within therapeutic communities.) However, conflict will, it seems, always occur, can be survived and can have positive outcomes. This needs to be carefully thought about.

Theorising Conflict

In order to begin to clarify our thoughts on conflict we turned to political and social theory. First, we needed to identify key salient points and polemics. Discussion here is limited by space constraints, but some understanding of the theoretical terrain is essential before we can begin to understand the evidence. The study of conflict is an integral part of the study of any human relationships. Some believe conflict to lie at the heart of human nature; others see it as a necessary part of the human condition. Some see conflict as profoundly dangerous (threatening stablity) others see it as something to be celebrated, as engendering change. There are dozens of different stances on conflict but, for the sake of expediency, and bearing in mind our core questions, they will be discussed here under two headings: conflict as dangerous, and conflict as desirable and/or socially useful.

Conflict as Dangerous

Many proponents of this view have been influenced by the work of Thomas Hobbes (1588–1679). For Hobbes, conflict is both inevitable and dangerous. It is an inevitable part of the human condition because human nature is self-serving, power-seeking and self-interested, 'every man's end being some good to himself' (*Human Nature*, Ch. 24). It is dangerous because competition and the quest for glory lead, in a world of scarce resources, to a state of war. This is fully fleshed out in *Leviathan* (1659), which imagines the consequences of unrestrained human behaviour in accordance with natural attributes and rights. In what is perhaps the most famous passage in political theory, Hobbes explains:

> In such condition, there is no place for Industry; because the fruit thereof is uncertain: and consequently no Culture on Earth, no Navigation, nor use of the commodities that may be imports by Sea; no commodious Building; no Instruments of moving, and removing such things as require much force; no Knowledge of the face of the Earth; no account of Time; no Arts; no Letters; no Society; and which is

worst of all, animal fear, and danger of violent death; And the life of man, solitary, poor, nasty, brutish, and short. (*Leviathan*, Ch. 14)

Competition, diffidence and the search for power and glory make co-operation impossible. Conflict, for Hobbes, is the outcome of unrestrained human interaction. Its consequence is fearfulness, war and death (*Leviathan*, Ch. 17). Only an authoritarian ruling body can control this.

This view influences fields as far flung as psychoanalysis, politics and the study of international relations. Sigmund Freud (1856–1939), for instance, in a letter to Albert Einstein (1880–1952) in 1932, wrote that:

Wars will only be prevented with certainty if mankind unites in setting up a central authority to which the right of giving judgement upon all conflicts of intent shall be handed over. There are clearly two separate requirements involved in this: the creation of a supreme authority and its endowment with the necessary power. (Qtd. in Burton and Dukes 1990, 7)

This view of conflict dominated the study of international relations for a long time (see, for example, Wright 1990).

Freud established a tradition in psychoanalysis that views conflict as primordial requiring restraint. For Jacques Lacan (1901–81), 'The Oedipus complex means that the imaginary, in itself an incestuous and conflict relation, is doomed to conflict and ruin' (Lacan 1993, 96). It follows that

In order for the human being to be able to establish the most natural of relations, that between male and female, a third party has to intervene, one that is a model of something successful, the model of some harmony. This does not go far enough – there has to be a law .... (Ibid.)

The law in question, for Lacan, is the 'law of the father', a symbolic order of language in which are inscribed rules and codes that establish 'normal' social relations. Points for us to note are that conflict has a negative role and requires restraint, order and control. The alternative is the total breakdown of interpersonal communication and relations. Unrestrained conflict threatens the social fabric.

Sociologists tend to take a nuanced approach to conflict but some nonetheless see it as broadly a 'bad thing' in that its effects are socially negative. Emile Durkheim (1858–1917), for instance, sought to understand and preserve social stability. Conflict over norms and values inhibits this (see Durkheim, *Division of Labour*). Talcott Parsons (1902–79) pursues similar ideas (Parsons, 1937), but the views of Durkheim and Parsons on conflict have nuance. Both accept that a certain amount of conflict is 'natural' or inevitable in human society. However, both desire to minimise this in the name of stability because unrestrained conflict contributes to social discord.

These approaches to conflict help us to understand how conflict in an intentional community can be destabilising. None of the communities visited were in a state of Hobbesian war of all against all, but members of most could recall at least one period of serious prolonged strife. They spoke of these times as unsettling, disruptive and distressing. These were times when co-operation ceased. This helps us to see the importance of conflict mediation, or management, which can bring a group back from the brink of social disintegration. We shall explore this further below in our discussion of real conflicts in actual communities.

Conflict as Desirable or Socially Useful

This position (again, broadly speaking) sees conflict as valuable, functional or socially positive. Again, due space constraints, we can only sample this attitude and will examine three key positions, those of Lewis Coser (functionalism), Ralf Dahrendorf (conflict theory) and post-Lacanian psychoanalysis.

Coser, drawing on Georg Simmel (1858–1918), saw conflict as a form of socialisation and, therefore, a necessary part of the human condition (Simmel 1955). Coser believes that conflict has positive functions, notwithstanding its (sometimes) negative effects. Some forms of conflict are more useful than others. For example:

> Internal social conflict which concerns goals, values or interests that do not contradict the basic assumptions upon which the relationship is founded tend to be positively functional for the social structure. Such conflicts tend to make possible the readjustment of norms and power relations within the groups in accordance with the felt needs of its individual membership subgroups. (Coser 1968, 151)

Conflict, in this reading, can permit the clarification of a group's ideas. It can also allow for changes in the balance of power and is a dynamic force.

> A flexible society benefits from conflict because such behaviour, by helping to create and modify norms, assures its [i.e. society's] continuance under changed conditions. Things that work against this are rigid systems and the suppression of conflict. (Ibid., 154)

Ralf Dahrendorf takes this further. In his 1964 essay, 'Out of Utopia', he challenged contemporary sociology which, he claimed, adhered to 'utopian', meaning undesirable and unachievable, values. The essay was an explicit rejection of H.G. Wells' essay on sociology (1905) in which Wells argues for utopia as the proper study of sociology. Dahrendorf's argument hinged on utopian desires for closure and perfection. This, he says, is a form of social death, against which he contrasts a dynamic view of society driven by conflict.

> The great creative force that carries along the model that I am trying to describe and that is equally ubiquitous is social conflict. The notion that whenever there is social life there is conflict may be unpleasant and disturbing. Nevertheless, it is

indispensable to our understanding of social problems … conflict can be temporarily suppressed, regulated, channelled, and controlled but … neither the philosopher-king nor the modern dictator can abolish it once and for all. (Dahrendorf 1964, 224)

Finally, the post-Lacanians also see conflict as creative. Like Freud and Lacan they view conflict as disruptive but, for them, this is exciting. Yes, they say, conflict it primordial and inevitable; yes it threatens order; but these are good things. Conflict is seen variously as transgressive, disruptive and transformative (see Sargisson 2000). Thinkers who assume this position include some of the so-called 'French' feminists, such as Luce Irigaray and Hélène Cixous. They build on Lacanian analyses to suggest that acts of transgression and deconstruction can generate conflict within the apparently hermetic system of the (deeply masculine) symbolic order. This, in turn may create new space in which femininity (the repressed Other) can be re-thought, re-articulated and re-enacted (for examples, see Butler [1989] and Cixous [1996]). Celebrations of difference (Butler, 1989) and pluralistic social interaction (Laclau and Mouffe, 1985) all derive from a perception of conflict as both inevitable and profoundly creative. Thinkers under this (loose) banner see the social world as a complex field of antagonisms. Conflict is something that can transform the social world.

Conflict in New Zealand's Intentional Communities

Intragroup conflict is an inevitable outcome of community life. It was identified by 98 per cent of interview subjects as a source of personal pain and anguish. For instance, when asked about the positives and negatives of life at the new community of Anahata (formerly Centrepoint) Chris Perkins replied:

> The negatives – there have been a couple of nasty incidents (I won't go into detail) where there were new people here and because of some of the things the kids did, they were angry at each other. There was some shouting and threats of calling the police and so on. That brought back old memories of old ways. On the other hand, it resolved itself and the police weren't called. (Chris, Anahata: 18 May 2001)

Even long-standing communities experience conflict. Joy is one of the early members of Riverside community, which recently celebrated its 60th anniversary:

> One of the worst things, I think, is the effect [of conflict] on relationships … In a community all relationships are interwoven and you can't shut the door and say 'They can go to hang', because you're going to be meeting them tomorrow and you're going to be going to a meeting and talking about your common needs and your common responsibilities and your common lives, and to feel seriously out of tune with somebody and disillusioned with them, or they with you, I think, is fairly

shattering. You can be irritated with another human being, and intolerant, but to lose your faith in yourself with other people or your faith in other people in your life, I find that shattering. Sometimes you accept it but you wish you could shake it off. (Joy, Riverside, 22 February 2001)

Whare speaks similarly of his childhood at Chippenham:

The worst thing was that I knew there was a problem between other people. I could feel it although I never really knew what the problem was. I knew there was some kind of tension going on between people in the house, and I found that hurtful in a way; I felt that I hurt because somebody else was kind of hurting inside. (Whare, Chippenham: 12 March 2001)

Conflict can destroy a community. Those that survive can take years to recover. We can see this by looking at an example. Chippenham, Mansfield and Gricklegrass are all secular communities founded in the 1970s by an organisation called Community Assistance Incorporated (CAI). CAI was committed to fostering co-operation and providing community support.

In 1994 conflict arose amongst members over the nature and future of CAI. They disputed the principles on which the communities were founded. This lasted for over three years, caused massive harm, damaged relationships, cost CAI dear in financial terms, and eventually led to the liquidation of its assets following a High Court judgement. CAI was wound up but the communities survived, under the banner of a new umbrella organisation, Heartwood Community Te Ngakau o te Rakau Incorporated (Heartwood).

They disputed the use of the communities' assets. CAI was financially secure and solvent with surplus resources. Given its commitment to community assistance, some members felt that assets should be realised by selling the (now valuable) properties and using the money to support co-operative and community projects. This group felt that the communities (and their members) were enjoying the benefits of CAI's assets and that this 'social good' should be more widely shared. Another group agreed that community and cooperative projects should be funded but did not feel that they needed to sell the properties. This would be better done, they argued, by managing CAI's existing resources more effectively. Factions formed in what became a bitter dispute and the communities were soon in constitutional crisis because the wording of CAI's constitution could be interpreted to support both groups. Mediation was tried and failed, and eventually the dispute went to litigation.

Feelings ran high and some are documented in Chippenham community's newsletter, *Chip'N'Away*. One writer expresses 'a sense of outrage that a very small group can so wantonly destroy the community's assets built up by so many; a sense of violation that the ideals upon which the community was founded can be so arrogantly trampled upon' (*Chip'N'Away*, Vol. 2, Issue 1, July 1996, 1). The communities survived, the properties were not sold but CAI was wound up. Its assets were in the hands of the liquidators who insisted a new management structure be created, and this is Heartwood. Heartwood consists of trustees who are former members, representatives from each community, and trustees from 'outside' (including a solicitor and member of another intentional community). Some members of the faction wanting to sell the properties left (one still remains). This created gaps and Chippenham took new members in haste – a decision it repented at leisure because these people were not committed to community living but rather wanted an easy life in a large and beautiful home. They were eventually asked to leave and further upheaval occurred. It took another three years for things to settle down at Chippenham, and at the time of my visits in 2001, Mansfield was still having problems recruiting and retaining members. In 2004, the communities are reaching a settled state, with a combination of new and old members. The effects of this conflict, then, have lasted for almost a decade and threatened the future of the communities as well as causing hurt, mistrust and pain to the parties involved. The impacts have been financial, emotional and structural.

This shows the irreparable damage to relationships that conflict can cause. It can lead to the dissolution of the group (Barker 1989). It can cause infighting, destabilise the value base, and threaten the social fabric. In short, this example supports the theoretical perspective that views conflict as having a negative function. Of course, one example does not provide sufficient material for a general theory. But people across the land say that conflict has threatened their group.

However, these communities have survived. And to establish that conflict is dangerous to an intentional community is not to prove that conflict has no useful function. Nor does this provide an answer to our question – why, given that New Zealand communities all experience conflict, have so many of them lasted for so long? It takes us some way towards answering some of our questions: it suggests that the literature on intentional communities is not wrong when it suggests conflict can be destructive. But it does not tell us why they have survived. We need to think further about actual conflicts in order to understand.

Three Kinds of Conflict

It is, of course, possible to have conflict about anything, but the fieldwork in New Zealand enabled us to identify three common kinds of conflict. These are conflicts over principles, domestic issues and relationships. We found conflicts over principles to threaten the value base and the social fabric. Disputes over domestic arrangements and relationships are more common. These too, we found, can threaten a group but not in the same way. We need to look at this further and also to see whether communities have devised effective strategies for dealing with these different kinds of conflict.

Conflicts of Principle

Conflicts over principle are the most difficult to survive. Intentional communities are formed by people who share a vision and want to put their principles into practice. A serious challenge to these principles from within the group challenges the community's reason for being, as it did with CAI/Heartwood. Another example occurred in the Buddhist monastery of Bodhinyanarama. Bodhinyanarama is set in a 500 acre valley of regenerating mixed and native bush. Like many communities in New Zealand, Bodhinyanarama is committed to environmental regeneration, reintroducing native species and removing non-natives. As a Buddhist community it is also committed to cause no harm to any lifeform. A few years ago, the community faced a dilemma: what to do with the possums? Possums are not native to New Zealand and have no natural predators here. They consequently breed prolifically and can decimate woodland with alarming speed and efficiency, which inhibits the regeneration of native species.

How could they cause no harm and permit regeneration of threatened native species? Two solutions were considered: one was an electric fence, which would keep possums off the property. This was quickly dismissed as the cost was prohibitive and the actual installation nigh-on impossible – the 500 acre valley is steep-sided, borders Department of Conservation land and is inaccessible to machinery. The second option, which was eventually agreed upon, was a conventional management programme, which would permit the killing of some possums. This decision caused much heartache, debate and conflict and, for a time, it appeared that the community might not survive the crisis. Some members left. The monks at Bodhinyanarama spoke openly about this dilemma and the pain it caused. Subsequently new members have joined, including the senior monk, Ajhan Sucitto, who said, frankly, that it was easier to live with the decision than to have made it.

The impact of conflicts of principle cannot be over-stressed. Intentional communities are usually founded in order to realise a vision of the good life. The object of commitment varies and may be an idea (Abrams and McCulloch 1967); a value system (Kanter 1972); or an alternative lifestyle (Metcalf 1989). They aim to realise utopia. Conflicts over these foundational commitments can be devastating.

Domestic Conflict

> The primary issue with which a utopian community must cope in order to have the strength and solidarity to endure is its human organisation: how people arrange to do the work that the community needs to survive as a group, and how the group in turn manages to satisfy and involve its members over a long period of time. (Kanter 1972, 64)

When people live together in a shared space, the division of labour and domestic chores can become a source of irritation. The issues are the same in any household. Individuals may leave (exit is a possibility in all households) and in extreme circumstances, the group itself can be threatened. Coser claims that small tightly-knit groups are especially vulnerable to interpersonal conflict, which they are inclined to suppress. This, he says is dangerous because suppressed conflict can become explosive:

> While they provide frequent occasions for hostility (since both sentiments of love and hatred have been intensified through frequency of interaction), the acting out of such feelings is sensed as a danger to such intimate relationships, and hence the tendency to suppress rather than allow expression of hostile feelings. In close knit groups, feelings of hostility tend, therefore, to accumulate and hence intensify. (Ibid.)

Conflict, for Coser, can and does have positive outcomes but this kind of conflict, he says, is negative. Intense hostility in a small group threatens the existence of the groups (as well as the safety of the members).

He identifies two causes of conflict under such circumstances:'realistic' and 'non-realistic'. These categories form accurate descriptors for the kinds of conflict observed in communities. Realistic conflict, so-called, is conflict over actual issues. 'Non-realistic' conflict is very real, in that it involves hostility, but occurs over a faux issue:

> The conflict doesn't just aim at resolving the immediate issue which led to the outbreak; and accumulated grievances which were denied expression previously are apt to emerge at this occasion. (Ibid.)

Conflict over domestic issues is often 'non-realistic'. Suppressed hostility can explode over such an issue as who does the dishes? The real issue may or may not be domestic. Somebody who persistently fails to clean up after him or herself after making lunch, for instance, can infuriate other people who share the kitchen. And so an explosion of anger can occur over one small pile of crumbs on a worksurface. The issue is not really this pile of crumbs, but rather perhaps responsibility for domestic hygiene.

Who cleans the toilet? Who buys the food? Who does the gardening? Who does the accounts? All of these are potential areas of dispute and resentment. This is sometimes explained in terms of frustration/aggression theory (see Bisno 1988, 27–28). This may appear trivial but these conflicts can generate serious problems in a community, such as the retention of new members. Mansfield community, for instance, at the time of my visits in 2001 was having difficulty retaining members. People would join readily – the house and gardens are lovely and existing members are friendly, committed and experienced at communal living – but they would not stay beyond the trial period. Mansfield, which had the potential to carry 15 people, was down to just two members and was under pressure from Heartwood to recruit, not least for reasons of financial viability. They had stopped having meetings because it seemed ridiculous to have a formal meeting of just two members. And so the problem drifted. However, during my stay they did sit down together and identified a key problem. Mansfield lacked clear procedures organising domestic space and work. Existing members had very clear ideas about how things should be done but these were not written down anywhere and so new members found themselves constantly and unwittingly stepping on toes. Timatanga had experienced something similar. In this case, conflict was triggered over the use of non-organic materials in the community garden. Some new members had used a weedkiller, unaware of the unwritten (but strong) rule prohibiting this. Both of these cases evoked resentment and anger. Both were avoidable. In both of these cases, the community has learned from the experience and set in place structures aiming to avoid its recurrence.

Some conflicts can be anticipated and avoided but some conflict will always occur in all communities. For instance, the oldest intentional community that I visited was the Community of the Sacred Name in Christchurch, an Anglican convent. Members here spoke of the difficulties that sometimes occur when living in close quarters with people whom you might not necessarily choose as friends. This was openly discussed and described as the challenge of 'learning to love someone whom you might not like very much' (Group Interview, 2 February 2001). The community sees this as primarily an individual responsibility, achieved through prayer and inner searching. Also, though, it provides clear structures for negotiating conflict and managing domestic issues.

During my stays at Chippenham Community, I observed effectively operating systems for the allocation of chores and responsibility. These are House Rules, administered through fortnightly community meetings. Membership involves working for the community (sweat rent) for two hours a week and logging your hours. People take responsibility for a specific area, such as general maintenance or for servicing bathrooms, kitchen, or gardens. Help can be requested at the house meeting or bilaterally. Big projects and all alterations are collectively agreed by consensus and members joked about the amount of time it can take to choose something like new carpets this way!

The system works well but as a last resort, there are sanctions available.

Residents who persistently fail to attend house meetings or abide by collective decisions; who fail to sustain required payment; who fail to carry out duties or show an interest and caring in the property; who disregard rules or flagrantly ignore behaviour codes collectively agreed upon; who act with disinterest or disregard for the vision, goals and practices of Heartwood Community Te Ngakau o te Rakau Inc., may be seen as unsuited to this community and by common agreement of a house meeting be asked to leave. It is the policy of the community to take appropriate legal action to recover any debts unpaid by vacating residents. (Chippenham Household Community Policy)

This formula was devised following the conflict of the 1990s. No system works across time without some problems and, during my stays at Chippenham, minor conflict occurred during a house meeting. One member was irritated with another who had not complied with the Rules and Agreements on domestic issues. It turned out that the person concerned had not logged their sweat rent. Discussion of the procedures occurred – perhaps they were overly bureaucratic? Perhaps it is not sufficient just to do the work but necessary also to log it? Perhaps problems in one party's personal life were clouding their judgement and perspective? The point is not that dispute occurred but rather that it was aired in an appropriate space and manner.

These rules were devised by consensus and members attribute their success to this. Chippenham has no 'leader' responsible for rule enforcement. Rather, the group enforces and revises its own rules. Agreements are collectively owned and individual participation produces collective autonomy and responsibility. Key factors here are open communication, willingness to participate and a clear process.

Conflict over Relationships

> Being here over time, the worst thing has been relationship problems and not being able to get away from them, or it being very difficult with somebody actually having to leave their home in order to escape from what they are feeling. (Arafelle, Earthspirit, 12 April 2001)

Problems with close personal relationships occur everywhere but can be particularly intense in intentional communities. The usual problems become magnified for a range of reasons, which have two causes. The first is structural: life is less private here than in the wider community. These people live together, sometimes in the same building; they see each other most days; and they form closely-knit groups. Arguments quickly become public knowledge and are played out in a (confined) public space. The second stems from the intensity of relationships within intentional communities. This derives in part from proximity but also and importantly from a shared sense of purpose. Intentional communities are formed in collective opposition to values and ways of life 'outside'. This creates a bond and even if members are not close personal friends they usually share a vision of the good life. Sometimes this bond forms around a leader or the community itself.

And so infidelities in monogamous relationships are all the more painful if all parties belong to the same group; betrayals of friendship hurt all the more when the person concerned is a member of your community; atmospheres can become intensely strained; and rifts and splits in relationships can affect everyone.

> When people have interpersonal difficulties, that affects the whole community; pretty much my problems are everybody's problems … And that's good and bad. (Graham, Anahata, 19 May 2001)

It is good because other members of the group notice problems and provide support. For instance, the group might offer to 'babysit' children for a few days in order to create an opportunity for a couple to have time together. It is bad because things can rapidly escalate. People who have lived for some time in community learn to distance themselves from other people's immediate problems. Chris, at Anahata, puts it like this:

> One thing I've learned about living in community is that if you get caught up in everybody else's crisis, then you do not improve it, you just magnify it.
>
> You have to allow them their process and we have some very clear guidelines on how you deal with process, with people, and about how it is not okay to be angry at someone and walk around them; you have to sit down and work out issues and if you can't do it on your own, you call in a third person, not to decide who is wrong and who is right, simply to make sure that each person is hearing what the other one is saying. (Chris, Anahata, 18 May 2001)

Some groups, like Tui Community, have become expert at negotiating interpersonal conflict. At the time of my visit, Tui had a mature, long standing and stable membership which had, in Tui's 18 year history, been through various shifts in close personal relationships. Former partners, wives and husbands now live with different partners, wives, or husbands, in a more or less stable situation. The community has devised a system of 'heart meetings' at which personal issues can be aired. These are rotated with regular business meetings. They employ a range of techniques for expressing anger in non-confrontational ways, for resolving conflict and for asking for help when it is needed. Some members of Tui are psychotherapists or counsellors. Building on their experiences of handling conflict within Tui, they now offer training to the wider community in Golden Bay. Personal trauma has thus yielded sustainable relationships, sustainable systems and income.

'Heart business' is often conducted in intentional communities by a process of 'sharing'. Communities worldwide have practices like this, devised as outlets for personal feelings. The Findhorn Foundation in Scotland pioneered 'sharing' and Riverside has a similar mechanism. We think this may date back to the practice of 'mutual criticism' at the Oneida Community. Sharing is a form of communication governed by certain rules. One person speaks at a time and usually in turn. A sharing is not a conversation but a statement of feeling. Each person airs feelings and personal issues if they want to. A sharing can be something like 'I feel happy this week because the carrots are starting to sprout', or something more contentious, such as 'I feel angry with Lucy'.

It is important, when sharing, not to attribute feelings to others, but rather to acknowledge your own feelings and responses. This takes practice. Suppose, for instance, a person stands up halfway through a meal and leaves the room and the door slams behind them. The 'wrong' way to share feelings about this is to say 'You upset everybody [accusatory: attributes blame and speaks 'on behalf' of others in the group] when you stormed out the room angry [interprets emotions] and slammed the door [inflammatory description]'. This generates blame, defence and attack. The appropriate way to share over this would be something like 'You suddenly left the room earlier today [uncontroversial statement of fact]. I felt confused and I'd like to ask you about it [statement of your own response and wants]'. This invites comment but does not attribute emotion to others and is not inflammatory or confrontational.

There is a widely held belief in these communities that issues need to be aired and not left to fester. At Tui, for instance, they use the following exercise as a 'pressure valve' for releasing tension between two parties who are angry with each other. A line is drawn between them. This line must not be crossed and no physical contact is made. The parties then shout – simultaneously and as loudly as they can – everything they feel about the other person. They shout until they have nothing more to say. The physical effort of shouting seems to help and the process appears cathartic. Such practices have been devised to permit the release of pressure. They are 'safety valves' and they minimise the build up of what Coser calls 'non-realistic' conflict. They channel antagonism into an appropriate space, permitting people to vent hostility and express dissent.

If conflict persists, then a facilitator is often chosen from within the community. This person's role is to permit the parties to hear each other's point of view and to help them find a way through the conflict. It is not her/his role to solve the problem or create a solution. It is certainly not their role to persuade or lead. The 'solution' comes from the people in conflict. Often a facilitator employs pre-agreed techniques. For example s/he may invite conflicting parties to 'step into each others shoes', to try to imagine and describe how the other feels. This aims to build empathy rather than antagonism. Again, rules of communication may involve cooling off time, breaks, or an agreement to openness. For deep, complex, or prolonged conflict, intentional communities sometimes call in an external facilitator or mediator. They also use external facilitators to help with constitutional change, or devising collective goals. The new community of Anahata, for instance, paid somebody to help them to devise and agree their community goals. Some people in communities work as professional facilitators and counsellors. Elaine Dyer, for instance, from Timatanga Community, has a national profile as a conflict facilitator and mediator.

Surviving Conflict

Conflict endangers communities and causes harm to individual members – to the direct participants and to those around them. When a community founded on common values experiences serious conflict about those values, the future of the group is in jeopardy. We have looked at two cases where communities have survived such conflict. Another is the shift from religious to secular at Riverside, discussed in Chapter 6. Surviving conflicts over principle is difficult and usually leads to one or more key members quitting the group.

This really hurts. People have a lot invested in group membership and leaving is very hard. This relationship is variously termed 'total personality involvement' (Coser 1968) or 'social identity' (Hogg 1992). Their sense of self may be wrapped up in their membership and leaving can problematise this. The group tends to distance itself from somebody who is leaving and that can hurt too. Through a process described by Hogg as 'social attraction', members model themselves closely on what they perceive to be the characteristics of the in-group. A new sense of self needs to be forged when circumstances change.

Some of these insights from social psychology are useful and can help us to see why groups stay together against the odds. An example is Muzafer Sherif's conception of 'superordinate goals' that bind a group in co-operative endeavour. Sherif was interested in intergroup conflict and co-operation. In his famous 'summer camp' experiments, he found that different (previously competing) groups would cooperate if they shared superordinate goals: 'Goals which are compelling and highly appealing to members of two or more groups in conflict but which cannot be attained by the resources and energies of the groups separately. In effect, they are goals attained only when the groups pull together' (Sherif 1958, 64). What makes different groups pull together is also, perhaps, what makes members within a group pull together. Likewise, theories of in and out-groups shed light on the nature of cohesion in intentional communities. It has been shown (in studies of intergroup conflict) that strong opposition from an out-group fosters strong ingroup loyalty and cohesion (Sherif 1958; Sumner 1906; Hogg, 1992). People in intentional communities do tend to see themselves as outsiders. The existence of an external 'other' helps to bond the group.

Conclusion

We have discussed a variety of possible explanations for group cohesion. We have also considered a range of procedures, structures and systems designed by actual communities to help avoid or manage conflict. Members of these communities generally see conflict as unpleasant but inevitable:

> So long as there is a world, we can never get rid of conflict. (Ajahn Viradhammo *The Resolution of Conflict* http://www.bodhinyanarama.net.nez/munindo1.htm)

> I remember once thinking 'community is about solving conflict' and that was true at the time but it doesn't take away from the good things about being in a community. (Trystan, Peterborough, 3 January 2001)

> Conflict is a natural part of being human; it's what you do after the conflict that makes a difference to how it all goes down later. What I think we have to learn from each other is how we manage to live with conflict. (Chrissie, Te Ora, 2 February 2001)

What is important to us is how they respond to conflict. One response is to stifle it. There is a tendency, when this occurs, for the repressed feelings to erupt over a faux issue and this is unpleasant. Anything can trigger anger at any time. Another response is to deal with the issue of conflict but to harbour resentment against the individuals concerned. In such circumstances somebody usually ends up leaving the community. Trust breaks down and people can no longer work together. Often conflict over broken relationships can leave a community in this condition – damaged but limping on until one or more parties leave and fresh people arrive. Or, nobody leaves and the community withdraws from collective projects and communal activities, becoming a group of people who share the same land but do not actually share a value base, trust or bond. Several of the communities visited during this research were in this condition of withdrawal. Sometimes this is a temporary phase. Sometimes it is not.

Groups that survive serious conflict and continue to operate as communities where people interact with goodwill and trust tend to be careful not to allow conflict to fester. Often, such groups have seen the damage that occurs when this is allowed to happen, felt at firsthand how bruising this can be, and are determined not to repeat the experience.

Instead, they devise ways of managing conflict. Some communities anticipate this and prepare for it by undergoing training in conflict negotiation or interpersonal communication. For instance, most members of Mamaki have been through Forum training and at Valley Farm, members are encouraged to learn Constructive Living techniques (http://www.anamorph.com/todo/cl.html/). This works well as long as all members share the same training and agree to and maintain the same rules and codes of communication. It can be difficult for new members who join later. Some communities devise codes of conduct and expectations about how to behave in a situation of conflict. Tui and Anahata have been discussed as examples. Otamatea and Earthsong also have similar sets of expectations.

The key, we think, lies is management and not resolution. Conflict need not be a 'bad thing' if it is managed carefully. This is apparent from research in the fields of social and political theory as well as social psychology, and also from our observation of intentional communities in New Zealand. It can be productive and evoke necessary change. It can produce a re-evaluation of the group's core values, as in the case of Chippenham Community. It can yield useful structures and processes, as we have seen above. It can function to establish, affirm and maintain group identity (Coser 1968). It can contribute to a dynamic and vibrant culture (Dahrendorf 1964). However, conflict can also lead to disruptive behaviour, harm and even to the dissolution of a group. And so we find ourselves treading a thin line between the polemical views identified in the theory of conflict, finding conflict to be both potentially dangerous *and* potentially useful. Living in an intentional community involves high levels of co-operation with committed people amongst whom there may be complex clashes, disputes and conflict. For this, procedures are necessary, and some of the most useful transferable initiatives and practices to come from intentional communities are the unintended outcome of learning to live together. We move on to consider more of these in the next chapter.

Note

1 Sections of an earlier version of this discussion appear in L. Sargisson, 2003 and is used with permission.

Chapter 9

Conclusion: What Have We Learned? Lasting Lessons from New Zealand

In this final chapter we identify and explore any lasting lessons from our research. What, if anything, can be learned from a study of intentional communities across a country which, for many, is thought of as lying at the end of the earth? Have these (usually small) communities scattered across this remote country anything to tell the rest of us? We think they do. What they have to tell us falls into three broad areas. Firstly, we have learned something about utopia – both the phenomenon of utopianism and the study of utopias. Secondly, we have learned important lessons about the study of intentional communities. And finally, our research sheds light on lessons that we can all share – these are lessons about living together.

Lasting Lessons for Studying Utopia

Good Place or No Place?

There exists within scholarship on utopias some tension between two interpretations of utopia. Both stem from the ambiguous etymology of the word. The scholarly Thomas More created a neologism and phonetic pun that combines three Greek words: *topos* (place), *eu* (good) and *ou* (no, or not). This creates an eternal tension in the concept of utopia because utopias are at once good places and no places. And so one interpretation focuses on the concrete utopia – the idea that utopia is an aspiration, something to be pursued and realised. Another places utopia always just over the horizon.

There are many variations and nuances on these two interpretations and most scholars combine them in some way. However, they have serious implications. The former view is the more straightforward. It leads people to experiment, to found communities, to change their lifestyle and to try to make their dreams come true. This impulse can be traced in advertising (eat this cereal and get the body you've always wanted, buy this car and you will be sexually attractive to women); travel (come to New Zealand and realise your potential); and politics (vote for me and I will make the world a better place). This is what takes utopians forward.

Utopia as noplace is more complicated. On the one hand, this view informs anti-utopians, like Karl Popper, who believe that attempts to realise utopia will create an authoritarian or totalitarian world. This is informed by an idea of utopia as perfect. A perfect world, it follows, is unchallengable. There is no room for dissent in such a place. To dissent would be irrational, mad, even, and so the dissenter would require treatment or elimination. Dystopias such as Zamyatin's *We* and Orwell's *Nineteen Eighty-Four* stem from this view. Our previous research has indicated that this view of utopia as perfection-seeking is a mistaken one (Sargent 1994; Goodwin 1980; Sargisson, 1996, 2000). Many contemporary scholars of utopia take a more nuanced view of utopia as the desire for something better, rather than something perfect (Levitas 1990; Moylan 1986, 2000). This means that utopia remains just around the corner, just over the horizon. The utopian ship sails ever onwards.

The material and knowledge gained from this research supports a view of utopia as *both* the good place and the noplace. Members of these communities often share a vision of the good life and are attempting to realise this in the here and now. However, the communities are not perfect. Their members view them as better than life in the mainstream, or life 'outside', not as utopia realised. It would probably be more accurate to describe them, as we do in Chapter 5, as utopias in process. Members feel that living collectively and exploring alternatives is better than remaining where they were. Often it is hard, physically, financially, emotionally and spiritually, but they say, it is worth the effort.

> All the things I've ever wanted to do, things I'd hadn't even dreamed of really, are possible at Gricklegrass. (Andrew, Gricklegrass, 6 January 2001)

> I think the most important thing has been to have the opportunity to try to live like this. I suppose looking at it from an outsider's point of view, it is actually a huge thing, to do something like this. (Arafelle, Earthspirit, 12 April 2001)

Communitarianism and Utopianism[1]

Throughout this book we have used language that assumes that there is a connection between communitarianism and utopianism. The old labels *utopian* community and *utopian* experiment should not be forgotten, and a more recent usage, practical utopia, indicates that some believe that the utopian nature of intentional communities should be made explicit. The so-called utopian socialists Étienne Cabet (1788–1856), Charles Fourier (1772–1837), Robert Owen (1771–1858), and Charles Henri Saint-Simon (1760–1825) all had direct connections with the establishment of intentional communities, and in the twentieth century intentional communities were founded based directly on the utopian novels *Walden Two* (1948) by B.F. Skinner (1904–90), *Stranger in a Strange Land* (1961) by Robert A. Heinlein (1907–88), and *The Harrad Experiment* (1966) by Robert Rimmer (1917–2001), among others. In the late nineteenth century, after the publication of *Looking Backward* (1888) by Edward Bellamy (1850–98), at least one community was founded based on Bellamy's novel, albeit over Bellamy's strenuous opposition. Also, in an article in 1989, Sargent showed that during the part of the nineteenth century when the establishment of intentional communities was at its peak in the US, the ideas put forth by their founders were generally paralleled by the ideas found in the utopian literature of the same period. Finally, in most cases the prospectus for an intentional society that was never founded is readily labelled a utopia, and fiction about intentional communities both actual and fictional is frequently listed among utopias.

Writers communicate their dreams by writing them down and publishing them; communards communicate their dreams by trying to put them into practice. All communities have constitutions, rules and regulations, and/or agreements (formal or informal) about how its members are to live their lives. Some of these agreements are not written down, but just as certain countries operate without written constitutions, the members most often understand the rules. If these documents and agreements had been fictions, we would call them utopias without question. In fact, most of them were fictions in the sense that they did not reflect any reality, even though that was not the intention of their authors. The forms of expression were different, but one motivation was held in common – the desire to communicate a social dream, a eutopia.

One of the reasons for not seeing the connection between utopianism and commmunitarianism is based on a misunderstanding of utopianism. Overwhelmingly utopianism is what Sargent has called 'social dreaming', dreaming of or desiring a better life, a life that corrects the worst problems of the present. In most cases utopias do not suggest that every problem will be solved; most utopias, and probably *all* contemporary ones, recognize that while the worst problems can be identified and radically improved, perhaps even completely solved, issues will remain that will need to be dealt with through the processes of education, the law, and political decision making.

To a large degree utopias are thought experiments, 'as ifs', trying out better ways of living on paper, and that experimental character connects utopianism with communitarian experiments. And one of the clear messages of this book is that in this one small country, people are carrying out a remarkable range of such experiments. All of these communities are experiments attempting to create what the founders and members believe to be a better life, not, certainly, a perfect life, but definitely a better one than they had or could have outside the community, and having found a better life, they are trying to make their communities even better.

Lasting Lessons for Studying Intentional Communities

Concerning Generalisations

While research on intentional communities has evolved from earlier work that was either largely antiquarian reports on individual communities or travelogues reporting on visits to a number of communities, it is still rarely comparative. Some contemporary scholars, such as Bill Metcalf (Metcalf 1996) and Yosef Gorni et al. (Gorni 1987) have studied communities in different countries but they make few comparisons. This is, perhaps, for good reason because, as our research has shown, those few generalised theories of intentional communities that do exist, such as Kanter's, are deeply flawed. Thus, while we say that our research contradicts much of the general understanding of communities, we base our statements on our wide reading in a literature that primarily focuses on individual communities.

We have found that communities are, in some respects, very much alike, so that comparison is possible, but we have also found that they differ profoundly, so that generalisations have to be made with great care. In questioning the assumptions that we believe are made and uncritically accepted and in making our own general observations based on our research, we hope to open debate and discussion with our colleagues in the field of communal studies over what generalisations can and cannot be made about intentional communities.

Most studies of intentional communities are based on communities in the US, UK, or Israel. We have shown conclusively that this is a mistake, that many of these generalisations are not universally applicable. While we now know that some of the best-known generalisations do not even fit the US (for example, Kanter's), it is equally clear that there are significant national differences, at least between New Zealand and the US (and between these countries and the UK and Israel). This suggests that scholars need to be very careful about generalising.

At the same time our study shows that most, if not all, intentional communities face common problems, ranging from the apparently trivial, like 'Do we allow dogs?' and 'Whose turn is it to clean up?' to the obviously fundamental, like 'What are our core principles?' We have also shown that there is no single answer to these questions; one size does not fit all. Nonetheless, the experience of communities can be useful to each other and we will explore this further in the final section of this chapter.

Classifying Communities

A methodological point that became clear during the planning stage for this book was that existing categories for organising communities were not going to be useful in this case. Often, scholars have organised communities into such categories as religious/secular, urban/rural, in order to have a descriptive and analytical tool with which to work. We have done this ourselves. In his article 'Three Faces of Utopianism Revisited', Sargent developed a taxonomy that was more useful than most. It asked about religious orientation, location, intent regarding longevity, property holding, political system, sexual orientation, source and interpersonal orientation (Sargent 1994). This is more complex than most taxonomies but even this did not form a useful basis for organising this research. Certainly, it asked questions we needed to answer and in order to begin to understand a community it is necessary to know these things. But it did not help us to explain the similarities and differences that cross these divides.

We opted then, for an approach that was based in the communities' understandings of their own aims. Why do they exist? What do they aim to achieve? What, in other words, is the utopia towards which members seek to move? The answers to these questions, we found, enabled us to develop the broad categories of religious and spiritual communities, co-operative communities and environmentalist communities. Within these categories we found wide variations and our accounts represent these variations.

Working this way has allowed us to glean and share information required by a traditional taxonomy and to give a real feel of the similarities and differences between and amongst communities that share a broad aim. It has also permitted us to be alert to phenomena that cut across our categories, such as conflict and conflict management. Methodologically, then the desire to sort, order and classify should, we feel, be tempered by the need to accurately reflect these communities for analytical discussion. Our categories are broad and fluid. Some communities, like Earthsong Eco-Neighbourhood and Tui Community, could be located in several places and we have tried to remain alert to this. No system of classification is ever going to fully represent reality and we feel it important to note this.

Measuring Success

Anyone who regularly reads the scholarly literature on intentional communities will have frequently seen such communities labeled a 'success', or, less often, a 'failure'. Since the publication of *Commitment and Community* in 1972, the basis for such judgments has tended to be the sole measure of longevity, defined as 25 years. While Kanter's definition of success was actually more complex than this, and no one would argue against the position that lasting for 25 years might be prima facie evidence of 'success', the 25 year measure has become a simplistic measure used to neatly divide intentional communities. Definitions of success were stated explicitly or implicitly in the classic studies of intentional communities prior to Kanter, and they generally used longevity in the sense that if the community no longer existed, it was judged a failure. Thus, Kanter's stress on longevity is part of a well-established tradition.

She justifies using longevity as a measure like this:

> One central issue is whether longevity is a necessary or sufficient measure of a group's success. With respect to nineteenth-century utopian communities at least, longevity is a valid criterion of success, not only because it is easily measurable but also because for many communities in the nineteenth century their over-riding goal was simply to exist – to establish a social order embodying all their ideals and to make of it a viable, stable, and permanent organization. (127–28)

Kanter's project, as suggested by her title *Commitment and Community*, is to discover the commitment mechanisms that create community, and she could not have undertaken the project without a definition that focused on longevity.

But even as Kanter's book was being published, others developed more complicated definitions of success. In a 1972 essay Robert S. Fogarty discusses five criteria, including whether the members saw the community as a success and whether the community was successful on its own terms. And after the tendency to use Kanter's one dimension was already apparent Jon Wagner (1985) developed seven possible measures, including Fogarty's and Kanter's. He provided a range of criteria that includes longevity but adds others that gives us a range of alternatives to consider. Wagner concludes that because it tries to apply a single measure to a multi-dimensional subject, we would be better off by dropping the concept of 'success' entirely.

Donald E. Pitzer (1989) has argued in his various essays on 'developmental communalism' that we need to understand communalism as a stage in a process with non-communal beginning and ending points. An intended corollary of his argument is that the measure of success should be applied to the whole movement rather than to the communal phase alone. Identifying communalism as a moment in a social movement is not particularly popular among believers in communalism as a solution to today's social problems, but Pitzer's argument clearly applies to the community that he has most studied, New Harmony, an immensely influential community that was a failure by almost any other measure.

Participants in a session on success at the 1993 meeting of the International Communal Studies Association suggested that we should ask the following questions:

To what extent do communities fulfill their own stated goals?
To what extent do communities fulfill the goals of the individual participants?
To what extent are communities capable of changing over time to adjust to the changed needs of the community and its members and to the outside?
To what extent do the goals and ideals of the community influence the larger society?

Some of the participants in the roundtable and members of the audience also argued that success and failure is simply the wrong subject. The subject should be the message that cooperation and community works for the members and that they provide preferable alternatives to competition. But, of course, as others pointed out, cooperation and community do not work for all the members; there are well-attested negative situations. Which raises the questions of whether we should consider a long-lived community that mistreats its members a success.

In a speech at the Ruskin Community, Henry Demarest Lloyd said,

Only within these communities has there been seen, in the wide borders of the United States, a social life where hunger and cold, prostitution, intemperance, poverty, slavery, crime, premature old age, and unnecessary mortality, panic and industrial terror have been abolished. If they had done this only for a year, they would have deserved to be called the only successful 'society' on this continent, and some of them are generations old. All this has not been done by saints in heaven, but on earth by average men and women. (Qtd. in Fogarty 1990, 235)

In other words, if you have done this for only a year, you are a success.

Concerning Homogeneity

There is a view amongst people who think about intentional communities that in order to survive across time they need to contain like-minded people who are similar in important ways. We have found this not to be the case. It is true that these communities contain mostly (though not exclusively) white skinned people. However, they come from all over the world and most groups contain a mixture of cultures from, for instance, Spain, Germany, Britain and South America as well as Pakeha New Zealand. Some members have mixed ancestry (for example, Maori/Pakeha). Moreover, members are often strong-willed and hold firm opinions. They may be like-minded in that they share a broad vision, but they do not all think in the same way.

> Yes, and I don't think that differences are suppressed in any way in communities. They are very opinionated places, well Chippenham is, and it has strong opinions about everything! That's part of the beauty of it, that you can actually voice your opinions ... They don't think 'That person's absolutely hideous, listen to what they're saying, I don't like them anymore', it's not like that. People don't think that, it's more 'Why do you think that?' The conversation here is wonderful. It's great having opinions from everyone. You might talk something over and eventually everyone will come to the same conclusion. There are so many things that I hadn't previously thought of, and I can see that there is a lot of validity in that. I love conversations here. (Fiona, Chippenham, 12 March 2001)

Diversity of opinion – and the ability to express this freely – generates dynamic communities, and these places are certainly dynamic. We revisit this below.

Lasting Lessons for Living Together

Decisions Need to be Legitimate as Well as Mutually Binding

Most of the communities that exist in New Zealand today are egalitarian. This excludes many of the religious communities but includes almost all of the secular ones. And nearly all of these egalitarian communities use some form of consensus decision-making in their business meetings. At least one person interviewed from each of these communities cited consensus as their most valuable process.

What is consensus? Consensus decision making is not majority-based system, where discussion culminates in a vote. Votes, it is said, create winners and losers. Rather, consensus seeks agreement. Consensus decision-making aims to enable people to deal with and live with conflict, to negotiate disagreements and to find collective solutions. In the management-speak of the modern university, participants fully 'own' decisions made by consensus. It is a fully egalitarian process and this is why we say that it mirrors the intent of the communities.

Why is consensus appropriate for egalitarian groups?

Consensus, we suggest, is the most appropriate way to make decisions in small egalitarian groups. When we say small, we include the larger groups of, say Anahata, and the Friends' Settlement, both of which were home to some 30 adults in 2001. It is appropriate for the following reasons: it mirrors the intent of the community and, as such, it is the most legitimate form of decision-making in this context. It effectively binds each individual to the decision and so it is the most effective form of making decisions in this context.

The wider world can learn a lot from intentional communities about how to make decisions by consensus. Like all democratic procedures, consensus is open to manipulation and abuse, and we have both seen it used to legitimise non-consensual decisions in the workplace. But done right, consensus is a marvelous tool. The making of decisions by real consensus is impressive. Solutions to apparently unsolvable problems emerge and the group bonds around them. It is a form of social magic.

Not all secular communities seek egalitarianism as their primary aim. Feminist, green, cooperative and co-housing communities seek equality as a secondary aim; equality forms part of their larger utopia. It is essential then in the interests of legitimacy and internal social justice that decisions affecting the group should be made by the group.

This contradicts the conventional wisdom about decision-making, which has it that people are incapable of making decisions that are not simply self-interested. This debate is ages old. Aristotle asked whether people could do this in *Politics*. Machiavelli, assumed not in *The Prince* (1513). Hobbes infamously and influentially assured us that they can not in *Leviathan* (1651). An influential view observable in both liberal and conservative traditions has it that the mass of humankind is generally self-interested and self-serving and requires government by others. There are a number of salient features to this view. Firstly, people cannot be trusted with the welfare of others and so checks and balances are required; this position rests in a theory of human nature. Secondly, most people are not competent to make decisions that transcend simple self-interest, and this justifies elitism.

This problem is nicely articulated in James Harrington's seventeenth century utopia, *The Commonwealth of Oceana* (1656). In a memorable passage Harrington says that it is too much to ask man to think in the common interest when sitting at a common table. He will be able to think only of his own appetites. He imagines two girls, sitting down to share a cake and asks: 'Who should cut it?' If the person who cuts is also the person who chooses, he suggests, she is likely to cut the cake unevenly and to choose the larger portion. The solution, he suggests, is as follows: '"Divide", says one to the other, "and I will choose; or let me divide and you shall choose"' (Harrington, 1992, 22). This has been the received wisdom in liberal conceptions of popular government ever since and it speaks of a separation of powers. The person who cuts the cake should not also be the person who distributes it. However, in these intentional communities, we have observed both in our visits and through painstaking work on archived minute books of meetings, that it *is* possible to be both the person who cuts the cake and the person who chooses *if they are one and the same*. In other words, these communities are working examples of participatory democracies in which everybody makes the decisions on everything. And this is possible only through consensus.

Why does consensus work in these groups?

Why does this work? How is it possible? Are the members of these communities especially virtuous? Are they evidence against widely held assumptions of human nature and competence? Well, perhaps they are, but we rather doubt it. They are, on the whole, ordinary people who have chosen to live extraordinary lives. But within this extraordinary context they behave much like everybody else. They sometimes feel jealous or greedy or covetous or selfish. There are, we think, three differences. One lies in their commitment to the group. This may be, as Kanter believed, commitment to the cause (she identified religious commitment as the strongest bond), or to the group itself. The second significant factor is an attitude of good will and trust. This is vital. We saw in the chapter above what happens when trust breaks down. A willingness to participate in the spirit of consensus is essential, and, because it is open to abuse, trust in others to do likewise is also essential. And thirdly is the ability to participate in an appropriate manner. Consensus decision-making is not easy and requires certain learned skills. There are two final points, which have little to do with the virtue or ability of members but a lot to do with why this works. The first is size. These groups are relatively small, they can feasibly meet to discuss issues face-to-face. The second is that members know each other, they are not a community of strangers. They are all 'on the same side', all a part of a particular 'ingroup' and further, are bound by their shared views of the world outside.

A certain amount of political education and socialisation is necessary for consensus to work and this is something that we can all learn from. Done wrong, consensus can generate an oppressive situation, which binds people to decisions they do not support: cabinet responsibility gone wrong. A persuasive speaker can sway people from their views, at least for the duration of the meeting. An articulate or confident person can dominate the debate. Lobbying can occur before the meeting. Done right, though, consensus is a fully inclusive, co-operative and non-hierarchical process structured in such a way as to permit all voices to be heard and all opinions respected. In order to do it right it is necessary to know how.

Some groups have induction procedures for training new members in consensus decision-making. Earthsong Eco-Neighbourhood, for instance, has a 'buddy' system, in which new people are given a mentor who guides them through the process. Others have written guidelines. Otamatea Ecovillage's guidelines can be found on their website (http://www.conserve.org.nz/ otamatea.html). In observations of meetings it is apparent that the hardest lesson to learn about consensus is not to do with the mechanics (although this can be complicated) but rather the attitude. It seems hardest to learn to want to make decisions for the group and not the individual. Again, this is long debated in the world of political theory. Jean-Jacques Rousseau is the most optimistic about this in his *Social Contract,* and once people have become immersed in the group they do seem to be able to think in terms of something approaching a general will.

Most groups use a facilitator to guide meetings. It is this person's responsibility to ensure that everybody has a fair say and that the system is not abused. Members usually perform this role in rotation. While the facilitator remains impartial the integrity of the process remains intact. We have observed that people step aside from facilitating when they are attached to one of the views articulated. The relationship between the facilitator and the group is important:

> Facilitation is where someone helps the group come to a solution by withdrawing from the discussion and focusing on the *process* of getting there. It is a role not a status. The facilitator makes suggestions about what to do, which the group may accept or reject, but never do they make decisions for the group. The authority stays with the group. (Swain 1996, 7)

The facilitator should not try to persuade or manipulate to yield a certain outcome. The group is the decision-maker.

Some ways of making decisions by consensus

Consensus is most effectively attained within a structured process in a space (that is, meeting) dedicated to that end. The process varies but the simplest form runs like this: the situation is described by the facilitator and issues are identified; views and opinions are heard (usually in a round to ensure full participation); problems are identified by the facilitator; suggestions are generated by the group and discussed in turn; proposals are summarised by the facilitator; proposals are refined, if necessary; and, finally, the decision is recorded. This is the process at many communities, including Peterborough Community, in Christchurch, where Trystan Swain lives. He is a trainer in consensus facilitation. Trystan is thus able to disseminate good practice and generate income though experience of communal life.

The decision-making process at the Quaker Community, Friends' Settlement, is consensus driven according to long-established Quaker practice:

> Our decision making method – widely called consensus – is an expression of regard for each person. All members, women and men, young and old, have an equal voice and responsibility. We do not take a vote. Instead, the Clerk (appointed by the Meeting to replace both chairperson and secretary of non-Quaker meetings) guides proceedings until he/she can feel unity in the sense of the meeting.
>
> The Clerk records a written minute which is then read aloud. If it is acceptable to the meeting, the next item on the agenda is considered. If not, individuals suggest changes to the minute, or discussion is resumed, or the meeting 'waits on the Lord' in silent prayer until a satisfactory way forward is found. (*Questions to Quakers*)

Business meetings at Friends' Settlement resemble their meetings for worship. Long periods of silence remain unbroken by the Clerk, and discussion is slow and deeply thoughtful. Solutions emerge.

Otamatea, Earthsong and Anahata Communities all use a card system to further structure meetings. This is a formal system through which discussion is structured. Each person taking part in the discussion has six coloured cards, one of which is raised at any time during the discussion to indicate a wish to speak. Each colour has special significance (Black: I have a personal/interpersonal difficulty that is preventing my full participation; Red: I have a process observation, for example, the discussion is off the subject (a 'point of order' under Robert's Rules); Orange: I wish to acknowledge someone or something; Yellow: I have a question or need clarification; Green: I can provide clarification and Blue: I have a comment or opinion).

Meetings are guided by a facilitator who calls first on the people showing black cards to state their difficulty and make suggestions about how to deal with the matter. The group can then decide whether this should occur within the group or privately. People holding red, orange, yellow, green and blue cards are then called on to contribute. Once a proposal has been clarified and discussed the meeting moves to the decision-making stage. For this each participant has five coloured cards, signifying varying degrees of acceptance,[2] which are taken in turn. This process is deeply formal and is particularly effective for people who are new to consensus.

Consensus is not appropriate for every community decision or even for every community but observation overwhelmingly confirms it the most legitimate process for making binding and legitimate decisions within egalitarian groups. It is possible for everyone to learn to do this with patience and practice and the result is worth the effort.

Regarding Change

We discovered during research for this project that change often takes people by surprise. Members of the older communities (who are best placed to reflect on this, spoke) for instance, of being unprepared for the eventuality of people leaving, or wanting to change the groups' initial aims. We learned that change can be difficult and even traumatic, but also that it is inevitable and survivable.

Radical change is possible without the destruction of the community

Many convents and religious houses have gone through radical change with some falling by the wayside, as have some other religious and secular communities. Many convents in particular have managed to incorporate significant changes into what was once quite a rigid structure. We found this, for instance, at the Community of the Sacred Name. This was once a large community of Anglican sisters, organised in a traditionally hierarchical manner. A Reverend Mother led the Community and made decisions for the group. Numbers are currently low because fewer women are seeking a contemplative religious life. The Pacific Islands are an exception to this trend and the younger members are Tongan. Some of the changes at the Community are a pragmatic response to this shrinkage in numbers. Some reflect the changed wants and beliefs of the sisters themselves. For instance, the community now contains an interesting mixture of hierarchy and democracy. Much of the physical space is still arranged to reflect a hierarchy. In the Chapel, for instance, the Reverend Mother's seat is slightly removed from the others and Novices and Supplicants sit at a distance on hard pews. Seating in the dining room is similarly arranged, a long table covers one end of the room, and chairs are placed behind the table to face down the room. Mother Judith's upholstered seat is placed in the middle and the nuns sit in a row on either side, in hierarchical order. The most senior sit closest to the Reverend Mother and the Postulants sit furthest away. Notwithstanding this formal hierarchy, decisions are made by a democratic process in which all members have an equal say; and the working life of the community is organised on egalitarian lines, according to ability. Everyone takes a turn at cleaning the bathrooms, for instance. The community has a weekly meeting, called a *confer*ence, at which day-to-day issues are discussed and decisions are made, disagreements go to a vote and a two-thirds majority is necessary to carry a decision.

In order to survive over time The Community of the Sacred Name has had to change. It may need to change more in order to adapt to the shrinking numbers. The large building, which is home to the community (ominous from the outside but beautiful inside) would no doubt convert into flats. The sisters may have to face leaving their traditional home and moving into smaller premises.

Riverside is New Zealand's oldest secular community. It is over 60 years old and amazingly has survived for all of that time as an income-sharing group. We know of none other like this. And yet Riverside has made enormous changes to its identity and goals over the years. It was founded as a Methodist Pacifist community during World War II and offered refuge to the wives of men interned for refusing to fight. In the 1970s it dropped its religious affiliation. This proved extremely traumatic and members who have been at Riverside for 50 years or more recall those days as difficult ones. It has also changed from being a community with, if not a leadership, then at least a strong core and when any strong person left this created a void. They self-govern by consensus and the minute books from their meetings have been lodged in the National Library. They make interesting reading and from them we can learn of the discussions that occurred during these transitional phases. The latest crisis, or crossroads, for Riverside concerns the income-pool, an issue that has been forced by two new members. Both high earners, they want to keep their income and some possessions (like a car) and yet want to belong to Riverside. In 2001 a compromise had been reached in which one partner belonged fully to the community and the other did not but lived as a tenant. The community was taking this challenge very seriously, and rather than taking the attitude 'don't join then!' was preparing to discuss the future of the pool. In part this is because Riverside has low numbers of full members at the moment. Of the 60 or so potential living spaces for people, more than half are rented out to non-members. Perhaps, they thought, new recruits were put off by the requirement to surrender all goods to the community and to live in relative poverty.

It is impossible to know how well founded this fear is. We have observed that new communities, like Otamatea, attract a mixture of people, including some professional people who do not want to give up either job or income and who desire a relatively high standard of living, whilst remaining committed to ecological sustainability. It is tempting to make generational claims here – perhaps the people in their 30s and 40s now have a different set of shared experiences and different expectations from those whose formative years fell in the 1930s and 1940s, or even the 1960s. This younger group would have had formative years under a government that destroyed the welfare state, ended free health care at the point of delivery, abolished child benefit and promoted a spending and credit boom. The 'Great Experiment' in New Zealand made Margaret Thatcher's Britain and Ronald Reagan's America look positively conservative (with a small 'c'). The radicalism and speed of the economic changes made during this time certainly changed practices drastically, perhaps it also shifted values. Whatever its cause, it is a fact that most people who enter communities today are of a different generation than those who are already there.

Change is necessary and difficult

Change, like conflict, is both difficult and necessary. Dynamism is necessary even in utopia and, as stated above, we do not adhere to the once-held belief that utopias represent (or even seek) perfection. There is always room for improvement, always another horizon about which to dream. Joy, a longtime resident of Riverside, spoke of this when asked to explain the longevity of this extraordinary community. She touches on many things in her reply, including determination and trust:

> I don't think it [Riverside] will collapse now, I think it will change. I know it needs to change, not fundamental beliefs. I don't know whether income sharing will continue, whether it's relevant today or even as important as we might have thought. It has been an important thing to the community, but it may go. You don't have to achieve all the things you aim at. As you grow into them, the level you aspire to changes, and you move on. It shifts – it's that maturity isn't it? (Joy, Riverside, 22 February 2001)

Change and adaptation to change are essential for a vibrant community.

There will always be a turnover of membership

People will come and go. None of the communities visited contained all of the original members. This itself is a cause of pain and distress and upheaval. Relationships in intentional communities tend to be intense and are different from friendships. Often, when a person is thinking of leaving (or even before they begin to actually consider it), there is a period of distancing. That person will withdraw, perhaps to his or her own living space and perhaps outside the group, to spend time with different people. They start to see the community differently, to be aware of its faults and flaws and not its strengths. Life can be quite uncomfortable while this occurs. And once the announcement is made, there is often a feeling of betrayal or sadness amongst those who are to be left behind. People have used the vocabulary of bereavement and abandonment to describe how it feels when somebody leaves the group.

In social terms then, the community has to adjust to this. But it can be even more difficult when there are also financial ties that bind a group together. Most of the communities in New Zealand involve some financial commitment for full membership. New members need to buy a home (Karuna Falls), or build a home (Awaawaroa), or purchase shares (Katajuta), or purchase a lease (Friends Settlement). Only in a small handful of communities are members all tenants. The older communes were unprepared for this eventuality and this is why some lie empty. Ophui members, for instance, have nearly all left the community to live elsewhere, either because their children grew up to want to be somewhere less remote, or because they sought work in the cities or for other personal reasons. They still meet at Ophui once a year but the (now quite valuable) land is mostly unoccupied. Sometimes members cannot afford to leave their stake in the community and want to be bought out, either by the collective or by a new person who will take their place. This has obvious difficulties – the existing group may not have the funds, or may not want just anybody to join them – and communities need robust agreements and how to divide the land and how to measure its value when people come and go.

We have encountered many examples of communities who have been unpleasantly surprised by what has happened when people leave. The story of Katajuta was wittily told but poignant. A new person came to Katajuta after it had been established for some years. After he had been with them for a while he appeared naked before them one day and proclaimed himself to be Jesus and demanded that they acknowledge him as their leader. Katajuta has always been very relaxed and had few formal rules at the time. They had none concerning the entrance of new members (no way of screening) and none regarding exit (no way of getting him to leave). The result was, by all accounts, a difficult period. Their current community agreements are included as an appendix, and it is apparent that much thought has gone into drafting the sections on issues of entrance and exit. Of the ten agreements, four concern entrance and exit and these are by far the longest and most explicit of all the rules.

People change

Sometimes, when people enter a relationship young they grow apart. Sometimes they grow together. Similarly, sometimes, people join an intentional community in their twenties and discover after some years that their needs and wants have changed. Indeed, this can happen at any age. Life changes, bereavement, divorce or separation, a new partner, aging children, illness, or simply growing older can all shift a person's priorities. This can cause problems in a community. It can lead to calls for a change in practices (such as the introduction of television or dedicated space for teenagers). It can lead to a shift in some members' core values (which can produce intense conflict). It can mean that the community is no longer an appropriate place to live. These changes need to be carefully negotiated and those communities that are flexible about practices seem most likely to adapt.

Intentional communities are places in which people experience change. Many people spoke of this during interviews. Often this is a consequence of living in the community:

> I think you go through some kind of metamorphosis if you live in one. If people haven't experienced living in one, they will go through some change, whether it is negative or positive. I'm aware that some people who have lived here had a bad time, basically because it wasn't on their wavelength, they just couldn't do it. I don't even know if I can do it, I'm not sure. (Whare, Chippenham, 12 March 2001)

> People come here and they last two days and crack up. The people who live here are used to it, they are used to people cracking up and bursting into tears. We don't know why but we think it has something to do with the land drawing people's emotions out. What I heard before I came to this community was that if you go to Tui you will see yourself and experience transformation. It does have an effect on people, so people who live here are quite skilled in helping people through their processes, not pushing them or trying to fix them. (Selma, Tui, 4 April 2001)

Often people decide to join an intentional community because they want to change; they seek self-discovery, development or improvement. Sometimes, though, these changes are less to do with the community and more to do with life itself. Transitions, such as the move from childhood to adulthood, youth to middle age, middle age to old age, all involve losses and gains and sometimes people become less committed to the group as a consequence. Similarly, a new relationship can be a major distraction and somebody who, for years, has been a linchpin in a group can become quite distanced and start to want different things. Size is a factor here. A small group will often struggle to accommodate these changes because in such communities each person has an established role (peacemaker, treasurer, ideas person) and the transition in the individual creates an unfillable gap in the group. In larger communities or ones with fluid membership these gaps are more easily filled by existing or new members.

Sometimes change (either to the individual or the group, or both) means that people leave the group and we met people who had moved from for instance Rainbow Valley to Riverside, Katajuta to Riverside, and Mamaki to Anahata. In the case of Katajuta, this came at a time when a single woman wanted a quieter life than was possible at the then rather wild community of Katajuta. Excessive drug use, an accusation of rape, and the general behaviour of some young male teenagers all contributed to her decision. Riverside offered a more committed, peaceful and spiritual way of life, and this suited her needs.

Sometimes a period in an intentional community is part of a transition in a person's life.

> In terms of the people living here, we've all changed a lot. I think when we leave this place we'll have gained a lot. I think it's a bit of a transitory place for a lot of people. People come here with something to sort out for themselves, and they leave having sorted it, ready to take the next permanent move in their lives or whatever. (Tess, Gricklegrass, 5 January 2001)

There are people across the land who have lived in an intentional community for a time. New Zealand has such a small population that these people represent a significant number, rather than an aberrant minority, and their contribution to the wider culture has been manifold. High profile former communards include Marion Hobbs, MP (in Cabinet in 2004) who was a founder member of Chippenham, and Tim Shadbolt, currently long-serving Mayor of Invercargill, who was a radical activist and commune founder. We have met radio and television presenters, MPs, academics, economists, accountants, builders, librarians, fishermen and artists who at one time lived in communities.

Children

Intentional communities are marvellous places for small children and the parents of small children

Many people speak fondly of their childhoods in intentional communities. There are, of course, exceptions. Many of the former Centrepoint Community children had seriously traumatic experiences and not all children in other communities had happy childhoods. But, on the whole, it is our observation that communities are good places in which to spend one's early childhood. In most, children receive plenty of attention from adults (there's usually somebody willing to read a story), consultative parenting in which children are involved in negotiating the rules that apply to them, and have other children to play with. Some communities were founded especially in order to create a different and better environment in which to bring up children. Timatanga was founded around a school and Robyn, from Rainbow Valley, cites 'the children's education' as the most important thing about her life in that community. Te Ora is very focused on Mountain Valley School, founded by its members as well as members of the nearby Graham Downs Community (also known as Renaissance). These alternative schools are based on Montessori learning methods in which the children decide what they want to learn each day. Observation of children inside intentional communities and community schools show them to be very mature when it comes to resolving disputes, making decisions and considering options.

They are less good for teenagers

Just as children leave home in the wider community, most people who spent their childhoods in an intentional community left in young adulthood. Sometimes this is because they wanted to 'do their own thing', be their own people and find their own path in life. Some return. Whare and his partner Charlotte had recently joined Chippenham Community when I first visited in January 2001. Whare had lived at Chippenham as a child and teenager and had left to return some five years later. Chippenham is city-based and lively, offering them a combination of security, belonging, a cooperative lifestyle, freedom and fun that they sought at the time.

Sometimes, though, the community itself and the nature of life inside an intentional community are intolerable for teenagers. This is especially noticeable in rural communities. Lack of easy transport, entertainment and other people of the same age can create real problems for young people. Generally, our observations indicate that teenagers experience the same range of problems inside communities as in the wider community. The usual teenage embarrassment about parents can be all the more intense if one's parents are ageing hippies. Boredom, rampant hormones and resentment remain much the same.

Some communities draw teenagers. This has been the case historically at Happisam, which has at times in its history been infamous for heavy drug use. The Minutes of community meetings at neighbouring Rainbow Valley show that this influx caused some concern. A large concentration of teenagers can create problems in a group. Often the founders of intentional communities are reluctant to lay down the law and tend to be permissive. Sometimes this works and teenage members work things out for themselves. Sometimes it does not and a community can spin out of control.

Balancing Needs: People Who Live in Intentional Communities Need to Learn How to Balance their Own Needs with Those of the Group

This is important. Members of intentional communities are people with everyday needs and wants. The group has collective needs and wants. We observed, through visits and close reading of minutes from meetings that one of two things can occur – both of which are destabilising and disturbing. The first is the free rider. The second is burn out. These are antithetical but both can be difficult. We discussed conflict at some length in the chapter above and free riding is a major cause of domestic conflict. Anger will flash over a pile of dirty dishes one day – the underlying issue is often a history of unequal input. Having discussed conflict and its management at some length above we do not intend to rehearse those debates here, but simply note that a free-rider is a leech on a group's collective energy. Sometimes a lazy person is tolerated because they contribute in other ways that are valued by members. They might, for instance, be lots of fun, or brilliant in one valuable aspect. Usually, however, they are eventually pressed to leave the group.

The opposite is also a problem. Kanter, in her seminal work, makes much of the positive function of commitment in intentional communities. It is, she says, the glue that binds a group and helps it to survive over time. It is our observation that too much commitment can be a bad thing. If people give too much to the group and neglect their own needs and self-maintenance, they become dysfunctional. This can lead to resentment, exhaustion and ultimately mental or physical breakdown. This can be found in all aspects of life – at the workplace, in the home and in any situation of group interaction. But it is dangerous to the individual and unhealthy for the group. The individual's physical health is at risk and the group's internal dynamics are unsustainable if it drains too heavily from its members. People need to give and to receive from the community in which they choose to live. The relationship needs to be one of mutual nurturance.

Sustainability. Intentional Communities Need to be Sustainable

Our research has identified four aspects to a sustainable community – financial, social, spiritual and environmental. The first two factors are essential. Members of some groups also feel that environmental and spiritual sustainability are necessary and these have been thoroughly discussed in chapters above. Often they are inseparable:

> I think community living is an environmental thing as well a social thing and I'd like [Chippenham] to focus more that way if we can – if people are interested.

People here do think about those things, they think about the world and the political situation in various parts of the country and the world. All these things are connected and you can't tackle one without the other. Even on a small scale. (Fiona, Chippenham, 12 March 2001)

Financial sustainability

For a community to be viable it needs to be financially sustainable. This has several aspects.

Earning a living Members need sufficient material sustenance. Even a group like Riverside, committed to voluntary 'poverty' needs to ensure that its members live comfortably and are fed, clothed and warm. This can be achieved collectively, through an income pool but more usually community members generate their own income. Some communities combine collective income and individual income. At Graham Downs, for instance, a cash crop of pine trees was planted some 20 years ago, which will soon be ready for harvest by the community.

Historically many communards have relied on state welfare benefits. These were cut in the 1980s, and some groups found themselves unable to continue. A culture of independence has evolved and nowadays few people in communities rely on benefits.

Earning money is more difficult in some locations than in others. Members of remote rural communities, for instance, can find this a real problem. However, the climate in most of New Zealand is good, and many communities grow most of their own food. Wilderland is probably the best known case. Gricklegrass aims to be self-sufficient as far as possible, buying in corn and rice. But in most cases people earn a living outside the community. We found people working in a wide range of occupations living in communities, which included university lecturers, computer consultants, firemen/women, teachers, counsellors, specialists in personal development and psychology, conflict mediators, spiritual guides, farmers, fishers, artists, including glass makers, painters, potters, weavers and mask-makers. Some have their own businesses producing calendars, providing eco-tourism, telesales, internet consultancy and web design, offering training in various aspects of ecological or social design and hosting B&B (for example, to the crew for *The Lord of the Rings*). Some work casually on local farms; some work away and come home at weekends. There is no model to follow and no one way of earning a living. Even within a community there will be a range of occupations, such as mussel farmer, academic, worker in a cooperative store and artist. What *is* necessary is that a living is generated.

The community needs secure tenure over its property On this issue the New Zealand communities face two problems. One is perennial: how to find enough land on which to base a sustainable community? Groups across the world face this problem. The other is particular to New Zealand and concerns legal restrictions on land use: how to own and occupy the land together legally? The perennial problem has been less of an issue in New Zealand where historically land has been cheap and plentiful. Nowadays this is not the case. There is plenty of space in New Zealand still but prices are inhibitive for many new groups. The particular problem is complicated. The two communities in this bicultural nation are subject to different land laws; which presents a problem to these communities: it is difficult for non-Maori groups to own and occupy land collectively. People in intentional communities have devised ingenious ways around New Zealand's restrictive laws on land use but often their occupancy is only marginally legal. Sometimes they live illegally on their land. This leaves them vulnerable to prosecution and so most tend to assume a low profile and not to publicise the numbers of people and houses on their plot of land. This has proved to be the single most serious problem to New Zealand's intentional communities and local solutions are worth a brief examination.

The main issue is not the ownership of land but rather its use and occupancy. Multiple ownership is possible (see Appendix II), though difficult, but at some point in their history most of the older communes have tried to expand. This has presented problems regarding the legal occupation of the land. In rural contexts, local planning regulations tend to prohibit multiple occupancy in 'Rural A' land. Farms are supposed to be self-sustaining financial units and the land, it is judged, cannot sustain more than one household. The communities, in order to gain original planning permission, often wrote their (required) Management Plans to accord with local regulations and included statements asserting their financial viability as working farms. Most of the older communes, however, did not really seek to 'farm' the land but rather to conserve it, permitting native bush and indigenous fauna to recover from generations of logging, sheep farming (involving clearance of plant life) and pine forestry.

The land these communities purchased was usually remote hill country and simply could not sustain more than one household, even if it were farmed conventionally. This presented a problem when communities (invariably) applied for permission to build further homes. Applications for expansion are assessed by local councils against the community's Management Plan. If a community was not found to be self-sustaining then it could not justify expansion.

Julie Sargisson's study of communities on the Coromandel Peninsula summarises problems of occupancy (Sargisson 1990). She suggests that the problems stem from assumptions embedded in Pakeha culture and manifested in laws of occupancy. It is assumed that non-Maori people should not live outside of nuclear families (where one household occupies and uses one section of land). She notes that the laws are threefold, concerning planning permission, building regulations and health regulations (6). Each of these restricts multiple occupancy. Current building regulations were imported from the UK in 1946 and are, she suggests, inappropriate to the contemporary economic and social context of New Zealand (9). Health regulations are concerned to prevent accidents and disease and assume this to be less likely through single-occupancy titles to land. The new generation of intentional communities wants to change the regulations rather than be forced to live illegally on their own land.

This could be resolved by turning to Maori land law. Pakeha land laws derive from the feudal 'Torrens' system, which grants 'titles', or sole entitlements to land. A landmark Act, the 1993 Te Ture Whenua Maori Act, permitted Maori communities five types of land owning trusts. These are Putea, Whanau, Ahu Whenua, Whenua topu and Kaitiaki trusts. The Act aimed to inhibit further alienation and fragmentation of Maori land. Some aspects of Putea and Whanau Trusts might transfer well to intentional communities of mixed of Pakeha ethnicity. Putea trusts are small, uneconomic interests [in land] pooled for the common benefit without individual dividends. They can be created to prevent further fragmentation and to assist cultural and social development, while at the same time retaining ownership of ancestral land. Whanau trusts are not dissimilar, preserving family links to particular land, turangawaewae, but without expectation of individual interests or dividends. Consent from all owners is required (Durie, 1998:136).

Intentional communities seek to own land in a way that permits collective management and ownership. It can be seen from this brief summary that this is possible, though difficult. Land ownership in New Zealand is complex but can be adapted to multiple ownership. The more intractable problems, as Sargisson points out, stem from rules of land occupancy and planning permissions. Owning the land is one thing, being allowed to build on it and occupy it is another.

Somewhere to turn to when the money runs out There is one organisation, Prometheus, without which many of the communities discussed in this book would not exist. Prometheus is an ethical financing company, which has provided loans to intentional communities across the country. Between 2001-2003, for instance, it leant money for projects in Orapui, Earthsong and Otamatea communities and to Mountain Valley School, which is not an intentional community but is connected to the communities of Graham Downs (also known as Renaissance) and Te Ora. They self-describe as 'banking with a heart' and support projects that are 'environmentally friendly and socially valuable' (http://www.prometheus.co.nz).

Prometheus assisted Earthsong by providing a short-term loan when their building contractors went into liquidation and, further, has provided loans to individual members in order to assist with the purchase of their homes by unit title:

> Prometheus is willing to look at factors other than strict income and equity ratios in approving loans. We were thus able to approve loans for some community members that more conventional finance organisations might not have.
>
> Of the four houses we have provided finance for to date [27 May 2003], two of these loans have enabled families into their eco-houses, and a third enabled

an individual to purchase a studio unit and join the community. The remaining loan was for a women's co-house with a formal partnership agreement specifying ownership shares between the three women co-owners. (Ibid.)

Social Sustainability

Physical space It is extremely difficult to maintain an intentional community unless the physical space meets the group's needs. One factor is location (it is difficult to meditate next door to a nightclub); another is the arrangement of space inside the community land. For instance, a group that wants to explore interpersonal relationships will have different requirements from a group that seeks individual spiritual development through quiet contemplation. The importance of physical layout is increasingly recognised within communities.

Earthsong has carried this to its limit, considering each aspect of spatial design in the light of its contribution to a viable social community. Older communities that adapt pre-existing buildings (like Chippenham, Mansfield and Earthspirit) were not able to design from scratch and have to make best use of existing structures. Nut, from Earthspirit, spoke about this in interview. Earthspirit has one large community house, which is currently home to one member. The others live in temporary dwellings on the plot. This layout has been one of the reasons that the community is not larger. Members discovered that they needed to live in separate homes, but inhibitive planning and building regulations made it impossible to build. This is a disincentive to people who might want to make Earthspirit their home:

> Space makes a big difference for me in a community – how the houses are set up. Earthspirit is not the way I would do it. I would have a bigger piece of land (which we didn't have the money for anyway) but have small separate houses. This is not set up for a bigger community. (Nut, Earthspirit, 11 April 2001)

The only way that Earthspirit could legally expand would be to use the main building as communal living space. After nearly 20 years of experimentation, the existing members know that this is not how they want to live:

> It could [expand] if it was really necessary, with smaller spaces for everyone [within the large house] with a community place. But then, probably if we did that, it would change again and I wouldn't want that, it would be something different, but I do know space wise it does make a difference how things are set up. I don't like us all spending money on our own firewood all the time, for instance, and it seems like a waste in some ways to just have three of us here. (Ibid.)

One group that thought about this in its early days was Peterborough. Peterborough is city based, near the centre of Christchurch and consists of several neighbouring houses that all have road frontage. Behind each house is a small semi-enclosed garden and behind these they have created a large open space that runs the length of the houses, which contains buildings and a large area where children can run and play. Here, at the back of the property, is the 'most communal' space.

Working from the back of the property forwards, one moves from 'most communal' to 'least communal' space. The large buildings at the back belong to the community and are available for collective use. At one time, they housed community businesses. They currently provide storage space and the community office is located in one of them. Then comes the strip of shared space, which is mostly used by the children – it is a place away from the road for riding bicycles, running and letting off steam. In front of this are the household gardens and in front of these (at the front of the property) are the houses. Gardens are laid out in such a way as to afford each household some privacy but they have no gates or fences. They are well maintained. In order to enter the houses, one has to walk around the back of the property to the backdoor. My first visit was in the evening and because the community was urban I had neglected to bring a torch! For this visit I had been invited to a community meal, which was 'pot luck' with everybody bringing some food. Within the houses, shared space is the first to be encountered. Some houses are home to single people and some to families. In the singles homes this space is an open plan kitchen/lounge and dining area. Behind this, at the furthest point from the 'most communal' space are people's private bedrooms. In this way Peterborough has adapted and designed space to maximise communal interaction whilst preserving private spaces.

Social structures Just as physical space can work for or against a community's aims, so can social structures and successful communities employ structures and processes in which form echoes function. Egalitarian communities require fully participatory structures. Other structures were discussed in Chapter Eight. These include agreed procedures for the management of conflict. Conflict will not disappear, but must be managed effectively if a group is to meet its members needs. A related component of a successful community is communication. Poor communication within a group can quickly lead to misunderstandings and resentment. Some groups, like Anahata, have agreed processes for communication. Others, like Valley Farm Ecovillage, have undergone training. Others, like Tui, have time dedicated in meetings to sharing 'heartbusiness'. Communication is essential for a community's sustainability across time.

Members' behaviour Other key factors in establishing a socially sustainable community involve the personal deportment or behaviour of members. A certain amount of commitment is necessary as is a willingness to negotiate, compromise and see the point of view of other people:

> If you live in a community, you have to have an ability to put yourself in somebody else's shoes and you have to understand that your values and views may differ

from your neighbours, and that it's their right as long as they keep it to themselves. (Bronwyn, Timatanga, 22 March 2001)

Many people cited respect for the right of others to hold differing views as an essential learned behaviour. This can take years of practice and is difficult because it is also necessary to be able to communicate your own point of view. Drawing on over 50 years of experience at Riverside community, Joy spoke of this:

> Of course if you are selfish or grasping or lazy, I don't think you would feel happy living like this, but if you are friendly and open and prepared to compromise sometimes and be compassionate and reasonably tolerant (I don't mean soft, you should stick to your principles and stick to your values), then you would be more likely to make a success of it.

She continues by expanding on the thought in parentheses. It is necessary, she says, to be able to do three things: firstly, to hold and express your own view. This requires a certain amount of strength. Secondly, to allow other people to express and hold their position, which may be different, or even operating on a very different level, to your own way of thinking. And thirdly, Joy identifies a need to balance the part of yourself that is a member of the group and the part of yourself who is a private individual with particular – perhaps selfish or antisocial but nonetheless strong – wants. If this tricky balancing act is achieved, she says, the community will be vibrant, full of necessarily strong personalities, bound to a common set of values and collective aims, and meeting their own needs. The result is a group with internal cohesion as well as diversity:

> [T]hat's the richness of the group. It depends on allowing people to be individuals
> ...
> As an individual, you do try and maintain two levels – yourself and what you believe and you as a member of the group. Somehow you have to function in a way that doesn't undermine the integrity of either. (Joy, Riverside, 22 February 2001)

The combination of internal heterogeneity and cohesion identified by Joy is an ideal, almost a utopia in itself. Certain measures can help a group to move towards this. For instance, in Chapter 8 we considered steps taken by groups to maximise communication and to socialise new members into the ways of the group. When the influx of new people arrived in 2001 at Anahata, the group needed to start building these systems and processes:

> There are slightly more children here than adults. It is challenging. For instance X's style of parenting is far more permissive than mine – she encourages children to express themselves. Sometimes that irritates me. When someone else's child does something you wouldn't let your children do, your children say 'Why do we have to go to bed – so and so doesn't have to go to bed?' Some of the kids don't go to

school [they are home educated] and so bed time isn't important because they don't have to get up in the morning. My children perceive that the others can play at home all day and they feel it's a rip off. We had a long discussion about food. You can't watch them all the time. Some of the parents didn't want the pantry locked because they wanted their children to be able to snack. You have to make compromises and integrate other people's style. Sometimes its really hard work and we all find it difficult sometimes. Other people interact with your children in a way that you wouldn't necessarily do … We stopped buying Nutella. You should have seen it when we first moved down here … I was horrified, they were gorging themselves on stuff that I thought was junk. (Lindsay, Anahata, 19 May 2002)

The picture conjured by this extract is chaotic. Clashes of different parenting styles, an uncoordinated food purchasing system in which the purchaser (one of the few non-parents) simply replaced supplies as they were used, an unlocked food pantry, combine with different rules over bed times and general comportment: little wonder that tempers frayed. By the time of my visit some of these issues had been resolved but the noise levels generated by the children in this community were extreme and continued late into every night.

The Need for Support

Finally, and in addition to internal financial and social sustainability, these communities require external support networks. This comes in a number of forms. We have already discussed Prometheus and the provision of financial support. Our focus here is on structural and cultural support.

Housing co-operatives are, as we saw in Chapter 6, under-represented nationally by the New Zealand Cooperative Association. This is regrettable, not least because of the need for changes in legislation regarding planning, building and multiple occupancy of land. An effective lobbying body could help with this.

The support networks that do exist are organised by communities themselves and provide contact and advice. The main one of these is *Chip'N'Away*, which started life as Chippenham Community's newsletter but which has now grown to be a national newsletter. This is funded by the Heartwood Trust and has survived not least because of the dedication of its editor, Dave Welch. Editions of *Chip'N'Away* are produced on a quarterly basis and are distributed to intentional communities across the country. Individual communities are encouraged to submit copy and the newsletter combines news articles from different communities with the discussion of broader issues that effect intentional communities. It is an invaluable source of communication and contact amongst communities.

There are also national non-governmental organisations, such as the New Zealand Eco-Village and Co-Housing Group, whose website offers practical advice about legal matters as well as links and news to and about individual communities. Communication is a key factor not only within communities but also amongst communities. Some of these communities are in remote locations and can easily become introverted. Contact with other, similar, groups can reaffirm their original vision, acting as a reminder that whilst everybody struggles sometimes with life in a community, it is being done for a wider reason.

This can help combat the loneliness of being different, the isolation of being a lone voice, a sole campaigner, maverick, freak or weirdo. Boundaries are important and difference requires a safe space in which to flourish. This is one of the strengths of intentional communities: they are generally safe and relatively contained spaces in which alternatives can be tried, tested and explored. However, this has its negative aspects, if experimentation occurs in a completely closed space, 'free' from scrutiny, interaction or observation, this can produce disassociation from conventional standards of right and wrong. Again, this can be useful. It can help people who want to escape materialism and to explore alternative ways of being. Also, though, it can permit abusive relations to seem the norm. This seems to have been the case at Centrepoint.

Once again, communication emerges as a key factor. Communication between intentional communities (or other spaces of difference) and the wider community has multiple effects. People inside the community are encouraged to reflect upon and perhaps articulate and explain their way of life, its codes and norms. People outside the community learn through contact with members about other ways of living. This happens casually, through contact in the workplace, as well as through participation in local projects, such as women's refuges, alternative schools and community gardens. Even so, life is not easy for those who choose to live differently:

> That is the worst part, and all the stresses that you have to deal with when you are doing something different and you haven't got support for it; you are isolated, and the world is not going where you want it to go; you are just hoping that you can hold a flame alight long enough until the world realises it needs it. (Chrissie, Te Ora, 2 February 2001)

Final Words

The story told in this book is one part of a long tradition of utopianism. New Zealand seems to draw social dreamers, people who find the modern world too fast, too crowded with unnecessary things, too materialistic, too full of constant questing for things that are not really necessary and so individualistic that people are lonely and isolated, even in a crowd. Life in the mainstream, we learn, is unfulfilling, lacks commitment, and has no soul.

The members of these communities are attempting to create something better, influenced by religion, spiritual beliefs, ideology and/or politics together with a deep sense of personal unease and a strong desire to do something about this. We have tried, in this volume, to begin to explain why so many people have been willing to put one life behind them and withdraw to try to live differently.

Joining a community is not something that people do lightly. It is a big commitment. It is difficult. And these places are not perfect. They do not solve all of life's problems. However, most often they are felt by their members to be worth the effort and better than the alternatives. They are ever-changing and dynamic. They have highs and lows, but (if they don't fold) they continue onwards in their neverending search for utopia.

Notes

1 Parts of the section on communitarianism are based on Sargent (1994).
2 Red: I am entirely against the proposal and will block the consensus; Orange: I have a serious reservation but I am not willing to block the consensus; Yellow: I have a question to be answered before I can make a decision; Blue: I am neutral or basically for it, with some slight reservation; Green: I agree with the proposal.

Appendix I: Katajuta Community Agreements

1. The ideal of the group is TO LIVE IN HARMONY WITH THE LAND AND THE PEOPLE LIVING ON THE LAND.
2. Every member is granted a sharehold in Katajuta Farm Ltd. This shareholding is non-transferrable.
3. Members must take responsibility for their own membership. Annually on our anniversary all residential members must reaffirm their support for the company by signing Katajuta Community Agreement.
4. Privies are paid to the company for the privilege of living on the land owned by the company and as a gesture of support for the company. Privies as at the 14th of February stand at $8.00 per week for members and $5.00 for tenants.
5. All members are required to bring building, fencing, tree removal, water access, access, burning off and earthworks proposals to the group for approval.
6. In the event of someone new wanting to become a member of the group (i.e., a shareholder) he/she must be sponsored by an existing member. That existing member must bring the proposed new member to a meeting and introduce them to the group. After two subsequent meetings that the proposed member does not attend a decision can be made as to their membership. That decision should be made not less than six months and not more than one year after the date of the first proposal.
7. We have to know and/or have the opportunity to get to know prospective members. While becoming members they have to live on Katajuta Farm or in the area.
8. Decisions on this and all issues are made by consensus. Meeting quorums are four.
9. If a member leaves she/he has two years to make a positive statement to the group about their continued involvement in the group. Shares may be removed by the group if the member fails to do this. In the event of a group deciding to evict a member that members loses his/her rights under the Companies Act for a maximum of one month during which time the remaining members will decide on the permanent status of that member.
10. Members will introduce any tenants to the group on whether to rent to this person. Once the person becomes a tenant there is a reevaluation in not less than one month and not more than two months. If members decide to remove the tenant the owner of the house/building will be contacted. The owners instruction may at that point be carried out by the group. We will

invite tenants to attend meetings or participate as much as they and we feel comfortable with.

Thanks to Ross Smith of Katajuta for providing us with this document.

Appendix II: Recognised Forms of Land Ownership in New Zealand

Partnerships

Agreements of partnership can be made over jointly owned land. This has drawbacks of inflexibility, changes of membership involves redrafting a new agreement. The onus for enforcement is on aggrieved parties.

Trusts

This is a common form of multiple ownership. Trustees manage property on the behalf of beneficiaries. The trust does not own the land but holds it in the names of the trustees. The main problem with trusts is that beneficiaries cannot control the actions of trustees. Usually in intentional communities the trustees are members and therefore also beneficiaries.

Charitable Trust

There are many different forms of these, the most common in communities being educational and spiritual. Other permitted *raisons d'être* are the alleviation of poverty or 'other charitable acts' (Charitable Trust Act). There are tax implications to claiming this status and it is quite firmly regulated. Many communities use this form of ownership but some find themselves 'forced' into hypocrisy (and unconstitutional practice) as constitutions are written primarily to comply with these specifications and often bear little resemblance to the actual community.

Incorporated Society

These stem from the Incorporated Society Act of 1908 and are designed to be non-profit making. Membership includes a fee and members cannot profit form the actions of the Society. Some intentional communities use this and membership involves a large fee which allows the purchase of land.

Limited Liability Company

These can hold land but are designed primarily to control business risk. They require directors and shareholders. A Companies Act of 1993 overhauled status of Limited Liability Companies and clearly delineates the responsibilities of directors. When used by intentional communities shareholders are usually also directors.

Freehold/Fee Simple

New Zealand operates the 'Torrens' land system of titles. Titles give an estate in land tenure and are a hangover from the English feudal system. Titles over land clearly identify the 'owner'. Titles are held over separate dwellings and land can be subdivided into unit titles (see below). Unit titles are popular in the wider community for the autonomy they permit: there is not need to consult one's neighbours regarding changes to ones property. Within intentional communities this autonomy is restricted by covenants which impose the community's land ethic. Households can co-own common land, as in the case at Otamatea, although this is quite complicated.

Unit Title

These were created by the Unit Titles Act in 1972. They provide a method of co-owning shared land whilst separately owning certain units. Common property is owned in undivided shares. These may be unequal and proportionate to the individual investment. Individual titles are issued following deposit of a unit plan with the Department of Land Registry. The whole area or development is owned by the Body Corporate, which is comprised of all unit owners. This form of ownership is used by some eco-villages. The biggest problem is that titles are issued only once building has reached a certain stage and so investors have to work on trust (build without ownership) in the first instance, or else founders have to be responsible for large loans. There are tax implications in this form of ownership as property development is seen as a business activity and is thus liable to taxation.

Tenants in Common

Tenants in Common co-own land in what is called an 'undivided' share. They may co-own unequal proportions of it and so some may invest more than others. The drawback for intentional communities is that planning rules usually permit only one home on each parcel of land. However, they are appropriate for communities that live under one roof.

Cross Leases

These are incredibly complicated and rarely used in intentional communities. In 1958, when they first emerged, a lease was not deemed a subdivision and so cross-leasing was developed to side-step the requirements of subdivision. Since the 1991 Resource Management Act, most have been changed to fee simple subdivisions. It is possible to use this system in such a way that leases are held on buildings in a restrictive covenant.

Flat Owning Companies

Here, the building or land is owned by a limited liability company, which issues 'licences to occupy' the premises. The company can sell shares, for example to those holding licenses to occupy. The property is managed according to the Articles of Association (or Constitution) which convey rights and obligations on shareholders. This can work well from the point of view of establishing coherent rules for managing the land but its drawback is that this form of ownership offers low financial security to the individual (adapted from Scott, 1998).

Works Cited

Abrams, Philip and Andrew McCulloch with Sheila Abrams and Pat Gore (1976), *Communes, Sociology and Society*, Cambridge, Eng, Cambridge University Press.

Anderson, Russell (1981), 'High-octane By Product Transports Christian Community', *New Zealand Truth*, 9 June, 16.

Bachelor, C.T. and Amy Rothstein. *On Conflict and Consensus: A handbook on Formal Consensus decisionmaking*, online book available from http://www.empowermentzone.com/consent.txt.

Barker, Eileen (1989), *New Religious Movements: A Practical Guide*, London: HMSO.

Barrington, A[rchibald] C[harles] (1952), 'Riverside Community', *P[eace] P[ledge] U[nion] Journal* (73), September–October, 7–11.

Baxter, James K. (1970), *Jerusalem Sonnets: Poems for Colin Durning*, Dunedin, The Bibliography Room, University of Otago. Also in his *Collected Poems*, in Weir, John (ed.), Auckland, Oxford University Press, 1980, pp. 455–74.

Baxter, James K. (1971), *Jerusalem Daybook*, Wellington, Price Milburn.

Baxter, James K. (1972), *Autumn Testament*, Wellington: Price Milburn. Rpt. Paul Millar, Paul (ed.), Auckland, Oxford University Press, 1997. Also in his *Collected Poems*, Weir, John (ed.), Auckland, Oxford University Press, 1980, pp. 537–68.

Baxter, James K. (1972), 'Elegy for Boyle Crescent', *Islands* 1 (1), Spring, 25–26.

Baxter, James K. (1979), 'The Ballad of the Junkie and the Fuzz', in his *Collected Poems*, in Weir, John (ed.), Wellington, Oxford University Press in association with Price Milburn, pp. 442–51.

Baxter, James K. (2000), *The Dictionary of New Zealand Biography. Volume Five. 1941–1960*, Auckland: Auckland University Press/Wellington: Department of Internal Affairs, p. 39.

Belich, James (1996), *Making Peoples: A History of the New Zealanders From Polynesian Settlement to the End of the Nineteenth Century*, Auckland, Allen Lane The Penguin Press.

Bennett, John W. (1963), *Hutterian Brethren: The Agricultural Economy and Social Organization of a Communal People*, Stanford, CA, Stanford University Press.

Bestor, Arthur Eugene, Jr. (1950), *Backwoods Utopias: The Sectarian and Owenite Phases of Communitarian Socialism in America, 1663–1829*, Philadelphia, University of Pennsylvania Press, 1950. 2nd enl. ed. Philadelphia, University of Pennsylvania Press, 1970.

Bickerton, Professor [Alexander W.] ([1895?]) *Morganeering Or, The Triumph of the Trust. A Fragment of a Satirical Burlesque on the Worship of Wealth*, Christchurch, Wainoni Publishing Co.

Bickerton, A[lexander] W. ([1898]), *The Romance of the Earth*, Christchurch, Wainoni Postal Publishing Co.

[Bickerton, Alexander W.] ([1899]), *A Federative Home. 'Wainoni'*, Christchurch, Ptd. at the *Lyttelton Times* Office.

Bickerton, Professor [Alexander W.] ([1903?]), *Mental Healing and Nerve Disorders*. Christchurch, 'Wainoni' Postal Publishing Co.

Bisno, Herb (1988), *Managing Conflict*, London, Sage.

Black, Veronica (1985), *The Spirit of the Coromandel*, Auckland, Reed Methuen.

Booth, General [William] (1890), *In Darkest England and The Way Out*, London, International Headquarters of the Salvation Army, 1890.

Borrows, J.L. (1969), *Albertland – The Last organised British settlement in New Zealand – An account of brave endeavour, disappointment, and achievement, North of Auckland on the shores of Kaipara Harbour*, Wellington, A.H. and A.W. Reed.

Bouvard, Marguerite (1975), *The Intentional Community Movement: Building a New Moral World*, Port Washington, NY, National University Publications Kennikat Press.

Braunfels, Wolfgang (1972), 'The St. Gall Utopia', in his *The Monasteries of Western Europe: The Architecture of the Orders*, London, Thames and Hudson, pp. 37–46.

Brem, Pnina (1981), 'A Study of Kibbutzim and the Lessons for New Zealand', unpublished Bachelor of Town Planning Research Essay, University of Auckland, 1981.

Brett, Henry and Henry Hook (1927), *The Albertlanders: Brave Pioneers of the 'Sixties*, Auckland, The Brett Printing Co.

Bryan, Mary (1974), 'Proposed Ohu Seen as a Place for solving problems', *Wanganui Chronicle*, 28 September, 12.

Buchanan, Alison (1976), 'Long dreamt-of community finally under way', *Wanganui Chronicle*, 31 July, 12.

Bunker, Sarah; Chris Coates; David Hodgson; and Jonathan How (eds) (1999), *Diggers and Dreamers 2000–2001*, London, Diggers and Dreamers Publications.

Burdon, R.M. (1956), *Scholar Errant: A Biography of Professor A.W. Bickerton*, Christchurch, Pegasus Press.

Burns, Kevin, P.P. and Pauline O'Regan, S.M. (2000), *Parish for the People in the Pews*, Christchurch, Glanmire Publications.

Burns, Malcolm C. (1982), 'Centrepoint and the Utopian Tradition', unpublished Bachelor of Town Planning Research Essay, University of Auckland.

Burton, John and Frank Dukes (eds) (1990), *Conflict: Readings in Management and Resolution*, London, Macmillan.

Butler, Judith (1989), *Gender Trouble: Feminism and the Subversion of Identity*, New York, Routledge.

Caley, Gordon (1981), 'Methane: An answer to your road fuel problems', *Mushroom* (22), January, 13–15.

Canterbury Papers Nos. 1 and 2. Information Concerning the Principles, Objects, Plans, and Proceedings of the Founders of the Settlement at Canterbury, New Zealand (1850), London, John W. Parker.

Canterbury Settlement. A Full and Accurate Report of the Public Meeting Which Was Held in St. Martin's Hall, On the 17th April, 1850, By the Association for Founding the Settlement of Canterbury, in New Zealand. The Right Hon. The Lord Lyttelton in the Chair (1850), London, Published for The Canterbury Association by J.W. Parker.

Carter, Marlene (1998), *Creekside Community* [On cover *The First 20 Years*], McLeod, Joy and Colin (eds), Christchurch, Creekside Community.

Chip'N'Away (1996), 2 (1), July, 1.

Cixous, Hélène and Clément, Catherine (1975), 'Sorties: Out and Out: Attacks/ Ways Out/Forays', in Cixous, Hélène and Clément, Catherine, *The Newly Born Woman*, trans. Betsey Wing, Minneapolis, University of Minnesota Press, pp. 63–132.

Clarke, W.H. (1894), *A Co-operative State Farm Scheme: A Means for Providing Remunerative Employment for All Surplus Labour; A Home for the Aged, Infirm, and Needy; Ways and Means for Teaching Trades, or Such Other Technical Education To Our Rising Generation As Will Enable Them To Earn Their Own Maintenance; and Totally Abolishing Poor Rates. In Three Parts*, Wellington, Samuel Costall, Government Printer.

Cleveland, Les (1979), *The Politics of Utopia: New Zealand and Its Government*, Wellington, Methuen New Zealand.

Colless, Brian and Peter Donovan (eds) (1980), *Religion in New Zealand Society*, Edinburgh, Scot, T. and T. Clark/Palmerston North, Dunmore Press.

Communities Directory: A Guide to Intentional Communities and Cooperative Living 2000 Edition (2000), Rutledge, MO, Fellowship for Intentional Community.

Community Comments (1977), 5 February and 1 July.

Coser, Lewis A. (1968), *The Functions of Social Conflict*, 2nd edn London, Routledge and Kegan Paul.

Coser, Lewis A. and Rosenberg, Bernard (eds) (1969), *Sociological Theory: A Book of Readings*, 3rd edn New York: Macmillan.

'Creekside Kids' (1980), *Mushroom* (20), April, 10–12.

Cummings, Michael S. (1996), 'A Tale of Two Communes: A Scholar and His Errors', in *Communities Directory: A Guide to Cooperative Living*, 2nd edn Langley, WA, Fellowship for Intentional Community, pp. 64–72.

C[unningham], R[obert] F[luke] ([1873?]), *Prospectus of The Aurelia Co-operative Land and Labour Association* [Thames].

Dahrendorf, Ralf (1958), 'Out of Utopia: Toward a Reorientation of Sociological Analysis', *American Journal of Sociology*, 64, September, 115–27. Rpt. in Coser 1969.

Donovan, Peter (ed.) (1996), *Religions of New Zealanders*, 2nd edn Palmerston North, Dunmore.

Durie, Mason (1998), *Te Mana, Te Kāwanatanga The Politics of Maori Self Determination*, Oxford: Oxford University Press.

Durkheim, Emile (1947), *The Division of Labour in Society*, New York, Free Press.

Edge, W.R. (1974), *Clarion Settlers per 'Kumara' 'Wakunui' 'Tokomaru' 'Paparoa' and 'Rakaia' in 1900*, Auckland, Author.

Ellwood, Robert S. (1993), *Islands of the Dawn: The Story of Alternative Spirituality in New Zealand*, Honolulu, University of Hawaii Press.

'Farewell Breakfast to Mr. and Mrs. Godley' (1852), *Lyttelton Times*, 25 December, 9.

Feuer, Lewis S. (1966), 'The Influence of the American Communist Colonies on Engels and Marx', *Western Political Quarterly*, 19 (3), September, 456–74.

Field, Louis H. (1979), 'Architectural Implications of Traditional and Alternative Lifestyles', unpublished BArch thesis, University of Auckland.

Finch, John (1844), 'Notes of Travel in the United States', *New Moral World*, 12–13, 13 January–6 July, 232, 233–34, 241, 249, 257–58, 265, 273–74, 281, 289–91, 297–98, 305–06, 313, 321, 329, 337–38, 345–46, 353–54, 361–62, 369–70, 418–19; 1–2, 10–11. 22 installments.

Fitzsimons, Barbara (1981), 'A Christian Community … (or God, Gas and Getting-it-together)', *Mushroom*, 22, January, 10–12.

Fogarty, Robert S. (1972), 'Success?', *Communitas* (2), September, 4.

Fogarty, Robert S. (1980), *Dictionary of American Communal and Utopian History*, Westport, CT, Greenwood Press.

Fogarty, Robert S. (1990), *All Things New: American Communes and Utopian Movements, 1860–1914*, Chicago, University of Chicago Press.

Free Church Colony of Otago in New Zealand. Powers of Local Self-Government Established by Act of Parliament, and Other Privileges, Conferred Upon the Colonists. – The Removal of Every By-Gone Obstruction, and a Free Call from the Authorities to Proceed With the Enterprise. In a Letter from Capt. Cargill to Dr. Aldcorn, of Oban (1847), London, Printed by Waterloo and Sons.

'"Freedom" School Is Seeking Recognition, But No Finance' (1964), *Waikato Times*, January, 1.

Freire, Paulo (1970), *Pedagogy of the Oppressed*, trans. Myra Bergman Ramos, New York, Seabury Press.

G.B. *Parliamentary Papers* (1852), 35, p. 570.

Gamble, Warren (2000), 'Dishonoured prophet will go – for a price', *New Zealand Herald*, 29 February, A9.

Gide, Charles (1930), *Communist and Co-operative Colonies*, trans. Ernest F. Row, New York, Thomas Y. Crowell/London, G.G. Harrap. Originally pub. as *Les Colonies communistes et coopératives*, Paris, Association pour l'enseignement de la coopération, 1928.

Gilman, Robert (1991), 'The Eco-Village Challenge' in *In Context*, Summer (Context Institute: http://www.context.org).

Goodwin, Barbara (1980), 'Utopia Defended Against the Liberals', *Political Studies*, 28 (3) September, 384–400.

Gorni, Yosef; Yaacov Oved; and Idit Paz (eds) (1987), *Communal Life, An International Perspective*, Efal, Israel, Yad Tabenkin/New Brunswick, NJ, Transaction Books.

[Gouland, Henry Godfrey] (1851), *Plan of a Proposed New Colony To Be Called Britannia*, Lyttelton, Printed by I. Shrimpton.

Graham, Judith (1992), *Breaking the Habit: Life in a New Zealand Dominican Convent, 1955–67*, Dunedin, John McIndoe.

Grant, David (1986), *Out in the Cold: Pacifists and Conscientious Objection in New Zealand during World War II*, Auckland, Reed Methuen.

Green, Brenda (1980), 'Shared House Life', *Quaker Acres*, 25, June, Wanganui Educational Settlement – Quaker Acres, MS-Papers-2597–26/2/1, Alexander Turnbull Library.

A Guide to Co-ops (1981), Auckland, Auckland University Environment Group.

Hansen, Dan (1975), 'The Wilderland Manifesto', in List, Dennis and Taylor, Alister (eds), *The 2nd New Zealand Whole Earth Catalogue*, Martinborough, Alister Taylor, p. 68.

Hardy, Dennis (1979), *Alternative Communities in Nineteenth Century England*, London, Longman.

Hardy, Dennis and Davidson, Lorna (1989), *Utopian Thought and Communal Experience*, Middlesex University Geography and Environmental Management Paper No. 24.

Harrington, James (1992), *The Commonwealth of Oceana and A System of Politics*, Pocock, J.G.A. (ed.), Cambridge University Press.

Harvey, D.D.C. (ed.) (1939), *Letters of Rev. Norman McLeod 1835–51*, *Bulletin of the Public Archives of Nova Scotia*, 2 (1).

Hayden, Dolores (1984), *Redesigning the American Dream: The Future of Housing, Work, and Family Life*, New York, W.W. Norton.

Hayward, Margaret (1981), *Diary of the Kirk Years*, Queen Charlotte Sound, Cape Catley/Wellington, A.H. and A.W. Reed.

Hebblethwaite, Margaret (1993), *Base Communities: An Introduction*, London, Geoffrey Chapman.

[Hennell, Mary] (1841), 'Appendix [– History of Cooperation]', in Bray, Charles, *The Philosophy of Necessity; or, The Law of Consequences; As Applicable to Mental Moral, and Social Sciences*, 2 vols, London, Longman, Orme, Green, and Longmans, 2, pp. 495–663. Repub. as *An Outline of the Various Social Systems and Communities which have been Founded on the Principle of Co-operation*, London, Longman, Brown, Green, and Longmans, 1844.

Hillery, George A., Jr. and Morrow, Paula C. (1976), 'The Monastery as a Commune', *International Review of Modern Sociology*, 6 (1), Spring, 139–54.

Hinds, William Alfred (1878), *American Communities: Brief Sketches of Economy, Zoar, Bethel, Aurora, Amana, Icaria, the Shakers, Oneida, Wallingford, and the Brotherhood of the New Life*, Oneida, NY, Office of the American Socialist. Exp. eds Chicago, Charles H. Kerr, 1902 and 1908.

History of Cooperation in the United States (1888), *Johns Hopkins University Studies in Historical and Political Science* 6, Baltimore, MD, Johns Hopkins University Press.

Hobbes, Thomas (1994), *The Elements of Law, Natural and Politics. Part One Human Nature*, Gaskin, J.C.A. (ed.), Oxford, Oxford University Press.

Hobbes, Thomas (1996), *Leviathan*, Gaskin, J.C.A. (ed.), Oxford, Oxford University Press.

Hogg, Michael A. (1992), *The Social Psychology of Group Cohesiveness: From Attraction to Social Identity*, London, Harvester Wheatsheaf.

Hogg, Michael A. and Abrams Dominic (2001), *Intergroup Relations: Essential Readings*, Philadelphia, Psychology Press.

Horn, Walter and Born, Ernest (1979), *Plan of St. Gall: A Study of the Architecture and Economy of a Paradigmatic Carolingian Monastery*, 3 vols, Berkeley, University of California Press.

Horsch, John (1931), *The Hutterian Brethren 1528–1931. A Story of Martyrdom and Loyalty*. No. 2 of *Studies in Anabaptist and Mennonite History*, Goshen, IN: Mennonite Historical Society. Rpt. Scottsdale, PA/Kitchener, Ont., Canada, Herald Press, 1977; and Cayley, Alb., Canada, Macmillan Colony, 1985.

Hostetler, John A. (1963), *Amish Society*, Baltimore, MD, The Johns Hopkins University Press. Rev. edn 1968, 3rd edn 1980, 4th edn 1993.

Hostetler, John A. (1974), *Hutterite Society*, Baltimore, MD, The Johns Hopkins University Press. New edn 1997.

Hursthouse, Charles (1857), *New Zealand, or Zealandia, The Britain of the South With Two Maps and Seven Coloured Views*, 2 vols, London, Edward Stanford.

Idyll of the Shipbuilders: Being a Brief Account of the Life and Migrations of the Families from the Highlands of Scotland that finally settled at Waipu, North Auckland ([192–]), Auckland, Clark and Matheson.

Infield, Henrik F. (1944), *Cooperative Living in Palestine*, New York, Dryden Press.

Infield, Henrik F. (1947), *Cooperative Communities at Work*, London, Kegan Paul, Trench, Trubner.

Infield, Henrik F. (1947), *Sociometric Structure of a Veterans Cooperative Land Settlement*. Sociometry Monographs (15), New York, Beacon House.

Infield, Henrik F. (1955), *The American Intentional Communities: Study on the Sociology of Cooperation*, Glen Gardner, NJ, Glen Gardner Community Press. Sociology of Cooperation Monograph (2).

Infield, Henrik F. (1955), *Utopia and Experiment: Essays in the Sociology of Cooperation*, New York, Praeger.

Infield, Henrik F. and Joseph B. Maier (1950), *Cooperative Group Living: An International Symposium on Group Farming and the Sociology of Cooperation*, New York, Henry Koosis and Co.

Infield, Henrik F. and Koka Freier (1954), *People in Ejidos: A Visit to the Cooperative Farms of Mexico*, New York, Praeger.

'Introduction' (1909), *The Forerunner* (1), May, 3.

Isaac, Skye (2002), *Tauhara: The Growth of a Educational and Spiritual Centre*, Hastings, Cliff Press.

Jones, Tim (1975), *A Hard-Won Freedom: Alternative Communities in New Zealand*, Auckland, Hodder and Stoughton.

[Joyce, Alexander] (1881), *Land Ho!! A Conversation of 1933, on the results of the adoption of the system of 'Nationalizing the Land of New Zealand', adopted in 1883*, Lyttelton, F.L. Davis.

Kanter, Rosabeth Moss (1972), *Commitment and Community: Communes and Utopias in Sociological Perspective*, Cambridge, Harvard University Press.

Karlovsky, Nicholas (1982), 'Living Alternatives: A Study of alternative lifestyles, the social processes behind them, their architecture, and their future implications', unpublished BArch Thesis, University of Auckland.

Kelsey, Jane (1995), *The New Zealand Experiment*, Auckland, Auckland University Press.

Lacan, Jacques (1993), *The Seminar, Book III The Psychosis (1955–1956)*, Miller, Jacques-Alain (ed.), trans. Russell Grigg, London, Routledge.

Laclau, Ernesto and Mouffe, Chantal 1985, *Socialist Strategy: Towards a Radical Democratic Politics*, New York, Verso.

Levitas, Ruth (1990), *The Concept of Utopia*, Hemel Hempstead, Philip Allan/ Syracuse, NY, Syracuse University Press.

LeWarne, Charles Pierce (1975), *Utopias on Puget Sound, 1885–1915*, Seattle, University of Washington Press.

Lineham, Peter J. (1977), *There We Found Brethren: A History of the Assemblies of Brethren in New Zealand*, Palmerston North, G.P.H. Society Ltd.

Lineham, Peter J. (1993), *Religious History of New Zealand: A Bibliography*, 4th edn, Palmerston North, Department of History, Massey University.

'Lives Apart' (1978), *Mushroom*, 14, September, 20–22.

Lovell-Smith, Margaret (1994), *Plain Living High Thinking: The Family Story of Jamie and Will Lovell-Smith*, Christchurch, Pedmore Press.

Macdonald, Gordon (1928), *The Highlanders of Waipu or Echoes of 1745: A Scottish Odyssey*, Dunedin, Coulls Somerville Wilkie.

Madgwick, Paul (2002), 'Hope, Faith, and Big Bucks', *The Press* (Christchurch), 17 August, D5.

Manning, Nick (1980) 'Collective Disturbances in Institutions: A Sociological View of Crisis and Collapse', *International Journal of Therapeutic Communities*, 1 (3), Fall, 13–35.

McArthur, Judith (1980), 'Why Are We Waiting', *Straight Furrow*, 41 (4), 21 March, 10–11.

McCamant, Kathryn and Charles Durrett (1994), *Cohousing: A Contemporary Approach to Housing Ourselves*, 2nd edn with Ellen Hertzman Berkeley, CA, Ten Speed Press.

McCarthy, Tara M. (1998), 'The Medium of Grace: Mutual Criticism in the Oneida Community', *Communal Societies*, 18, 92–106.

McCormick, E.H. (1955), 'The Happy Colony', *Landfall*, 9 (4), 300–34.

McCrank, Lawrence J. (1997), 'Religious Orders and Monastic Communalism in America', in *America's Communal Utopias*, Pitzer, Donald E. (ed.), Chapel Hill, University of North Carolina Press, pp. 204–52.

McKenzie, N.R. (1952), *The Gael Fare Forth: The Romantic Story of Waipu and Her Sister Settlements*, 2nd edn, Wellington, Whitcombe and Tombs.

McPherson, Flora (1962), *Watchman Against the World: Story of Norman McLeod and his people*, Christchurch, Whitcombe and Tombs.

McSporran, Malcolm (1975), 'The Sunburst Community or the divine light can hardly be seen for the trees', in *The 2nd New Zealand Whole Earth Catalogue*, List, Dennis and Taylor, Alister (eds), Martinborough, Alister Taylor, p. 29.

Metcalf, William (1989), 'Utopian Thought and Communal Experience in Australia: A demographic analysis' in Hardy and Davidson (eds), pp. 60–67.

Metcalf, Bill (ed.) (1995), *From Utopian Dreaming to Communal Reality: Cooperative Lifestyles in Australia*, Sydney, NSW, Australia, UNSW Press.

Metcalf, Bill (ed.) (1996), *Shared Visions Shared Lives: Communal Living around the Globe*, Findhorn, Forres, Scot., Findhorn Press.

Miller, Timothy (ed.) (1991), *When Prophets Die: The Postcharismatic Fate of New Religious Movements*, Albany, State University of New York Press.

Minehan, Mike (2002), *O Jerusalem. James K. Baxter: An Intimate Memoir*, Christchurch, Hazard Press.

Mollison, Bill (1979), *Permaculture Two: practical design for town and country in permanent agriculture*, Stanley, Tasmania, Tagari Books.

Mollison, Bill (1992), *Permaculture: A Designer's Manual*, 2nd edn, Tagari, Australia.

Mollison, Bill and Holmgren, David (1978), *Permaculture One: A perennial agricultural system for human settlements*, Sydney, Corgi Books. DLC has Melbourne: Transworld Publishers.

Molloy, Maureen (1991), *Those Who Speak to the Heart: The Nova Scotian Scots At Waipu 1854–1920*, Palmerston North, Dunmore Press.

Morrison, Murdoch Daniel (1933), 'The Migration of Scotch Settlers from St. Ann's, Nova Scotia, to New Zealand, 1851–1860', *Nova Scotia Historical Society Collections*, 2, 72–95.

Moylan, Tom (1986), *Demand the Impossible: Science Fiction and the Utopian Imagination*, London, Methuen.

Moylan, Tom (2000), *Scraps of the Untainted Sky: Science Fiction, Utopia, Dystopia*, Boulder, CO: Westview.

Murdoch, Norman H. (1983), 'Anglo-American Salvation Army Farm Colonies, 1890–1910', *Communal Societies*, 3, Fall, 111–21.

Mutual Criticism (1876), Oneida, NY: Office of the American Socialist.

Naess, Arne (1973), 'The Shallow and the Deep, Long-Range Ecology Movement. A Summary', *Inquiry*, 16, 95–100.

Naess, Arne (1989), *Ecology, Community, and Lifestyle: Outline of an Ecosophy*, trans David Rothenberg, Cambridge: Cambridge University Press.

National Association for Promoting Special Settlements in New Zealand ([1861]), *New Colony for Non-Conformists in connection with National Association for Promoting Special Settlements in New Zealand*, 2nd ed. Birmingham.

Neill, A.S. (1960), *Summerhill: A Radical Approach to Child Rearing*, New York: Hart Publications.

New Zealand's Great Want. Organisation of Labour (1894), Gore, Published by J.A. Forbes.

Nordhoff, Charles (1875), *The Communistic Societies of the United States; From Personal Visit and Observation: Including Detailed Accounts of the Economists, Zoarites, Shakers, The Amana, Oneida, Bethel, Aurora, Icarian, and Other Existing Societies, Their Religious Creeds, Social Practices, Numbers, Industries, and Present Condition*, New York, Harper and Brothers.

Noyes, John Humphrey (1870), *History of American Socialisms*, Philadelphia, Lippincott.

'NZ Yearly Meeeting' (1974), *NZ Friends Newsletter*, June, 2–10.

Oakes, Len (1986), *Inside Centrepoint: The Story of a New Zealand Community*, Auckland, Benton Ross Publishers.

Oakes, L[en] D. (1988), 'Power and Finance in a Communal Psychotherapy Cult', in *Money and Power in New Religions*, Richardson, James T. (ed.), Lewiston, ME, Edwin Mellen Press, pp. 365–83.

Oakes, Len (1997), *Prophetic Charisma: The Psychology of Revolutionary Religious Personalities*, Syracuse, NY, Syracuse University Press.

OECD database http://www.economist.com.

O'Farrell, Patrick (1976), 'Millenialism, Messianism and Utopianism in Irish History', *Anglo-Irish Studies*, 2, 45–68.

'Ohu' ([1974]), *Mushroom*, 1, 7.

'Ohu' (1976), *Mushroom*, 5, Autumn, 15.

Ohu: Alternative Lifestyle Communities (1975), Wellington, Published for The Ohu Advisory Committee by the Department of Lands and Surveys.

'Ohu Where To Now?' (1976), *Mushroom*, 4, Summer, 11.

O'Regan, Pauline (1986), *A Changing Order*, Wellington, Allen and Unwin New Zealand in association with Bridget Williams Books.

O'Regan, Pauline (1991), *Aunts and Windmills*, Wellington, Bridget Williams Books.

O'Regan, Pauline and Teresa O'Connor (1989), 'An Experience of Christian Community', in their *Community: Give It a Go!*, Wellington, Allen and Unwin New Zealand in association with Bridget Williams Books, pp. 113–24.

Parr, Arnold R. (1994), *The Development of Collective Ownership and Control by an Intentional Community: An Analysis of the Organisation of Riverside Community in New Zealand*, Working Paper (14), Sociology Department, University of Canterbury, Christchurch.

Parsons, Talcott (1937), *The Structure of Social Action*, New York, Free Press.

Pearson, Lynn F. (1988), *The Architectural and Social History of Cooperative Living*, London, Macmillan.

Pemberton, Robert (1854), *The Happy Colony. Dedicated to the Workmen of Great Britain*, London, Saunders and Otley.

Peters, Victor (1965), *All Things Common: The Hutterian Way of Life*, Minneapolis, University of Minnesota Press.

Pitzer, Donald E. (1989), 'Developmental Communalism: An Alternative Approach to Communal Studies', in *Utopian Thought and Communal Experience*, Hardy, Dennis and Davidson, Lorna (eds), Geography and Planning Paper (24), Enfield, School of Geography and Planning, Middlesex Polytechnic, pp. 68–76. Also in *The Guide To Communal Living: Diggers and Dreamers 94/95*, Coates, Chris; How, Jonathan; Jones, Lee; Morris, William; and Wood, Andy (eds), Winslow, Buckinghamshire, Communes Network, 1993, pp. 85–92.

Porter, Frances (1989), *Born to New Zealand: A Biography of Jane Maria Atkinson*, Wellington, Allen and Unwin/Port Nicholson Press.

'Proposed Wanganui Settlement' (1973), *NZ Friends Newsletter*, October, 5.

'Quakers Have Established Model Community' (1983), in *Bush, People and Pasture: The Story of Waitotara County 1884–1984*, Melody, Paul (ed.), Whanganui, Waitotara County Centennial Committee, pp. 336–43.

Questions to Quakers (2000), booklet produced by The Religious Society of Friends, New Zealand Society Yearly Meeting.

Rain, Lynn (1991), *Community: The Story of Riverside 1941–1991*, Lower Moutere, Riverside Community.

Reeves, William Pember (1902), *State Experiments in Australia and New Zealand*, 2 vols, London, George Allen and Unwin.

Regardie, Israel (1937–40), *The Golden Dawn: An Account of the Teachings, Rites and Ceremonies of the Order of the Golden Dawn*, 4 vols, Chicago, IL, Aries Press.

Riverside Community: 'The Evangelism of Togetherness' (1960), Lower Moutere, Nr. Motueka, Riverside Community.

Roberts, Betty and Norman Roberts (comps.) (1991), *Old Stone House 1870–1990 and the Cracroft Community Centre 1972–1990*, Christchurch, The Cracroft Community Centre.

Roberts, J.P. (1980), 'Destructive Processes in a Therapeutic Community', in *International Journal of Therapeutic Communities*, 1 (3), Fall, 67–90.

Robertson, Peter (1974), 'Uncertainty covers ohu path while spring nears', *Zealandia*, August 25, 20.

Robinson, Neil (1952), *Lion of Scotland: Being an account of Norman McLeod's forty years' search for a land where he and his followers could live as they wished; of the voyage, in 1817, from the Western Highlands to Nova Scotia; to Australia in the 1850's; and finally to New Zealand. And how they built a community for themselves*, London, Hodder and Stoughton. [2nd edn] with subtitle *An account of Norman McLeod's forty years' search for a land where he and his followers could live as they wished; of the voyage, in 1817, from the Western Highlands to Nova Scotia; to Australia in the 1850's; and finally to New Zealand. And how they built a community for themselves*, Auckland, Hodder and Stoughton, 1974.

Robinson, Neil (1997), *To the Ends of the Earth: Norman McLeod and the Highlanders' migration to Nova Scotia and New Zealand*, Auckland, HarperCollins New Zealand.

Robinson, Peter (1974), 'A Visionary Pragmatist Tackles Modern Ills: Kirk's Kibbutz Stimulus for New Zealand's Nation-Building', *Australian Financial Review*, 3245, 2 October, 2.

Rockey, J.R. (1981), 'An Australasian Utopist: Robert Pemberton F.R.S.L. The Last of the Self-Confessed Owenites and the Last of the World Makers', *New Zealand Journal of History*, 15 (2), October, 157–78.

Roth, H[erbert] (1957), 'The New Zealand Socialist Party', *Political Science*, 9 (1), March, 51–60.

Roth, Herbert (1959), 'The Labour Churches and New Zealand', *International Review for Social History*, 3, 361–66.

Sargent, Lyman Tower (1994), 'The Three Faces of Utopianism Revisited', *Utopian Studies*, 5 (1), 1–37.

Sargent, Lyman Tower (1996), 'The Ohu Movement', *New Zealand Studies*, 6 (3) November, 18–22.

Sargent, Lyman Tower (1997), *New Zealand Intentional Communities: A Research Guide*, Occasional Paper (97/2), Wellington, Stout Research Centre for the Study of New Zealand Society History and Culture, Victoria University of Wellington.

Sargent, Lyman Tower (1999), 'The Ohu Movement in New Zealand: An Experiment in Government Sponsorship of Communal Living in the 1970', *Communal Societies*, 19, 49–65.

Sargent, Lyman Tower (2000), 'Utopianism and National Identity', *CRISPP: Critical Review of International Social and Political Philosophy*, 3 (2 and 3) (Summer/Autumn, 87–106). Vol. also published as *The Philosophy of Utopia*, Goodwin, Barbara (ed.), London, Frank Cass, 2001, pp. 87–106.

Sargent, Lyman Tower (2001a), 'Cooperation and Utopianism', *Utopian Studies*, 12 (2), 246–50.

Sargent, Lyman Tower (2001b), 'Utopianism and the Creation of New Zealand National Identity', *Utopian Studies*, 12 (1), 1–18.

Sargisson, Julie (1990), *Multiple Occupancy and Low Cost Housing on the Coromandel*, Hamilton, Housing Corporation of New Zealand.

Sargisson, Lucy (1996), *Contemporary Feminist Utopianism*, London, Routledge.

Sargisson, Lucy (2000), *Utopian Bodies and the Politics of Transgression*, London, Routledge.

Sargisson, Lucy (2003), 'Surviving Conflict: New Zealand's Intentional Communities', *New Zealand Sociology*, 18 (2), 225–50.

Scott, Peter (1998), 'Types of Ownership in New Zealand', http://www. converge.org.nz/evcnz/legal.html, 5 December 2003.

Shanahan, Mary (1992), 'Blessed by the Sun', *Next*, 12, February, 16–21.

Shenker, Barry (1986), *Intentional Communities: Ideology and Alienation in Communal Societies*, London, Routledge and Kegan Paul.

Sherif, Muzafer (1958), 'Superordinate Goals in the Reduction of Intergroup Conflicts', in Hogg and Abrams (eds), 64–70. Originally published in *American Journal of Sociology*, 63, 1958, 349–56.

Siers, Judy (1991), *James Walter Chapman-Taylor in the Hawke's Bay 1913–1922*, Napier, Hawkes Bay Cultural Trust.

Simmel, Georg (1955), *Conflict*, Glencoe, IL, The Free Press.

Sisters, Servants of the Immaculate Heart of Mary, Monroe, Michigan (1997), *Building Sisterhood: A Feminist History of the Sisters, Servants of the Immaculate Heart of Mary*, Syracuse, Syracuse University Press.

Slessor, Richard (1982), 'The Yeast in Architecture: Co-operative Housing as a Development of Self-Help Community Architecture in New Zealand', unpublished BArch Sub-thesis, University of Auckland.

Smithells, Philip (1975), 'Inaugural Tree Planting at Wanganui Settlement', *NZ Friends Newsletter*, August, 10.

Smithells, Philip and Olive (1976), 'Friends Wanganui Educational Settlement', April, Wanganui Educational Settlement – Quaker Acres, MS Papers 2597–26/1/1, Alexander Turnbull Library.

Spence, Clark C. (1985), *The Salvation Army Farm Colonies*, Tucson, University of Arizona Press.

Stace, Hilary (1998), 'Faith and Persistence Win Through: The School of Radiant Living in New Zealand and Its Appeal, Particularly to Women', unpublished Research Essay, Victoria University of Wellington.

Stover, Sue (1976) ['Quaker Acres'], *NZ Friends Newsletter*, June, 5.

Sumner, William Graham (1906), *Folkways: A Study of the Sociological Importance of Usages, Manners, Customs, Mores, and Morals*, New York, Ginn.

Swain, Trystan (1996), *Liberating Meetings: Facilitating meetings using consensus decision making*, Waitaha, Vegan Books.

The Times (London) (1838), February 10, 5.

Tolerton, Jane (1992), *Ettie: A Life of Ettie Rout*, Auckland, Penguin Books NZ.

Trollope, Anthony (1873), *Australia and New Zealand*, 2 vols. London, Chapman and Hall.

Utopianz: A Guide to Intentional Communities and Communal Living in Aotearoa/New Zealand (2004), Christchurch, Straw Umbrella Trust.

Wagner, Jon (1982), 'Sex Roles in American Communal Utopias: An Overview', in *Sex Roles in Contemporary American Communes*, Wagner, Jon (ed.), Bloomington, Indiana University Press, pp. 1–44.

Wagner, Jon (1985), 'Success in Intentional Communities: The Problem of Evaluation', *Communal Societies*, 5, 89–100.

'Wanganui Educational Settlement: A Progress Report' (1976), *NZ Friends Newsletter*, 1–3.

[Ward, John] (1842), *Nelson, The Latest Settlement of the New Zealand Company*, by Kappa [pseud.], London, Smith, Elder and Co.

Webb, Larisa Ingrid (1999), 'Living together? Change and Continuity of a Living New Zealand Intentional Community', unpublished MA thesis, University of Auckland, 1999.

What We Believe (1989), Rangiora, The Christian Church at Springbank. The Hostetler Papers indicate that the author was Fervent Stedfast.

Whitehead, Marian (1980), 'Alternative Communities and Rural Planning', unpublished Bachelor of Town Planning Research Essay, University of Auckland.

Why Christian Community (1956), Lower Moutere, Riverside Community.

Wood, Andy (1989), 'History and Overview', in *Diggers and Dreamers: The 1990/91 Guide to Communal Living*, Ansell, Vera; Coates, Chris; Dawling, Pam; How, Jonathan; Morris, William; and Wood, Andy (eds), Townhead, Dunford Bridge, Sheffield, Communes Network, pp. 6–16.

The Word, Letters from Raymond E. Hansen (June 1957), 89 (September 1948), 139.

Wright, Quincy (1951), 'The Nature of Conflict', in Burton and Dukes (eds), pp. 15–34. Originally published in *Western Political Quarterly*, 4 (2) (June 1951).

Wunderlich, Roger (1992), *Low Living and High Thinking at Modern Times, New York*, Syracuse, Syracuse University Press.

Zablocki, Benjamin (1980), *Alienation and Charisma: A Study of Contemporary American Communes*, New York, Free Press.

Zalewski, Patrick J. (1988), *The Secret Inner Order Rituals of the Golden Dawn. With the approval of Israel Regardie*, Lisiewski, Joseph (ed.), Phoenix, Falcon Press.

Manuscripts

Some material was provided to the authors by various communes and much of this material is undated and does not have the usual publication information.

Ahu Ahu Ohu, 1992 Information Sheet.

Alexander William Bickerton (1842–1929), 27/57, Folder 17, item 354a, manuscript of a novel. Canterbury Museum, Christchurch, New Zealand.

Archives New Zealand (ABWN 6095 W5021 22/5340).

Bodhinyanarama Guest Leaflet.

'Chippenham Household Community Policy'.

Chippenham Community, *Information for Guests and New Residents*.

Community Assistance, Incorporated, 'The Commune School'.

Community Assistance, Incorporated, 'Objectives'.

Droescher, Werner Otto. 'Wilderland – an Alternative?' In his 'Toward an Alternative Society', Unpub. MS, 1978. Werner Otto Droescher Papers, University of Auckland Library.

Gifford-Bickerton Papers (MS-Papers-0259–094) Alexander Turnbull Library.

Hansen, Raymond Ernest, 1910–1985. Papers, 84–204 Alexander Turnbull Library,

John Hostetler Papers, University Archives, The Pennsylvania State University Libraries.

Jonathan Hunt Papers, Department of Politics, University of Auckland.

Katajuta Community Agreements.

National Radio of New Zealand, *Country Life* Programme (27 January 2001).

Otakaro Land Trust Deed: Peterborough Charter.

Otamatea EcoVillage Booklet.

Riverside Community Papers. Canterbury University Macmillan Brown Library.

Riverside Community. MS-Group-0283 and MS-Papers–0439, Alexander Turnbull Library.

Web Sources

As anyone knows who uses web sources regularly, such sites are unstable. All these sites were accurate and in existence at the time the manuscript was submitted.

http://rndm.tripod.com/NewZealand.htm
http://www.anamorph.com/todo/cl.html/
http://www.anth.org.uk
http://www.bodhinyanarama.net.nz/munindo1.htm)
http://www.catholic.org/newzealand/fms
http://www.cohousing.org
http://www.cohousing.pl.net
http://www.cohousing.pl.net/infobook/principles.html
http://www.conserve.org.nz/evens/otamatea.html
http://www.gentleworld.org
http://www.hoc.org.nz
http://www.karmel.at
http://www.nzca.org
http://www.planet-hawaii.com/gentleworld/VEGAN/vegan.html
http://www.prometheus.co.nz
http://www.purenz.com/indexnz.cfm
http://www.purenz.com/wilderness.cfm
http://www.titoki.nz.co/Newsletter/html
Valley Farm EcoVillage Website http://www.ecovillage.co.nz

Index